# GREED, Inc.

*Also by Wade Rowland*


GALILEO'S MISTAKE
A New Look at the Epic Confrontation
Between Galileo and the Church

OCKHAM'S RAZOR
A Search for Wonder in an Age of Doubt

SPIRIT OF THE WEB
The Age of Information from Telegraph to Internet

# GREED,
# Inc. WHY CORPORATIONS RULE OUR WORLD

## WADE ROWLAND

Arcade Publishing
New York

FIRST U.S. EDITION

First published in Canada by Thomas Allen Publishers, a division of Thomas Allen & Son, Limited

*Library of Congress Cataloging-in-Publication Data*

Rowland, Wade.
 Greed, Inc. : why corporations rule our world / by Wade Rowland.
  —1st U.S. ed.
  p. cm.
 Includes bibliographical references and index.
 ISBN 1-55970-794-1 (alk. paper)
 1. Business ethics. 2. Social ethics. 3. Corporations—History.
 4. Corporations—Social aspects. I. Title.

HF5387.R69 2005b
174'.4—dc22                                        2005029293

Published in the United States by Arcade Publishing, Inc., New York
Distributed by Time Warner Book Group

Visit our Web site at www.arcadepub.com

10 9 8 7 6 5 4 3 2 1

Designed by API

EB

PRINTED IN THE UNITED STATES OF AMERICA

*For Christine Collie Rowland,*
*enlightened owner and CEO of a convivial business corporation*
*called Blue Cat Design*

*The greatest task before civilization at present is to make machines what they ought to be, the slaves instead of the masters of men.*

— Havelock Ellis

*The corporation is a machine for making money.*

— Anonymous

# Contents

# Introduction

Until quite recently, most people who spent time thinking about what we now call economics were in agreement that human beings had an inborn ethical leaning and aptitude, and this was what allowed markets to function. It seemed obvious that if everybody tried to get the better of everybody else, the system would simply collapse. Of course, the greedy have always been with us, but they tended to be looked upon with disgust, both for their personal depravity and the damage that did to the goal of fairness in distributing the earth's bounty — which is what economics was all about.

Adam Smith, the eighteenth-century moralist who invented modern economic theory, assumed that the entrepreneurs who flourished in the primitive capitalist markets of his day had limits to their avarice just like everybody else. Their innate sense of what was right and proper would steer them clear of excess, and, if their moral compass temporarily wobbled, the censure of their peers would soon put them back on course.

Early in the twentieth century the love of money for its own sake was colorfully described by the influential economist John Maynard Keynes as "a somewhat disgusting morbidity, one of those semi-criminal, semi-pathological propensities which one hands over with a shudder to the specialists in mental disease." In plain English, a sickness.

*Introduction*

Compare those viewpoints with the postmodern perspective of the likes of Gordon Gekko, a fictional character so well drawn by Oliver Stone in the 1987 movie *Wall Street* that his words continue to reverberate: "The point, ladies and gentlemen, is that greed — for lack of a better word — is good. Greed is right. Greed works. Greed clarifies, cuts through, and captures the essence of the evolutionary spirit. Greed, in all of its forms — greed for life, for money, for love, knowledge — has marked the upward surge of mankind. And greed — you mark my words — will not only save [this company] but that other malfunctioning corporation called the U.S.A."

The Gekko speech (delivered by Michael Douglas) is taken by many to be a creed for contemporary market capitalism, a factual description of the way the world works — and *ought to* work. I note, for example, that the Whitman College (Washington) Republicans display the speech on their Web site, adding the comment: "His character may have been a creep, but his speech was 100% correct."

Gekko's real-life counterparts, whose triumphs and misadventures are chronicled daily in the pages of the business press, are a far cry from the ideal entrepreneur imagined by early-twentieth-century economists like Keynes, let alone the Protestant moralists of the eighteenth and nineteenth centuries who built the theoretical foundation for capitalism and its markets, a remarkable body of work that still exerts a tidal influence on economic thought. And they, along with most of our ancestors, would look with horror on the unabashed greed and selfishness that is fundamental to our current consumer culture.

Why the change?

I propose in this book that the recent switch in our economic perceptions, attitudes, and behavior is a reflection of the rise of a new social phenomenon that I call the modern business corporation (defined in detail in chapter 7). Virtually unknown until the mid-twentieth century, these very large, publicly traded, and professionally managed corporations now dominate global economic activity. They have evolved out of earlier generations of the corporate species, of which it could accurately be said that human managers were in charge. The modern business corporation has matured to a stage of sophistication in which, I will argue, it must now be thought of as an autonomous, self-regulating entity that employs human "managers" merely as components or appliances. The corporation itself, as a self-contained entity, is in charge of its own destiny.

The most obvious clue that corporations have begun to operate independently of human control is the frequency with which their actions violate the human interest. These actions may be legal, and frequently are, but most people would call them immoral. What demonstrates more clearly than anything else that the autonomous corporation is in its essence inhuman, or alien, is its complete and demonstrable lack of the moral intuition and judgment that is an integral part of what it means to be human.

I recognize that for some readers this will seem less than obvious. While off-the-cuff *moralizing* abounds in our culture, genuine *moral argument* is rare and unexpected. And that is why I have carefully built my argument, starting at the beginning, with a defense of the moral certitudes that shaped economic thought from the ancient Greeks right down to the middle of the last century. In the current intellectual milieu it is sadly necessary to demonstrate first that moral values have real existence, and second, that they have application in understanding economic doctrine in general, and the corporation in particular.

That's for later. Right now I merely want to suggest that what passes for legitimate activity undertaken by many of our largest and most highly evolved business corporations is often by any sensible standard both immoral and antihuman. The examples I use will no doubt be familiar, if not in detail then certainly in kind, because they have become so commonplace. The American automobile industry, which has for half a century mightily resisted every government initiative to force it to improve fuel-efficiency and safety standards, is, at this writing, fighting to undermine legislation that would improve passenger survivability in highway rollover accidents.[1] Such accidents, and the associated deaths, have become epidemic since the introduction of truck-based sport-utility vehicles, SUVs. Introduced, bewilderingly, at about the time it became widely realized that oil supplies were finite and therefore in need of conservation, these famously gas-greedy vehicles are an invention born not out of any necessity or even any existing demand but in the cunning minds of marketers who saw some shadowy need in the American psyche that could be served by cars that had the virile appearance of urban assault or bushwhacking safari transport. They are so heavy (and hence gas-hungry) and sit so high off the ground that in avoidance maneuvers on the highway they tend to flip. When that happens passengers who are not ejected (due to faulty door locks on some of these behemoths, which is another story) are liable to die anyway, having had their heads crushed or necks broken when the roof collapses on them. When the National Highway Traffic Administration proposed new standards for roof strength, the industry circled its wagons in a well-practiced defensive strategy that resulted in a substantial watering down of the legislation. It was, naturally, far less than what many safety advocates had hoped for.

In 2005 there were about ten thousand rollover deaths on U.S. highways. In that same year the NHTA estimated that six hundred people wearing seatbelts died and another eight hundred were seriously injured in these crashes due to roof collapse. General Motors Corp. and the Ford Motor Co. both argued strenuously and not a little ingenuously that whether a vehicle's roof collapses in a rollover makes little difference to whether passengers survive, the fatal injuries mostly occurring when people are thrown against the roof prior to the car's impact with the ground. Independent experts pointed out that this defies both common sense and crash-site data, and Ford's own Volvo division stressed the importance of roof integrity when it launched its new SUV in Sweden.

The standards ultimately acceded to by the American auto industry will have only a small effect — it's thought somewhere between thirteen and forty-four deaths will be prevented. On the upside, in Ford and GM management-speak, they'll cost the vehicle makers only about $11 per unit to implement.

What is significant about this case history is not its novelty, but its depressing normalcy. This is the way business is done and has been done for at least the last fifty years in corporate capitalist market economies, the *ne plus ultra* of which is to be found in the United States. It's hard to imagine Henry Ford behaving this way, with respect to either wasteful fuel consumption or public safety, and it's even harder to understand how such calculating callousness is rationalized by today's auto executives, some of whose own family members will surely be at risk thanks to their failure to behave responsibly.

Similarly outrageous is the recent record of the corporate drug industry. The most current examples of egregious behavior involve pharmaceutical giants Pfizer, GlaxoSmithKline, and Merck.

A California lawsuit filed in 2004 alleges that Pfizer, the world's largest drug company, deliberately suppressed evidence that its antidepressant drug Zoloft had proved no more efficacious than a placebo in four out of five of the company's own trials, and that it concealed direct evidence that users of the drug were committing suicide and other violent acts at an alarming rate. Other side effects, such as convulsions and psychosis, the lawsuit alleged, were also concealed or downplayed.

A few months earlier Pfizer had pleaded guilty in U.S. federal court to criminal fraud charges and had agreed to pay a $430 million settlement in connection with the drug Neurontin. Neurontin, developed initially as a treatment for epilepsy (a small and inelastic market), was "repositioned" by Pfizer as being effective in treating a host of other "off-label" (non FDA-approved) conditions including migraine, bipolar disorder, nerve pain, and neuropathy. Sales rocketed from $97 million in 1997 to $2.7 billion in 2003. The government prosecutors charged that Pfizer flew doctors to lavish resorts, paid them kickbacks in the form of consultants' and speakers' fees, and fired salespeople if they didn't recruit enough doctors to prescribe Neurontin for nerve pain. The government also said Pfizer suppressed a study revealing the drug to be less effective than a placebo in treating bipolar disorder, leaving both doctors and patients in the dark.

The New York attorney general in 2004 filed suit against U.K.-based GlaxoSmithKline alleging that the corporation suppressed potentially sales-damaging knowledge about its multi-billion-dollar seller Paxil, especially in relation to its use in treating depressions in children and adolescents. The suit alleges that GSK conducted at least five studies on the use of Paxil in children and adolescents, but it only published and disseminated one, which showed mixed results on efficacy. The lawsuit accuses GSK of suppressing the negative results of the other studies, which failed to demonstrate that Paxil is effective and that suggested an increased risk of suicidal thinking and acts.

GSK is also said to have failed to disclose this information in "Medical Information Letters" that it sent to physicians. Glaxo denied the charges.

The scandal surrounding the painkiller Vioxx and other similar drugs being aggressively marketed in this hypercompetitive sector climaxed in August 2005 when a Texas jury awarded the wife of a heart attack victim $253.5 million in a judgment against Vioxx's manufacturer, Merck. It included $229 million in "exemplary damages." Jurors said later they had settled on this figure because it was the amount of profit Merck made by delaying its recall of the drug for four months after it was cautioned by the FDA. (The settlement was reduced on appeal.)

Before Merck pulled Vioxx from the market, twenty million Americans were taking the drug — about one in twelve people. An FDA study published in the British medical journal *Lancet* estimated that Vioxx has resulted in between 88,000 and 140,000 serious cardiovascular events. Several thousand lawsuits have now been filed, alleging that Merck knew of the potentially fatal side effects for years, but concealed the information from physicians and the public so as to sustain the drug's $2.5 billion annual sales.

A deliberate failure to prevent hundreds of avoidable highway deaths or thousands of deaths from drug side effects is a tragedy and a crime. But on another scale altogether is the calculated undermining of international efforts to mitigate what is perhaps the biggest threat ever to have faced humankind — global warming. ExxonMobil, the world's largest oil company, has been doing exactly that for more than a decade, its ultimate goal being to dissuade the U.S. Congress from signing on to the Kyoto Protocol or in any other way seriously interfering with current fossil fuel production and consumption patterns.[2] The carefully crafted strategy has been to undermine the science behind warming predictions, in the same way that big tobacco sought for decades to call into question the research linking smoking with lung and heart disease.

The tobacco industry campaign is exhaustively documented in the mass of incriminating correspondence made public as a result of hundreds of lawsuits. A much publicized Brown and Williamson tobacco company memo from the late 1960s is particularly enlightening. It said: "Doubt is our product since it is the best means of competing with the 'body of fact' that exists in the mind of the general public. It is also the means of establishing a controversy." In 1998, the *New York Times* published an internal memo of the American Petroleum Institute, the industry lobby group in which ExxonMobil is naturally a dominant player, outlining an almost identical strategy to invest millions to "maximize the impact of scientific views consistent with ours with Congress, the media and other key audiences." The document stated: "Victory will be achieved when . . . recognition of uncertainty becomes part of the 'conventional wisdom.'"

ExxonMobil has sought to create doubt in the face of worldwide scientific agreement on the impact of human activity on global climate, of which D. James Baker, the former administrator of the National Oceanic and Atmospheric Administration, has said, "There is a better scientific consensus on this than on any other issue I know — except maybe Newton's second law of dynamics." That the campaign, aided and abetted by a handful of other American fossil fuel producers, has enjoyed substantial success is attributable to its sophistication. ExxonMobil itself avoids blatant misrepresentations, and it instead funds scores of lobby groups, industry think tanks, and other front organizations that in turn churn out critical commentary on any and all scientific research that supports the established global warming consensus.[3]

But this critical "analysis" would be of little use if it were not widely seen, and so the second arm of the strategy is to harass media outlets with demands for "balance" in their coverage of each and every newly published scientific report. The media, mostly corporate-owned and increasingly bereft of highly educated and thus expensive science specialists, is with few exceptions inclined to comply with these demands both out of a desire to avoid problems with current and potential advertisers — and often their own corporate owners — and simple ignorance of the facts and issues at play. Thus ExxonMobil-sponsored criticism, frequently wholly specious, tends to receive equal play with legitimate scientific data.

The tens of millions of dollars ExxonMobil has invested in this campaign of misrepresentation have paid off handsomely, sowing doubt and confusion and a concomitant public apathy. And it is this apathy that makes it possible for ExxonMobil and its corporate cohorts to shape the legislative agenda in Washington in the face of much diminished resistance. That the fate of the planet is at stake matters not at all.

The litany of corporate misdeeds could easily fill this book and many more volumes. And that is the main point I want to make here in these introductory pages: corporate crime and immorality are not exceptional behavior, they are the norm. What has been described above is simply the way the modern business corporation does business.

The mystery I hope to shed light on in this book is why this should be the case. Why do big corporations behave like sociopaths? It is an important question because the behavior of our large corporations shapes society at large in a thousand ways.

Given the breadth of that impact, though, it's clear that the problem can only be fruitfully examined in the wider context of the kind of society we in the West have built for ourselves in the twenty-first century. It might be said of our time, as Charles

# *Introduction*

Dickens said of late-eighteenth-century France, that it is the best of times and the worst of times. Liberal democracy is spreading, triumphantly, throughout the world. Fact has everywhere vanquished superstition. Technology has revolutionized transportation, communication, access to information. Medical science has extended our lives and made them less harrowing, thanks in no small measure to those very drug companies that seem to put sales before safety. Consumer society affords instant gratification of our every material desire. Progress is on the march.

At the same time there is an undeniable melancholy at the core of it all. Something seems amiss. For one thing, we are making a mess of the planet. For another, the eternal goals of justice and equity seem to be receding, and at an accelerating rate. Not just progress, but meanness, obsessive self-interest, a callousness toward others increasingly reflected in our public institutions, seems to be on the march. Mental illness and spiritual malaise are endemic.

Social theorists and other commentators routinely identify capitalism as the source of society's ills. No doubt it is, but where does that get us? How does one alter the foundational precepts of society — how do we reform capitalism? It seems an overwhelming, impossible task. And what would we replace it with?

I want to propose here that there is indeed something that can be done, but that we first need to clearly identify the nature of the structural problem we face. It is not capitalism, or market capitalism, that is the real problem. It is *corporate* capitalism. It is capitalism hijacked and dominated by the modern business corporation.

In a nutshell (and as I'll describe in more detail later), the men who designed the market economy — the dominant social institution of the late-modern era — and adapted the ancient legal instrument of the corporation to operate within it were militant believers in the idea that morality is not innate but is generated by social institutions. Selfishness and greed were confidently asserted by the newly minted social sciences of the eighteenth and nineteenth centuries to be defining, universal, and irrepressible characteristics of human beings. This was accepted as a law of nature. The challenge facing the early designers of the market and the corporation was to work with this "fact" and create an ethical system in spite of it. Thus both were designed as mechanisms to *automatically manufacture social good out of individual vice.* They are machines for synthesizing ethical behavior.

Just as the most elegant of bridges will collapse if the engineers get their physics wrong, social constructs like the market and the corporation will fail, often in dramatic and surprising ways, if they are built upon mistaken assumptions about human relations. This is what has happened with the corporation: it is an engineering project gone amok.

The trouble with corporations is that they were designed to reproduce only one aspect of the multifaceted human psyche — in a word, greed. They seek only profit, and there is no end to their avarice. By design, they reflect none of the redeeming human qualities that are products of the moral impulse. As the dominant factor in our preeminent societal institution — the market — the corporation embodies and amplifies the profligate side of human nature, and it does it so successfully that it has reshaped the broad outlines of Western society in its one-dimensional image.

It wasn't supposed to be that way — the market was supposed to perform its alchemy and turn corporate greed into public welfare, but somewhere along the road to the present, corporations got the upper hand and took charge. Knowing how and when that happened is the first essential step toward righting this historic wrong.

# Part I

## How Morality Was Hijacked by Economics and Why It Matters

*It may be said that the "means" that a man uses are far more impor-
tant than the "ends" which he pursues, for they express more fully his
spirit. If a man strives for freedom by means of tyranny, for love by
means of hatred, for brotherhood by means of dissension, for truth by
means of falsity, his lofty aim is not likely to make the judgment of him
more lenient. I actually believe that a man who worked for the cause of
tyranny, hatred, falsity and dissension by means of freedom, love,
truthfulness and brotherhood would be the better man of the two.*

— Nikolay Berdyaev, *The Destiny of Man* (1937)

# 1

## A Pilgrim's Progress

Highway 401 undulates through the gentle Northumberland hills skirting the northeast shore of Lake Ontario, just a few miles south of where I live. There is nothing gentle about the highway itself — it's said to be North America's busiest, and you can get a pretty good idea of the state of the world by driving it. Over the years, and especially with the North American Free Trade Agreement, it has seen an enormous increase in truck traffic, huge juggernauts rocketing along at 80 mph regardless of the weather, hauling everything from car parts to chemical waste, from lumber to snowmobiles, from garbage destined for landfills hundreds of miles distant to fresh produce all the way up from Mexico.

Doing their best to stay out of the way of the bullying tractor-trailer rigs are tens of thousands of passenger vehicles driven by white-knuckled commuters heading to and from jobs in the city and its environs, occasionally finding themselves boxed in alongside trailers crammed with terrified livestock and poultry on their way from crowded feedlots and factory farms to the city's slaughterhouses.

Just south of the highway, closer to the lake, the country's rail backbone runs along twinned tracks, and you can occasionally see the pathetic little blue and yellow Via Rail trains, three or four coaches long, representing the national passenger rail service. Many if not most of the automobile commuters would prefer to take the train, but the service is too infrequent and unreliable and expensive to make sense. Closer to the city, where the highway begins to widen from six to eight and ultimately sixteen lanes, you can catch a double-decker commuter train, but over the years these trains, placed in service by the provincial government of another era, have seen their subsidies shrivel, and service hasn't kept up with demand.

I have done the commute from my bucolic surroundings to the city, where I worked for many years, thousands of times, writing off two or three hours of my life each trip, alone in my car.

I always had plenty to think about. There was a lot in my life that made me happy, more than my fair share. But over the years it got harder to stay cheerful, because there was so much about the trip that I found disturbing. I was disturbed at the whole idea of commuting sixty miles each way in a gas-sucking, smog-spewing automobile; disturbed at the pitiful lack of public transit as an alternative and what that said about society; disturbed that so many others were doing the same thing as I was; disturbed at the malignant sprawl of subdivisions oozing steadily across the verdant landscape that separates the big city from my little rural homestead, and what that said about our impact on the planet.

I often reflected that in my lifetime there has been a dramatic shift away from concern for public welfare and community goals and values to a focus on the individual — the "me first" attitude that famously characterized the '80s, but which had been steadily acquiring respectability for the previous three decades or more. Institutions that reflected our noble and generous side were withering on the vine, subsisting on bake-sale budgets, while those that represented the venal in us flourished and raised secular cathedrals of glass and steel in our downtown cores. A puzzle.

When I permitted myself to dwell on it, I was even more disturbed at the thought of what my job required me to do when I reached my place of work. On those days my conscience would tell me that the news, as I was packaging it for a national television audience every night, was doing a great deal of harm by inciting groundless fears, oversimplifying the intrinsically complex, pandering to vulgar curiosities, treating politics like a sporting event, presenting the speculative as factual, painting a cartoon image of the world and its actors, and pretending that what it did not cover was of no importance. I engineered myself a promotion from the newsroom floor to the executive suite, thinking I would be able to improve things, but found I had less, not more, functional control.

There had been a big change in senior management toward the end of my career as a news executive. The network president, an old television hand with deep knowledge of production, was pushed out, and the VP of the news division, a man of long journalistic experience in print and a pioneer of television news, retired. Determined to replace the CEO with one of the new breed of corporate managers being churned out by high-profile university management schools, the corporation's directors spent a large chunk of money on a corporate headhunter and interviewed several candidates, settling eventually on our ambitious, well-intentioned neophyte. Its new CEO in place, the network launched into the cyclical "rationalization" process so fashionable in the '80s and '90s, with wave after wave of layoffs and new hires, and endless reorganizations of departments and divisions, including mine.

I began to see how naive my colleagues and I had been. We

had thought that the news was essentially and honorably an altruistic enterprise, financed out of the vast resources of the network in the public interest as a way of repaying society for the privilege of using the public airwaves for private profit. Believe it or not, that's the way most network TV journalists thought about their work prior to the late '80s, when my own network began to itch for "modern" management and higher profit margins.

It was in the same tidal wave of modernization and rationalization in North American business that ABC, CBS, and NBC were all sold to American megacorporations, the ax fell on their respective news divisions, and everything changed forever. From that time forward, news was thought of as just another corporate division, and it was expected to make a profit. Journalistic notions of quality were replaced by accounting metrics as the measure of the news divisions' success or failure. I imagine it was much the same in a lot of other industries: no doubt there were plenty of people in the shoe manufacturing business who had thought their role in life was to produce the best shoes possible before the ax fell and their jobs were shipped to Third World sweatshops.

By the end of my tour of duty in the executive suite, I had attended enough new-regime management committee meetings to see that, if quality for its own sake had ever been the goal, it wasn't any longer, and that it was now all about increasing revenue and cutting costs. News and current affairs managers and producers had begun to experience, for the first time, serious pressure from the marketing division and its ad sellers, who were looking for such policy concessions as "brought to you by" sponsorship of the flagship nighttime newscast and proprietary sponsorship of segments within the magazine-style morning show. A drug company, for example, could be charged a premium for its advertisements if they appeared in the context of the program's health reports, and even more if the reports were billboarded as "brought to you by" the advertiser.

Staff at all levels were being pushed too hard. The product was incidental to profit margins, and might even be deliberately degraded — frequently was, in fact — if that could be shown on somebody's spreadsheet to result in extra income. Everything was cheapened, and although it showed for those who paid close attention, it tended to slip past the casual uninformed viewer (a category that included all of the new senior corporate managers brought in by our CEO), thanks to the fact that all of the competing network news operations were undergoing the same process at the same time. Though absolute quality had nose-dived with mass layoffs and dramatic budget cuts, *relative* quality remained about the same. Everybody was missing the same stories, closing the same foreign and regional bureaus, laying off the same class of very expensive but thoughtful and talented reporters and producers. News was becoming a generic product, with the networks covering the same safe stories in the same "cost-effective" ways, differentiating themselves not through content, but through their attractive anchors and a few "star" reporters.

It got so bad that eventually I quit. Or rather, I provoked my own dismissal. In retrospect, I'm reminded of the motorcycle trip I took as a young man to Yellowknife in Canada's Northwest Territories. It was an exceptionally hot and dry spring for the sub-Arctic, and my passenger and I had been skirting disaster for days. I was pushing the bike as hard as I dared through the foot-deep gravel and blinding dust of the Mackenzie Highway, more than once outrunning curious or hungry black bears — we weren't sure which — just emerging from hibernation. We were plagued by a mysterious electrical problem that, until we finally solved it, stranded us for a full day hundreds of miles from the nearest help. Each morning we would emerge from our tiny tent with faces massively swollen by mosquito and black fly bites to endure another endless day of heat, choking dust, and tension. I found myself, in my exhaustion, hoping we would crash simply to end the suspense, to get it all over with. The continuous stress of dealing with a near-impossible situation had made me a danger to myself, not to mention my companion.

At the network, the official story was that my position of "Director of Policy and Development for News and Current Affairs" had been organized out of existence, declared redundant in one of a continuing series of corporate "restructurings." And while I was told by my delegated corporate executioner that I was being let go "with regret" because my position no longer made sense in the latest organization chart, we both knew that the reason for my dismissal was that I had clashed with suicidal recklessness with a newly appointed network president and CEO. We disagreed about nearly everything, which is perhaps only natural because he knew absolutely nothing about journalism or, for that matter, television.

One rainy Friday afternoon I was told to hand over my keys and corporate ID, to leave my office suite by the back door, not stopping on the way out and not taking anything with me. I was introduced to an "outplacement consultant" who, I was told, would "look after everything." It was a more or less conventional corporate disappearance, as I had come to think of these events, professionally orchestrated and executed. To my surviving colleagues, I simply vanished, like so many of us had in previous downsizings, and many more would in the future.

The entire experience left me besieged with questions. What exactly is a conscience and why did mine insist on getting me fired? What was it that caused so many workplace colleagues to meekly acquiesce in what we all saw as the destruction of an important institution? What was it about corporate life that made good people do bad things? What was it that made the corporation that employed me deliberately debase the quality of a vital commodity like the news? How on earth had the board of directors seen fit to hire a CEO whose only experience had been in the cigarette and fast-food industries, to run a television network? What was *that* all about?

When I looked at those questions later on in the relative tranquility of the academic environment, I saw that I would make little or no headway trying to find answers within the economic and sociological framework that had provoked the questions in the first place. As someone has said, we're not sure who discovered water, but we're pretty certain it wasn't a fish. To learn anything really useful, I would need a new perspective, one that captured but was not confined to the economics and sociology of the corporation. I would have to step outside that frame of reference, into the wider, richer purview of moral philosophy.

And as soon as I did that, I could see that my many questions resolved themselves into two more or less distinct areas of concern, both related to the rather large question of the nature of morality and what constitutes ethical behavior. The first question concerns conscience, and the role it plays in human ethical behavior. More broadly, this boils down to a series of questions about the nature of morality itself. Is morality merely a set of societal conventions or customs, varying with time, place, and circumstance? Or is it a set of universal principles that are valid at all times, in all places, and in all circumstances? If it exists, what is its source?

A second question involves the moral status of the modern business corporation, and of the people who work within it. Is the corporation itself a moral agent, or do its actions merely reflect the moral perspective of those who work within it? This is a new and important line of inquiry, because the corporation has evolved in the past half-century into an institution of unprecedented power and influence.

These two issues — the moral status of corporations and the question of moral relativism — are linked in a way that makes it impossible to make sense of the corporate question this book is asking without first understanding the relativism problem. The reason for this is that the modern corporation, with all its power and influence in our lives, is the concrete realization of a deliberately designed and constructed *moral system* whose assumptions undergird market society. That moral system was concocted by Rationalist thinkers and policymakers of an earlier era, whose outlook and attitudes were shaped by the blossoming of modern science in all its youthful vigor and self-confidence.

*Rationalism* was and is the theory that the exercise of reason — as opposed to philosophical or religious testimony and authority, or spiritual revelation, or instinct and intuition, or even evidence supplied by the senses — is the *only* valid and reliable source of knowledge. Science, as a product of reason and built on mathematics and logic, is thus a superior source of knowledge of the world and the way it works — superior, specifically, to religion, which is a product of revelation, authority, and spiritual insight.

The Rationalist avant-garde saw religion as irrational superstition, and its insistence on the real existence of such unweighable, unmeasurable invisible phenomena as conscience and the soul as literal nonsense. At the same time, they recognized the need for a firm moral foundation on which to construct society. If not the Church and its moral teachings, then *what?* The goal was to find a Reason-based scientific rationale for moral behavior, to build a moral system rooted not in religious tracts or teachings, but anchored scientifically, in "laws" of human nature and thus more appropriate to a supremely self-assured era that came to look upon itself, in contrast to the earlier medieval epoch (the Dark Ages, they called it), as supremely enlightened.

The Rationalist era that produced so many of our important institutions and ideas covers, roughly, about three centuries from 1600 to 1900. It incorporates what historians call the Scientific Revolution, which begins with Galileo and the philosophers René Descartes and Thomas Hobbes. It includes as well the era known as the Enlightenment, which is formally dated from the last decades of the 1600s when Voltaire, Johann Sebastian Bach, and George Frederick Handel were born, and Louis XIV, the Sun King, was on the throne at Versailles to the carnage of the French Revolution of 1789. It is the era of the satirist Jonathan Swift, literary giant Johann Wolfgang Goethe, the great political philosopher Jean-Jacques Rousseau, the economist and moral philosopher Adam Smith (whom we've met), Jeremy Bentham and the Utilitarian philosophers, and the fomenters of the American War of Independence. Captain James Cook sailed around the world and James Watt patented his improved steam engine. Rationalism was the supreme intellectual fashion of the time, a narrow, computational Reason, which the French religious philosopher and mathematician Blaise Pascal, a lonely voice in this respect, opposed with his advocacy of the "knowledge of the heart."

With the 1790s came the Romantic era's counterattack against the excesses of Rationalism's sometimes fanatical commitment to reason and logic. The Industrial Revolution was under way, and while Rationalists cheered on the engineers and industrialists Romantics lamented the despoiling of nature and the human toll evident in the era's widespread social disruption, regimentation, poverty, and despair. The English mystical poet William Blake published his *Songs of Innocence* the year French revolutionaries stormed the Bastille; William Wordsworth and Samuel Taylor Coleridge both published major collections of lyric poetry just a decade later.

But by then the scientific Rationalist ethos had been deeply embedded in Western society — *institutionalized* by the work of the Utilitarian philosophers (of whom more later) and the great classical theorists of market capitalism. It would receive fresh authority from Darwin's revolutionary theories on natural selection (first published in 1859) and the new behavioral sciences, and it would dominate the politics and economics of the Victorian era, which spans most of the nineteenth century.

If I had undertaken an inquiry similar to this one into our social roots on the other, earlier side of this historical watershed, I would have been faced not with corporations and the market but with three great "estates" of medieval society — the Church, the nobility, and the commoners. It is sometimes said that in the capitalist societies of today, the place of the Church has been occupied by the corporation. Market capitalism is our theology, liberal economic theory is its dogma, and the corporation is the administrative vehicle for spreading the gospel and insisting that dogma and its rituals are observed. It is an appealing analogy, when one considers that capitalism is a system that has as its goal the welfare of humanity, as does Christianity. And just like Christianity it has its well-defined views of the role of the individual person within the wider social system, and of what constitutes good and bad behavior.

But, of course, the two ideologies have very different views of the nature of Good and the ingredients of human welfare, among other things — so much so that I think it is more accurate to see the corporation as a kind of *anti*-Church. Not in the sense of being opposed to the Church, but in being its converse, as a mirror image is to the object it reflects. Certainly market capitalism, as theology, is the antithesis of Christian doctrine as it was promulgated for the fifteen centuries prior to the scientific revolution, and thus may be called an anti-theology. That would make the "chiefs" of the corporate world — the chief executive officers and chief operating officers and chief financial officers and their scrubbed and suited acolytes — the anti-clergy of our time. They in turn call on the great advertising and public relations firms and corporate think tanks like the Cato Institute and the Fraser Institute and the Conference Board for support in propounding and disseminating dogma in the way the Roman Church called on the Holy Office and the holy orders and the college of cardinals.

No one has better captured the essential difference between the old and the new than the historian R. H. Tawney:

> The most fundamental difference between medieval and modern economic thought consists . . . in the fact that, whereas the latter normally refers to economic expediency, however it may be interpreted, for the justification of any particular action, policy, or system of organization, the former starts from the position that *there is a moral authority to which considerations of economic expediency must be subordinated.*[1]

In other words, the questions *Is it right? Is it Good? Is it in the human interest?* took absolute priority over considerations of efficiency and expediency.

What I have been speaking of as a watershed, then, is really more akin to a looking glass. On one side is otherworldly medieval society with its Christian values leavened with the ferment of humanism and classical Greek moral philosophy. On the other side we have the mirror image — modernism — defined by market capitalism; science, with its inviolable laws; the ethics of self-interest; and an obsession with the material — all of which would eventually find their supreme manifestation in the modern business corporation.

# 2

# The Fable of the Bees

IF THE CREDIT — OR BLAME — FOR THE METAMORPHOSIS of Europe from medieval cocoon into bustling modernism were to be assigned to one individual, it would have to be the English philosopher Thomas Hobbes. A man of moderate habits, razor wit, and imposing height, he was the son of an illiterate and pugnacious rural pastor who, following an altercation with a fellow clergyman at the church door, was encouraged to leave town. A brother, a well-to-do glover, assumed care of wife and three children, including the precocious Thomas, who (as he would later write) had been born prematurely when his mother was caught up in the panic caused by the sighting of the Spanish Armada off England's coast in 1588. Hobbes used to say that with him was born a twin, Fear. "I have a feminine courage," he joked.

As a gifted student, Hobbes at fifteen was sent to Oxford, where he was instructed in the Latin and Greek classics and the standard Scholastic teachings, overlaid with the aggressive Puritanism newly in vogue at his college, Magdalen Hall. By his own account he was bored and turned his attention to astronomy and, especially, to maps and charts of the world and the astonishing accounts of the exploits of Francis Drake and other intrepid seafarers of the time. He came late to philosophical inquiry, but if ever a man's thinking could be said to be a reflection of his age, it is Hobbes's pessimistic view of humanity, summed up in a sentence from *Leviathan:* "So that in the first place, I put for a general inclination of all mankind, a perpetual and restless desire for Power after Power, that ceaseth only in death."

Hobbes imagined a savage beginning for humankind, a hellish existence in which everyone was at war with everyone else, and life was "nasty, brutish, and short." And no wonder: a partial list of the calamities that marked his adult life includes the bloody and devastating Thirty Years' War, which broke out in his thirtieth year (1636); the English Civil War and Cromwell's dictatorship, a period of turmoil and terror that he endured from age fifty-four to seventy-two; the Great Plague of London (1665) in which 60,000 perished from the Black Death; and the Great Fire of London the following year that burned down two-thirds of the city.

For much of his life he owed his livelihood to the patronage of the noble Cavendish family. Through them he met such luminaries as Ben Jonson, after Shakespeare the greatest playwright of the age, and Francis Bacon, an early and influential proponent of science and its methods. As tutor to the Cavendish children and other aristocratic youths, Hobbes took several trips to Europe. On one of those continental sojourns, in 1636, he met with the great Galileo Galilei at the astronomer's picturesque Arcetri villa, just outside the walls of Florence. Galileo was living out his waning years in indifferent health, drafting his great scientific opus on the laws of motion, under loose house arrest for having defied the pope's injunction against promoting Copernicanism. This was the by now widely accepted notion that the sun, and not Earth, was at the center of planetary motions, a theory Galileo had all but confirmed with his telescopic observations. But it was his imperious insistence that science trumped all other sources of truth that landed the astronomer in hot water with Urban VIII, and led to the trial that defined the faith versus science debate for the next 350 years. Galileo and Hobbes had in common an immoderate admiration for their own admittedly remarkable intellectual capacities, and a violent disdain for the science of Aristotle that had been the received wisdom in universities throughout the Middle Ages.

It is not known what they talked about, or for how long, but it may be imagined that much of the conversation centered on the new mechanistic, materialistic view of nature that the two, along with René Descartes, their contemporary and mutual correspondent, were in the process of unleashing upon an unsuspecting world. It was Descartes whose radical modernization of philosophical inquiry had given mind a privileged position over matter in his famous *cogito:* "I think, therefore I am," he had concluded, thus making thought and the mind the philosophical precursor to things material. This in turn made it possible, even inescapable, to conclude that disembodied Reason reigned supreme as a source of knowledge and truth. Descartes as a philosopher, Galileo as a physicist and astronomer, and Hobbes as a social and political theorist had set out to change the world and were to achieve a degree of success that would have astonished each of them.

What Galileo and Hobbes especially shared was a confidence, new to history, that it was within the grasp of human reason to know everything there is to know about the world and existence — to know, as Galileo put it, what God knows. In retrospect, we see in this the birth of the scientific worldview, one of the most important intellectual landmarks in all of human history. Humankind, in the cold light of science no longer at the center of the universe and no longer confident in the divinely ordained benevolence of nature, from now on had to take responsibility for its own destiny. And, it was believed by the scientific avant-garde with increasing confidence, it was perfectly capable of doing so. Clerics, with their mealy-mouthed appeals to divine providence as the chief source of human welfare, should stick to their knitting — theology and moral philosophy — and let science get on with unraveling the mysteries of the universe and putting that knowledge to work on behalf of progress in the struggle against nature.

According to the new worldview, only what was physically tangible, weighable, and measurable had real existence. God, through most of recorded history the object and the illumination of all philosophical inquiry, was for the Rationalist thinkers, of whom Hobbes and Galileo and Descartes were among the prototypes, merely a benign clockmaker, reduced to passively watching His invention run through its endless routines. Living creatures were nothing but complex machines that operated according to mechanical principles — the lone exception being humans, whom God had accessorized with a soul, the "ghost in the machine." The once universal notion that people had been made in the image of God, and were kin to the angels, was replaced by mechanical metaphors that described humanity in terms of the latest and most advanced technologies, from the mechanical clock to the steam engine.

The disengagement of science from religion and the divine, while liberating in one sense, had a darker side. With the excitement of new understanding came a growing existential anxiety. For the first time in history, philosopher-scientists began to question the assumption that nature provided in ample measure everything humans needed for a comfortable life, and that the only problem for human society to resolve was the fair and equitable distribution of that God-given bounty. For these new thinkers, the workings of natural systems could no longer be taken for granted in their beneficial outcomes. No longer could we assume, as Aristotle had, that there was purpose in nature's

workings, and that purpose was the achievement of Good —
that Good was the engine that made the universe run. For Aristotle, all natural motion, which included all growth and decay,
was movement in the direction of Good, in the direction of the
ultimate fulfillment of things.

Rationalist thinkers for the first time began to worry about
previously undreamed-of terrors such as overpopulation, the earliest references cropping up in Thomas Moore's 1516 *Utopia*,
Francis Bacon's 1597 *Essays*, and from Hobbes himself, in *Leviathan*. Nature was coming to be seen in an entirely new way, not
as God's bountiful gift to humanity but as a potentially endan-
gering environment that needed, urgently, to be understood and
then conquered, as one might conquer and then administer a
subject people. Life was seen, increasingly, in terms of a struggle
for existence in which science was an indispensable ally. At the
same time, there was enormous confidence that nature *could*
be managed, if only rational thought were liberated and given
free rein.[1] Alexander Pope's famous epitaph to Newton, who
was born in the year of Galileo's death, captures the optimistic
aspect of the times in verse: "Nature and nature's laws lay hid in
night: / God said, Let Newton be! and all was light."[2]

These two factors, the loss of faith in the beneficence of nature and the new confidence in our ability to understand and ma-
nipulate nature, led naturally to the idea that the powers of
science and reason, once applied to the problems of human society, could produce results every bit as dramatic as those demonstrated in the physical sciences by the likes of Galileo and
Newton. Thinkers turned their attention to the workings of the
economy, a topic of some urgency in a world in which nature
could no longer be counted on to provide for human needs without careful human management.

But early economic theorists had a problem. They found

themselves confronted with a series of rules and principles that had governed economic life in Europe throughout the Middle Ages and that were still operative in their own times. These precepts seemed clearly to be in urgent need of a thorough Rationalist overhaul to bring them more into line with the realities of emergent capitalism, itself a beacon of the potential of Rational order to serve human interests. R. H. Tawney, in his classic *Religion and the Rise of Capitalism,* has summed up those ancient principles this way:

> Their fundamental assumptions . . . were two: that economic interests are subordinate to the real business of life, which is salvation, and that economic conduct is one aspect of personal conduct upon which, as on other parts of it, the rules of morality are binding. Material riches are necessary; they have a secondary importance, since without them men cannot support themselves and help one another. . . . But economic motives are suspect. Because they are powerful appetites, men fear them, but they are not mean enough to applaud them. Like other strong passions, what they need, it is thought, is not a clear field, but repression. There is no place in medieval theory for economic activity which is not related to moral end, and to found a science of society upon the assumption that the appetite for economic gain is a constant and measurable force, to be accepted, like other natural forces, as an inevitable and self-evident *datum,* would have appeared to the medieval thinker as hardly less irrational or less immoral than to make the premise of social philosophy the unrestrained operation of such necessary human attributes as pugnacity or the sexual instinct.[3]

A central moral problem of capitalism — perhaps *the* central problem — was thus succinctly stated by Saint Paul in his warning that "the love of money is the root of all evil." (1 Timothy 6:10). This negative view of avarice is one of the central pillars of the Judeo-Christian tradition on which Western medieval civilization was constructed. At the same time, the love of money and pursuit of material wealth were suspected by the Rationalists to be the indispensable, scientifically validated motivating forces that fuel the great engine of the capitalist market economy.

This disturbing moral paradox of emergent modern capitalist economies was laid bare in a provocative way by Bernard Mandeville, a Dutch physician who had settled in London in the late seventeenth century. His *Fable of the Bees*, a potboiler first published in 1705, typified the Rationalist thinker's unflinching commitment to look at things as they really are, rather than as they ought to be. It stirred up a storm of condemnation, but was nevertheless widely influential. At over 400 lines, it is too long to reproduce here, but it begins:

> A spacious hive well stocked with bees,
> That lived in luxury and ease;
> And yet as famed for laws and arms,
> As yielding large and early swarms;
> Was counted the great nursery
> Of sciences and industry . . .
> These insects lived like men, and all
> Our actions they performed in small:
> They did whatever's done in town,
> And what belongs to sword, or gown:
> Though the artful works, by nimble slight;
> Of minute limbs, escaped human sight
> Yet we've no engines; laborers,
> Ships, castles, arms, artificers,
> Craft, science, shop, or instrument,
> But they had an equivalent.

It was the vice, and the satisfaction of its demands, that made their economy flourish:

> The root of evil, Avarice,
> That damned ill-natured baneful vice,
> Was slave to Prodigality.

That noble sin; whilst Luxury
Employed a million of the poor,
And odious Pride a million more:
Envy itself, and Vanity,
Were ministers of industry;
Their darling folly, Fickleness
In diet, furniture, and dress
That strange ridiculous vice, was made
The very wheel that turned the trade . . .


Such were the blessings of that state;
Their crimes conspired to make 'em great;
And virtue, which from politics
Had learned a thousand cunning tricks,
Was, by their happy influence,
Made friends with vice: And ever since
The worst of all the multitude
Did something for the common good.


Mandeville's thesis was that virtue is nothing but hypocrisy, a fiction introduced by rulers and philosophers of old as a propaganda tool for simplifying governance. In fact, said Mandeville, virtue is actually detrimental to the causes of commercial and intellectual progress, for it is the vices — the selfish, greedy, lustful impulses of people — that lead to the circulation of the money and capital that support luxurious living, which in turn enriches society and encourages cultural and intellectual activity.

The absence of self-interest is the death of progress, says Mandeville, and in his *Fable* he sketches what happens when the hive is one day smitten with righteousness, "blest with content [contentment] and honesty." It falls into apathy and economic paralysis, and is quickly depopulated:


As Pride and Luxury decrease,
So by degrees [traders] leave the seas,
Not merchants now; but companies

Remove whole manufacturies.
All arts and crafts neglected lie;
Content the bane of industry,
Makes 'em admire their homely store,
And neither seek, nor covet more.

In a concluding commentary on his poem, Mandeville minces no words:

> After this I flatter myself to have demonstrated that neither the friendly qualities and affections that are natural to man, nor the real virtues he is capable of acquiring by reason and self-denial are the foundations of society; but that what we call evil in this world, moral as well as natural, is the grand principle that makes us sociable creatures, the solid basis, the life and support of all trades and employments without exception: That there we must look for the true origin of all arts and sciences, and that the moment evil ceases, the society must be spoiled if not totally dissolved.[4]

Mandeville's writing might easily be dismissed as flippant social satire: Samuel Johnson said that every young man of the time had a copy on his shelves, in the belief that it was a wicked book. But it was meant as serious commentary, and it had been deeply influenced by the work of another Dutchman who ranks among the most influential of the philosophers of the early modern era. His name is Baruch (Emmanuel) Spinoza and, together with Descartes and Galileo and Hobbes and other heavyweight thinkers of the day, he set Europe on the path of philosophical materialism and scientific Rationalism that has been the defining trait of Western civilization ever since. His system of metaphysics (really a kind of anti-metaphysics) has been called the most consummate in the history of philosophy. He was perhaps the ultimate mechanistic theorist, going further even than Descartes in his clockwork view of nature, in asserting that life was mere mechanism, and that everything we experience as mind is but a side effect, a spin-off, of mechanical action. All of nature, including human relations, was thus available for Rational disclosure and description in the same way as one could disassemble a machine and analyze the purpose of its components, and in this way gain a complete and definitive understanding of it.

There was of course no place in such a system for conventional notions of morality: "My view," Spinoza writes in his *Ethica* (1677), "is that nothing happens in nature which might be attributed to any defect in it." In other words, everything that happens in nature happens for a purpose and is necessary. That being the case, it is pointless to call some actions good and others evil. He defined Good simply — and in the view of many of his contemporaries, scandalously — as "that which we certainly know to be useful to us." For Spinoza, once the nature of human passions were completely understood, social relationships would be no more mysterious than the motions of the planets.

Thus the proper philosophical attitude to so-called human vices is not to criticize them, said Spinoza, but to discover their purpose. And fundamental to that purpose, he believed, was the politicizing of humankind for the purpose of putting vice-driven behavior — "passionate" behavior, he called it — to good social use. This was achieved by a very mechanical cause-and-effect linkage between the passions of self-preservation and everyday vices of self-interest. "How it can happen that men who are necessarily subject to passions, inconstant and changeable, should be able to [bring about] each other's safety and form a community, is clear . . . everyone refrains from inflicting injury through fear of receiving greater injury himself. . . . This is the law according to which a society will be established."

A hundred years after Spinoza and seventy years after Mandeville, Adam Smith, the father of modern economics, would write in *Wealth of Nations* (1776) of the wondrous mechanical processes of the capitalist market: "Without any intervention of law, therefore, the private interests and passions [i.e., self-interest and vice] of men naturally lead them to divide and distribute the stock of every society, among all the different employments carried on in it, as nearly as possible in the proportion which is most agreeable to the interest of the whole society."

What had been rejected in Spinoza by contemporaries as the scurrilous railings of an atheist and in Mandeville the scribblings of a vulgar satirist had become the solid orthodoxy of economics, the newest and most influential of the sciences of society. What had happened to evil? What became of immorality? They were reprocessed into virtue by the machinery of the market. Private avarice is converted through the market's automatic processes to public good. A vice on one side of the looking glass, it becomes a virtue — more than that, a social *necessity* — on the other.

The great moral paradox of capitalism had been conjured out of existence. And a space had been cleared in the deep forests of moral thought in which the modern corporation could hatch and flourish.

# 3

# Machine-Made Morality

A MERE CENTURY AFTER THE TÊTE-À-TÊTE between Galileo and Hobbes in Arcetri, Western philosophers and scientists would be claiming to have cracked the code to understanding human nature itself and to have divined the underlying imperatives of human social institutions. "It is our happiness," wrote one Victorian anthropologist, "to live in one of those eventful periods of intellectual and moral history when the fast-closed gates of discovery and reform stand open at their widest."

The impact of Rationalist thought on the theory of how social institutions ought to be organized was nowhere more strikingly exemplified than in the writings of French philosopher and socialist Henri Saint-Simon (1769–1825). A new world order was dawning, Saint-Simon confidently stated, in which society would be governed with unprecedented efficiency by scientific principles based on the natural order of things and therefore absolutely independent of human will. Politics, with all its inconsistencies and contradictions, would be replaced by scientifically engineered institutions as the "grand device for transforming human irrationalities into rational behavior."

Auguste Comte (1798–1857), pioneering sociologist and friend and ally of Utilitarian philosopher John Stuart Mill, also famously believed that social interaction must be governed by invariable natural laws. He called his sociology "social physics."

This Rationalist revolution was well established in the human sciences by the time Charles Darwin's watershed theory of evolution was published in his *Origin of Species* in 1859, near the middle of Queen Victoria's long reign. He had combined the now-fashionable idea of life as a struggle for existence with earlier notions of evolution, his own grandfather's among them, to produce a mechanism for the development and branching of species that was completely convincing to scientists.

The mechanistic worldview that characterized the scientific revolution would henceforth be reinterpreted in terms of interlocking *biological* processes rather than the meshing of cogs, gears, and cams, as it had been imagined in Descartes, Spinoza, and Hobbes. But the one was no less *deterministic* than the other. In both cases, nature operated with a blind, methodical inexorability that was ultimately explainable in mathematical algorithms.[1] If one knew enough about the machine and its initial state, one could predict future outcomes: Galileo's vision of a definitive knowledge of nature within the grasp of human reason, through science, seemed closer than ever to realization.

The Utilitarian philosopher James Mill (1773–1836) made a bold foray into human psychology, attempting to analyze all experience in terms of primary "sense atoms" that interacted according to fundamental physical laws. Affection, aesthetic feelings, "moral sentiment," and belief were all described by Mill as compound atomistic states that could ultimately be resolved into measurable units of pleasure and pain. Mind, the unobservable enigma, was reduced to behavior, which could be observed by all. Mind did not cause behavior — the reverse was true. In this, he was in agreement with Spinoza: mind was a kind of epiphenomenon — an interesting but ephemeral and ultimately irrelevant spin-off — produced by physical actions, which were determined by physical circumstances. Mind was the motion picture by which we experience our lives, which are determined in reality by immutable physical facts and circumstances.

Rationalism was by now morphing into Behaviorism, and out of such ideas would grow the Behaviorist theory of psychology initiated by the Russian Ivan Pavlov (1849–1936), who experimented with conditioned reflexes in animals. Reflexes — sneezing, scratching, responding to a doctor's diagnostic tap on the knee — are bodily actions that take place in the absence of conscious thought, that is, in a purely mechanical way. Behaviorists found them an exciting field of study because they were thought to represent, in pure form, the actual mechanism of human conduct. In a famous experiment, Pavlov was able to train a dog to salivate at the sound of a bell, by first associating the bell with food. On such slim evidence he extended his theories to cover all of human behavior, including language use.

Human psychology was in this way mechanized to the satisfaction of the Behaviorists. But before the social theorists of the era could account in scientific terms for the historical emergence of human *societies*, a problem would have to be solved. Darwinism and the idea of the "law of the jungle" had resurrected a long-standing and very difficult question in evolutionary garb: How did the collectivist social sense — community and civilization — arise out of the individual's single-minded, Darwinian struggle for survival? As allegedly machine-like creatures whose behavior is determined entirely by our physical makeup and environmental circumstances, how did we leap from savagery to civilization?

Here, Hobbes had already provided his famous answer, which he had detailed in his great work *Leviathan*. In it he had pictured the origins of human society in a primitive world so harsh, dangerous, and bestial that people had come together out of fear and desperation in a social contract that placed their governance in the hands of an absolute despot. They traded individual liberty for collective peace and security.

But for the "enlightened" nineteenth century, this was far too abstract an idea — what was needed was something more soundly based on nature, its systems and rules of operation.

The widely accepted answer was found in a combination of Behaviorism and evolutionary theory: social behavior was said to be the result of generation after generation of conditioning by reward and punishment, of behavior that favored cooperation within the group. Who survives and who succumbs in the great Darwinian struggle was determined not simply by particular physical traits of the individual, but also by the "fitness" of the community, its ability to collectively cope with its environment. That, in turn, was to be measured by the community's ability to control its members, to exercise what was called a "salutary discipline." This amounted to a more scientific expression of Hobbes's philosophical wool-gathering about the beginnings of society as a wary coming together of frightened individuals in search of security and safety.

Remembering that this notion of social beginnings was being promulgated in the age of worldwide European imperialism, it is easy to account for its popularity among social and intellectual elites. Implicit in it was a moral justification for colonialism, among other profitable injustices of the time. The Europeans were obviously, in this interpretation of evolutionary theory, racially and morally superior to those groups they had subjugated — the evidence of this was provided by the fact of the subjugation. The circularity, and essential emptiness, of this reasoning (subjugation might be, and in fact was, a result of factors other than race and moral fiber) was typical of the Behaviorists' attempts to jam the round pegs of complex psychological and sociological phenomena into the square holes of cause-and-effect interactions among perceived "laws" of nature.

Early social scientists of the late eighteenth and early nineteenth centuries, while increasingly interested in research for its own sake, saw their primary role in terms of social engineering, constructing scientifically based rational institutions for the management of human affairs. These institutions, particularly economic institutions, were to be designed to complement Darwinist evolutionary imperatives by reinforcing the kind of "salutary discipline" within communities that enabled them to prosper. Where common sense might envisage social institutions as the bottom-up, organic product of evolving communal convention and rite, based perhaps on innate moral consciousness and logically beginning with the family, Behaviorist thinkers thought of them as top-down social *technologies* — tools consciously designed for the furtherance of human welfare, even human evolution. Human imagination, coupled with the unlimited powers of reason, could and should devise technologies that would complement natural law by rationalizing — correcting "errors" and inefficiencies in — the evolutionary process. Behaviorist social engineering was reason compensating for perceived inadequacies in nature.

In this time of rapid industrialization with its accompanying dislocation and misery, it is only to be expected that the Behaviorist ideology would be recruited as a justifying rationale for the economic policies that were creating such social havoc. The "salutary discipline" that was the evolutionary salvation of Hobbes's nervous savages was reimagined as the *work ethic*, which sought to counteract two irritating realities about humans — their natural inclination to be content with what they saw as sufficient wealth, and their preference for activities other than work.

John Stuart Mill, a leading Utilitarian thinker and social engineer of the nineteenth century, complained that, in the absence of the coercion of rationally organized social institutions, most people will attempt to avoid work beyond what is necessary to support tolerable material comfort. "We look in vain among the working classes in general for the just pride which will choose to give good work for good wages; for the most part, the sole endeavor is to receive as much and return as little in the shape of service as possible." Why this should be seen as aberrant or in any way problematic behavior is a puzzle whose answer must be sought in the topsy-turvy moral world of market capitalism.

According to the work ethic, as first promulgated in the early industrial era, one must always give first, in order to receive. This was a moral as well as a practical axiom, and it denied the previously dominant Roman Catholic/humanist view that people are of value in themselves, that their worth is not dependent on their contribution. The work ethic asserted further that it was both wrong and wrongheaded to be satisfied with what one had. As long as there was the possibility of having more, one was morally obliged to do the work necessary to get it. This also contradicted not only Christian but earlier Classical and humanist presumptions that beyond some level of sufficiency and comfort, additional material wealth was a serious spiritual handicap.

"Work is the normal state of all humans; not working is abnormal," was the work ethic's presumption, and an important corollary was derived from that: "Most people fulfill their duty [to work], and it would be unfair to ask them to share their benefits or profits with others, who could also fulfill their duties but for one reason or another fail to do so." A further, very significant conclusion could be teased out of the logic of the work ethic, which was that "it is only such labor that has a value recognized by others — labor which commands salaries or wages, which can be sold and is likely to be bought — that has the moral value the work ethic commends."[2] Work, as it was understood in the work ethic, amounted to what we would call "the job," a new and for most, unwelcome entity in the world. It was not work itself that was being endorsed and encouraged (and resisted), but work on behalf of capital: wage labor.

The so-called salutary discipline imposed on workers by the industrial regime — the harsh regimen of factory toil — was in this way endowed with ethical content: workers who submitted to it, either willingly, or, more frequently, through coercion, were "bettering" themselves. Those who did not were behaving immorally. To ensure that the majority of the potential factory labor pool made the "right" choices, Poor Laws in Britain were revised in 1834 on the advice of Utilitarian theorists and laissez-faire liberal economists to make certain that the unemployed were no longer able to live in the modicum of dignity previously afforded by relief payments. It was necessary that conditions of life for the unemployed be both physically and emotionally intolerable. That was the stick. The Factory Act passed a year earlier at Westminster had limited the hours of work for children aged nine to thirteen in textile factories to nine hours a day, and for children from fourteen to eighteen to twelve hours a day. A decade later, further reforms limited the factory work week for children under eighteen to sixty-nine hours. That was the carrot.

Of all the new sciences of people and society, it was economics that made the most rapid progress in reducing the complexities of the real world to the kinds of mechanical, arithmetical relationships so admired by the Rationalists. Economists to this day tend to model the market economy as a cybernetic system — a set of mechanical relationships automatically regulated through information feedback in the way a thermostat regulates the temperature in a room, or a steam engine governs its own speed.

An early and instructive illustration of this kind of thinking predates the modern science of cybernetics by nearly a century and a half. It is David Ricardo's "iron law of wages" (1820), an excellent example of a tightly reasoned rationalization of the subsistence wage levels that kept the average worker and his family in a state of precarious near-starvation. Ricardo argued that labor was doomed to living on the brink of destitution due to a long chain of mechanical relationships that ensured that capitalists must reap profits if there is to be progress; landlords get rich no matter what; and the worker is doomed to life at the margin.

As Ricardo said, "The natural price of labor is that price which is necessary to enable the laborers, one with another, to subsist and perpetuate their race, without either increase or diminution." Though there might be periodic fluctuations, brief periods of plenty, the iron law of wages would remorselessly push workers back down to bare subsistence. Despite this endemic misery, Ricardo concluded with the quintessentially Rationalist observation, "These, then, are the laws by which wages are regulated, and by which the happiness of far the greatest part of every community is governed. Like all other contracts, wages should be left to the fair and free competition of the market, and should never be controlled by the interference of the legislature."

Ricardo, as we know him from his biographers, was anything but a misanthrope. The harshness of his theories he saw as realism, a clear-eyed look at the way things have to be. He was in this deeply influenced by his friend Rev. Thomas Malthus, who famously argued that, since population expands faster than agricultural land can be developed (the one growing exponentially, the other arithmetically), humans are doomed to live on the edge of starvation unless stern limits on reproduction are put in place. He concluded that such limits are fortuitously imposed by the automatic feedback relationships of the market. Left to itself, in other words, the wretchedness of poverty would limit population growth through relatively high death rates. (And it was Malthus's idea of food scarcity and its effects that inspired Darwin to see the struggle for survival in a world of limited resources as the key to evolutionary theory.) All of this gloom and doom prompted the essayist Thomas Carlyle to dub economists "respectable professors of the dismal science."[3]

In the same mechanistic vein, Jean Baptiste Say proposed a Law of Markets (c. 1830), which holds that an economy always provides sufficient demand to purchase its own output (significantly, regardless of whether workers are paid a fair wage). Revenue produced by production would either be spent, or it would be saved and used for investment, in which case it would also be spent. There could never be any shortage of purchasing power. The obvious implication, once again, was that legislative interference in the market was unnecessary and counterproductive. Say's Law represented consensus opinion in economic theory for more than a century, well into the Great Depression of the 1930s, at which time it was discovered to have absolutely no relationship to the real world.[4]

Within this system of so-called natural law lay the intellectual, political, and moral justification for the laissez-faire market system, an allegedly self-regulating miracle of economic efficiency. For the later Rationalists of the Victorian era, celebrated "laws" of social and economic behavior more often than not were merely rationalizations contrived, consciously or otherwise, to defend the existence of current social conventions and power relationships. This ensured that the formal social structures built up around the laws were invariably supportive of the prevailing power structures in society.

The process had a self-reinforcing circularity that could be found even in so scientifically authoritative a theory as Darwinian evolution. Biologist Richard Lewontin says that "what Darwin did was take early nineteenth-century *political* economy and expand it to include all of *natural* economy," so that his theory of evolution bore "an uncanny resemblance to the political economic theory of early capitalism." Moreover, its theory of sexual selection was remarkably similar to the gender relations in Victorian society, where "the chief force is competition among males to be more appealing to discriminating females."[5] In this recursive system, Darwinian "law" as perceived (through Victorian eyes) in nature was then read back into social institutions as a way of analyzing them and as guidance for social policy. This produced the so-called social Darwinism that lent scientific credibility to the moral credo of the work ethic and extended the Rationalist policy prescriptions of Ricardo and Malthus well into the twentieth century and beyond, to the neoliberal revival of today (often misidentified as neoconservativism). The whole complex system was a tissue of circular argument existing, as it were, in thin air, with little or no tangible connection to the real world.

By the nineteenth century Rationalism had transformed itself from a philosophy into an ideology, from a method of inquiry to a political doctrine resting on a foundation of rhetoric. This is a particularly ironic turn of events, given that Rationalism started out in the 1600s as an uncompromisingly scientific way to uncover truth.

Yet as ideology, as a set of ideas about the relationships that humans can and should have with one another, it was inevitably concerned with the moral and ethical. It could be said that Rationalist undertakings in social engineering were motivated by the perception that machines were more efficient than humans in carrying out the essentially mechanical processes that, it was believed, lie at the heart of all properly organized social institutions — processes such as those involved in reaching and sustaining the delicate equilibria among market forces that are necessary to economic stability and health. There was a sense in which machines were much more rational than humans, in the predictability of their operations and their steadfast devotion to the single purpose for which they were designed. With the nineteenth century this notion attached itself to moral action as well as to other aspects of human endeavor: presumably, a machine-made morality could be similarly robust and reliable.

By cloaking itself in the authority of science, and in particular the language of Darwinism, economics, more than any of the other social sciences, was able to attribute a natural inevitability to the processes it described. In the face of that authority, those who reacted with ethical outrage at the devastating social effects of nineteenth-century industrial capitalism with its "dark satanic mills," child laborers, and squalid living conditions were seen to be both selfishly contemptuous of the wider social utility being served, and just plain ignorant.

Not much has changed: neoliberal ideologues of the twenty-first century react in much the same way to the kinds of concerns expressed in these pages.

# 4

# The "Science" of Selfishness

WHEN I WAS STUDYING ECONOMICS in the 1970s almost all the
available courses at my university were ones that looked into how
the market system worked, either at the macro or the micro level.
There were also one or two courses on why the market is organized as it is, how it came into being, that were offered as economic
history. These were very small classes. There were no courses on
whether the market *ought* to function the way it does. The un-
spoken assumption was that the market economy is a fact of life,
a force of nature, as immune to ethical challenge as gravity or in-
ertia. Much attention was paid to the mechanics of the creation
of wealth, but almost none to its just distribution. No reputable
economist taught about the impact of economic systems on those
who worked in them, or about effects of consumerism and mass
marketing: that was for sociologists, or for the nascent and scarcely
credible discipline of cultural studies. Economics had by then
thoroughly washed its hands of untidy, emotive questions of
morality, equity, and justice.

For a young, socially conscious man bent on doing something useful with his life, sociology or cultural studies did not
seem to be viable options. What could one do with such a degree?
I stuck it out in economics as long as I could, but faced with a
solid wall of required courses in statistics and econometrics, I

finally dropped out, in the fifth year of an honors program, and went to work for a newspaper.

I tell this story because it seemed then, as it seems now, deeply ironic that a so-called science that was founded by a moral philosopher who was interested in spreading ethical behavior throughout society by means of economic institutions should wind up being essentially hostile to moral questioning.

That founder, of course, is Adam Smith.

A story is told of the early childhood of Adam Smith (1723–90) that is breathtaking in its latent potential for history. When he was four years old, living with his widowed mother in the Scottish fishing village of Kirkcaldy near Edinburgh, Smith was abducted by a band of Gypsy tinkers. A pursuit was hastily mounted, and the young lad was abandoned by his captors, and returned to his mother. Smith's earliest biographer, a man of wry humor, was no doubt accurate when he commented, "He would have made, I fear, a poor gypsy." One cannot help but wonder, though, if Smith had taken up the violin and bandana rather than devising the framework for laissez-faire economics, how the world would have turned out.

Smith received a university education in moral philosophy at Glasgow and Oxford at a time when, strange though it may seem today, the discipline encompassed not only ethics and the fundamentals of religion, but also law and political economy. He came to see economics and ethics as being so closely related as to be inseparable, and he published important works in both fields. The first of these was *The Theory of Moral Sentiments*, which he wrote while teaching moral philosophy at Glasgow University. In it he outlines the principles of "human nature," which, in keeping with the thinking of his time, he took to be elements of natural law. From these principles human behavior and the workings of social institutions could be deduced, as the trajectory of a missile can be predicted from physical data.

A central question the book addresses concerns the origins of moral behavior: given what science said was the overarching power of the instinctual drives of self-interest and self-preservation, how is it possible for people to make moral judgments on their own actions and those of others? Why should this be a concern? Smith's eventual answer is that each of us has within us an observer (today we would call it the superego) who acts as an "impartial spectator," observing and judging, and communicating through an inner voice that could not be ignored. Less than entirely satisfying as a solution, Smith's hypothesis would be disregarded by later Rationalist and Behaviorist thinkers, who preferred to ignore the question altogether as "metaphysical" and therefore nonsensical.

Nevertheless, Smith's perception of the dual nature of people, their compelling, instinctual passions on the one hand and their ability to reason and to feel sympathy, on the other, would provide the cornerstone of his later economic thought. The drives of passion were regulated and harnessed for good largely through social institutions that served to channel aggressive, combative, competitive "natural" instincts into socially beneficial outcomes. (The similarities to Mandeville's much more primitive *Fable of the Bees*, though indignantly denied by Smith, are impossible to ignore.) As he said, and would repeat in his great work on economics, self-interested people are "led by an invisible hand . . . without knowing it, without intending it, [to] advance the interest of the society."

Like Hobbes before him, Smith became the beneficiary of the enlightened sponsorship of an aristocratic family, whose scion he was hired to tutor and with whom he journeyed to the continent for the mandatory Grand Tour. He was already acquainted with many of the prominent figures of the time on his side of the English Channel — chemist Joseph Black, James Watt of steam engine fame, businessman and merchant trader Andrew Cochrane, and the great philosopher David Hume, and he would later establish friendships with political philosopher Edmund Burke, essayist Samuel Johnson, and historian Edward Gibbon. It is thought that he was also an acquaintance of Benjamin Franklin.

On the continent Smith was to meet many of the leading lights of the so-called Age of Reason, or the French Enlightenment. In Geneva he conversed with Voltaire, and in Paris he mingled with a group of social reformers and theoreticians who called themselves *les économistes*, and who are known to us as the physiocrats. The group's leader was François Quesnay, court physician to Louis XV, who is credited with writing the first systematic analysis of an entire economy. Steeped in the contemporary theories of natural law and natural justice (the term *physiocracy* means the rule of nature), Quesnay and the physiocrats also believed in a natural economic order and were violently opposed to regulation, inappropriate taxation, and other forms of interference. Their famous watchword was *"laissez faire, laissez passer."* They proposed the elimination of all taxes except an *impôt unique* on the net income from land, which they regarded as the true source of all wealth. The precise extent of the physiocrats' influence on Smith's own economic thinking is controversial, but it is known that he was a sincere admirer of Quesnay, to whom he had intended to dedicate his own economic opus prior to the doctor's death.

Smith's monumental *Inquiry into the Nature and Causes of the Wealth of Nations*, completed on his return from France and published in the year of the American Revolution (1776), was devoted primarily to demonstrating how self-interest can produce social welfare through the "institutional direction of passions." As had his earlier book, it argued that social institutions channel human vice toward socially beneficent results. Both books assume, without much thought given to anthropological or historical evidence (which was in any case scanty), that social and economic relationships, as they were presumed to exist in their pure, natural state, are natural phenomena. As such, it followed that these relationships function best when left alone. Government interference in economic institutions in the pursuit of public good is therefore misguided and likely to be self-defeating.

In its influence on individual entrepreneurs, market capitalism with its rich competition was presumed by Smith to strongly discourage unethical or otherwise antisocial behavior while at the same time reinforcing the "propriety" necessary for orderly commerce. In highlighting competition as the crucial institutional mechanism, Smith writes: "The real and effectual discipline which is exercised over a workman . . . is that of his customers. It is the fear of losing their employment [to competitors] which restrains his frauds and corrects his negligence."[1]

Much of *Wealth of Nations* is devoted to describing in detail how the "invisible hand" operates. Mutual competition among innately self-interested people, who are instinctively driven to barter and trade, constantly forces the prices of commodities down to their "natural" level, which is determined by the cost of production. Smith explained how wages and rents and profits, which are all costs of production, are each in their turn subject to competition, and therefore held to their "natural" levels.

Smith was anxious to explain how economic growth could occur within this self-regulating mechanism, and his explanation is both ingenious and dangerously in error. When manufacturers who have accumulated capital wish to expand production, they hire on new workers. (Smith was writing just prior to the looming Industrial Revolution.) When they do this they bid up wages, according to the law that says that increased demand for an existing supply means higher prices. All things being equal, the higher wages ought to spell disaster for the manufacturers (higher costs make them less competitive), but there is a loophole. Higher wages for workers increase their numbers (mainly, Smith presumed, through decreases in infant mortality) and with more workers bidding against each other for jobs, wages fall. Profits and capital accumulation increase and the cycle can repeat itself. In this way, the economy could notch its way up, step by step, to a level where even those at the bottom of the economic ladder could be made relatively prosperous.

Smith's analysis depicted a smoothly running, self-regulating machine perfectly attuned to the mechanistic, deterministic mindset of his age. It also incorporated an idea his era had invented — progress. This was defined as a steady improvement in material living standards through the conquest of nature, without, however, much thought being given to ultimate goals or to defining "improvement," or even to establishing what is meant by standards of living.

While Smith, the economist, is universally granted his proper place in the pantheon of modern social thinkers, his moral philosophy has been sadly neglected. As both an economist and a teacher of natural theology working at the heart of what has been called "the Scottish Enlightenment" in Edinburgh, Smith was infused with a belief in the divine order of nature on the one hand, and in the supreme power of Reason on the other.[2] Combined, these led him, and other thinkers and policymakers of his era, to en-

gage in what seemed to be the chief challenge facing the educated classes: to find ways to use the natural order of things to
bring about a better, more Eden-like world.

His theories constitute nothing less than the genesis of an
ambitious program for the synthesizing of moral behavior, for the
supplanting of innate moral sense — unreliable, if not wholly
fictitious in the Rationalist view — with self-sustaining, self-
regulating processes within institutions.

Ironically, and despite his undoubted good intentions in describing what he believed was an automated, naturally occurring
system for producing moral outcomes, Smith set the stage for the
eventual marginalizing of authentic moral discourse, making
ethics a matter for our "private" lives only.[3] In public life, morality was institutionally managed. In a practical sense, this would
eventually mean that actions taken within these institutions
were morally neutered, in that each action was merely one in a
long chain of causality leading to distant, rational objectives. Bad
outcomes were "operational errors" — unintended side effects
that were nobody's fault — rather than ethical failures. Morality
was reduced to rules of procedure, which in the economic context were measured according to standards, not of right and wrong,
but of efficiency.

Revolutionary though his ideas may seem, Smith was in some
respects a dinosaur in the environment of intellectual ferment
and experimentation in which he lived and worked. His piety
and his acknowledgment of some residual altruism in people
(the "impartial spectator" within each of us, capable of some
semblance of objective moral reaction) was out of step with the
more ideologically flamboyant and outspoken Rationalist thinkers,
notably the Utilitarian philosophers, all of whom moonlighted as
economists. According to Utilitarian theorist and jurist Jeremy

Bentham (1743–1832), "human beings . . . are deficient in altruism and therefore require the threat of coercion to encourage them to seek majority interests rather than their own." Bentham and the Utilitarians set about rewriting British penal law within that vision (the pain of imprisonment ought to outweigh the pleasure gained from the crime); David Ricardo (1772–1823) and John Stuart Mill (1806–73) buttressed Smith's economic science with up-to-date Utilitarian ideas, establishing the pursuit of pleasure and avoidance of pain as the principal economic motivators.

Where Smith had posited a more or less traditional view of humans as morally sensitive, though in need of institutional encouragement, the Utilitarians tended to the increasingly dominant view of people as essentially self-serving creatures. What people wanted most, Utilitarians asserted, was pleasure, and what they most wished to avoid was pain, and life was mainly a process of achieving and maintaining as favorable a balance between the two as circumstances allowed. If moral sense was not innate, no matter: the wonderful human capacity for reason could supply a substitute in the form of a complex scheme of reckoning that worked more or less like arithmetic.

According to Utilitarian ethics, that action is Good — morally correct — which creates the greatest balance of pleasure over pain for the greatest number. In other words, Utilitarian morality defined itself exclusively in terms of observable outcomes, regardless of the means used to reach those ends, or of motive or intention. (Indeed, Rationalists tend to argue that humans are incapable of genuinely altruistic or selfless motivation, and engage in what we call "moral" acts only to further their own ends.) Serious efforts were made by the Utilitarians to list various pleasures in ranking order, and even to assign numerical values to them, so that ethical quandaries might be solved by math.

The twentieth-century British philosopher Bertrand Russell succinctly captured the essential emptiness of Utilitarianism as moral philosophy. He notes that philosopher and economist John Stuart Mill, in his classic *Utilitarianism* (1861), "offers an argument which is so fallacious that it is hard to understand how he can have thought it valid." Russell had in mind Mill's assertion that pleasure is ultimately the only thing desirable and that all other desires are subordinate to it, in that they all relate to gaining pleasure in one way or another. Russell parses Mill's argument this way: "He says: *Pleasure is the only thing desired: therefore pleasure is the only thing desirable.* He argues that the only things visible are things seen, the only things audible are things heard, and similarly the only things desirable are things desired. He does not notice that a thing is 'visible' if it *can* be seen, but 'desirable' if it *ought* to be desired. Thus desirable is a word presupposing an ethical theory; we cannot infer what is desirable from what is desired." Russell goes on to point to another major problem in Mill's argument: "If each man in fact and inevitably pursues his own pleasure, there is no point in saying he *ought* to do something else. Kant urged that 'you ought' implies 'you can'; conversely, if you cannot, it is futile to say that you ought."[4]

Despite its manifold inadequacies as both science and philosophy, Utilitarianism, a pinnacle of progressive Rationalist thinking, was one of the foundations on which the stately edifices of political liberalism and laissez-faire market capitalism were erected in the nineteenth century.[5] The great liberal economist William Stanley Jevons (1835–82) defined economics as "the mechanics of utility and self-interest," adding that "to satisfy our wants to the utmost with the least effort — to procure the greatest amount of what is desirable at the expense of the least that is undesirable — in other words, to maximize pleasure, is the problem of economics."[6]

Jevons was truly a man of his times. He was born into a family of wealthy iron merchants in Liverpool, where his father had been a pioneer in the construction of iron-hulled ships. The young Jevons shared his father's interest in engineering and the physical sciences, studying chemistry and mathematics at the Liverpool Mechanics Institute. For five years he served as chief assayer to the newly established Australian mint, then returned to London to continue university studies in higher mathematics and economics. He was a fervent believer in free markets, and opposed compassionate welfare reforms: "A poor law must be harsh and niggardly if it is not to undermine the sources of our welfare," he said.[7]

He opposed unions, in which "workers [are] led by ignorance to arrest the true growth of our liberty," that is, the laissez-faire market. The solution to the problem of organized labor, he said, was to begin educating working-class children at an early age to "impress upon them the simple truths" of the laws of economics, "which they cannot escape from, and must ultimately obey. They must learn that there are natural laws which they cannot break." Those laws, he believed, were part of the divine order of nature, just as were the laws of physics or chemistry. "Just as in Physical Science there are general and profound principles deducible from a great number of apparent phenomena, so in treating of Man or Society there must also be general principles and laws which underlie all the present discussions and partial arguments."

As an economist, Jevons wrote, he wished to aid in the reform of abstract social science, making it as disciplined as physics, but at the same time, he said, "I would join science to morals and religion. I would try to show that they are not antagonistic." God's moral law, in Jevon's mind, was written in the laws of nature that governed human social behavior, primarily through the market economy. He thought of his own mind as "a machine." Following Bentham and the Utilitarians, he said, "I regard man in reality as essentially selfish, that is, as doing everything with a view to gain enjoyment or avoid pain. This self-interest is certainly the main-spring of all his actions."

In seeking to put economics on a thoroughly mathematical footing based on the kinds of "ideal" assumptions routinely made by the so-called hard sciences, he theorized a market of perfect competition, perfect knowledge, and perfect selfishness, analogous to the frictionless world of idealized physics. The approach became the gold standard, and spawned the modern science of economics.

If Jevons is remembered for a single contribution, though, it is the concept of marginal utility, which linked Utilitarianism directly to market prices through an ingenious formula, and in so doing significantly expanded and deepened the impact of Utilitarian thought on social institutions. In an idealized market of one buyer and one seller, as people acquire units of any commodity or service (say, sandwiches) each new acquisition will have less subjective value than the one before (less marginal utility). Demand for the product or service will thus be reduced, and that will force the price down, until the point is reached when the consumer has so much of the commodity or service that a further unit will cause no added happiness. At that point, the price will have fallen to zero, because demand has evaporated. "Value," Jevons asserted, "depends entirely upon utility." (Readers may see here a problem similar to the one pointed out by Russell with respect to Jeremy Bentham's ideas: the fact that something is demanded has nothing necessarily to do with whether it is worthy of being demanded. That is another question, and it goes directly to deeper issues of human welfare. It is an issue to which I will return.)

\*     \*     \*

But Utilitarianism is not the only ethical philosophy at work in modern market capitalism. Lurking deep in the system's theoretical structure as conceived by Smith, Jevons, and their successors is a more primitive premise called ethical egoism. It is the basis for Jevons's idealized assumption of perfect selfishness in economic actors, and a foundational assumption of Utilitarian thought.

Ethical egoism is based on a psychological theory called *psychological egoism*, which proposes that people are genetically disposed *always* to seek their own welfare, or, in Utilitarian terms, *always* to choose the course of action that will provide them with the greatest personal balance of pleasure over pain. The theory of psychological egoism is of course incompatible with the concept of an innate moral impulse, and that was doubtless part of its attraction for Rationalist social engineers. It is a notion that seemed, to its advocates, to find powerful validation in the Darwinist idea of survival of the fittest, the suggestion being that those individuals within a species who succeed in getting what they want are more likely to survive and to procreate. In a world of psychological egoism, the meek inherit nothing, and have no descendants.

The baseline assertion of psychological egoism, then, is that all human action must ultimately be explained in terms of concern for personal welfare — selfishness. The physicist and mathematician John von Neumann, a father of the atomic bomb and creator of a theory of automata (robots) that has been enormously influential in modern economic theory, asserted, without feeling any need to provide supporting evidence, "[It] is just as foolish to complain that people are selfish as it is to complain that the magnetic field does not increase unless the electric field has a curl. Both are laws of nature."[8]

But does this make sense? What about the case of the weary office worker who gives up his seat on the subway to a pregnant woman? Or the torture victim who refuses to betray her comrades? Or the doctor who forgoes wealth and comfort to serve the destitute in some far-off land? Or the activist who risks imprisonment to campaign for justice? Or any number of other cases that might be cited as examples of altruistic, or other-directed, behavior?

The Behaviorist's response is likely to be that in each case, there must be a sense in which the individual actually wants to perform the action more than not, or else he wouldn't do it. The torture victim, for example, wants to protect her comrades more than she wants the pain to stop. But this response shifts the grounds of the argument in a significant way, from making a claim about what *is*, to what *must be* the case. It is no longer a claim about nature, but a claim about necessity — the action *must* flow from the desire or it will not be performed. Thus, the critique assumes its own truth in defending its truth: "We know that psychological egoism is the case because, if it were not, altruistic actions would be unexplainable." It is a circular argument and thus devoid of meaningful content.

In contriving to make moral philosophy out of "natural law," economic thinkers of the nineteenth century piled error upon error, in a tangled web we have yet to unravel. Psychological egoism's claim that we always act in our own self-interest is leveraged into a philosophical doctrine, *ethical egoism*, which rests on an assertion that people *ought* always to act in their own best interest. The reason why people ought always to behave egoistically is that, it is alleged, they *naturally* do — that in their "natural state" (whatever that may be) people behave selfishly unless forced to do otherwise. As we'll see in a moment, there is no credible evidence for this. Nevertheless ethical egoism makes the further claim that *all* people ought *always* to behave this way: the universalizing move is necessary to transform what would otherwise be a simple (if erroneous) observation into a moral theory.

This may seem a strange moral philosophy, one that must inevitably lead to a kind of Hobbesian hell in which everyone is constantly at war with everyone else.[9] Ethical egoism painted itself into a logical corner from which there was no obvious route of escape. How does a world of selfish people organize itself into societies and civilization? The question may have a familiar ring — it is the one asked by Adam Smith in his *Theory of Moral Sentiments*, and before him by Hobbes in *Leviathan*. The only conceivable solution for the Rationalist economist was some kind of mechanism that would miraculously synchronize the self-interest of each individual with that of his neighbors to ensure that no conflict arose — to ensure that it could never (or rarely) be the case that my satisfying my self-interest made it impossible for my neighbor to do the same.

What was needed was some alchemy that would ensure that, in pursuing their individual selfish ends, people were at the same time acting in the interest of general welfare. And Adam Smith had supplied it with his "invisible hand."

# 5

# Ethics and the Market

THE ASTRONOMER AND GEOGRAPHER OF SECOND-CENTURY EGYPT we know as Ptolemy was convinced that only perfection and order could be found in the heavens, and he contrived to find an explanation for the seemingly chaotic movements of the so-called wandering stars, or planets. He devised such an explanation (inventing trigonometry along the way), based, as he believed it had to be, on perfectly circular orbits. His calculations of the movements of the planets are still used by those few remaining mariners who find their position at sea not with GPS gadgets, but with sextant, clock, and ephemeris tables giving the positions of the planets according to date and time. Like all the best scientific theories, Ptolemy's was a system that was both explanatory and accurate in its predictions, and it lasted fourteen hundred years, until Copernicus came along with a better solution. But it was based on an erroneous assumption — that is, that the earth is stationary and orbited by the sun.

Adam Smith's "invisible hand" is a device that might have been conceived by Ptolemy. We find the magical automatic coordinating mechanism which makes selfish individual actions result in social Good fully realized in what is perhaps the most famous passage in his *Wealth of Nations*. Smith begins by observing that while in their natural state animals are independent and have little need of the help of other animals, the human being has almost constant occasion for the help of his brethren, and it is in vain for him to expect it from their benevolence only. He will be more likely to prevail if he can interest their self-love in his favor, and show them that it is for their own advantage to do for him what he requires of them. Whoever offers to another a bargain of any kind, proposes to do this. Give me that which I want, and you shall have this which you want, is the meaning of every such offer; and it is in this manner that we obtain from one another the far greater part of those good offices which we stand in need of. It is not from the benevolence of the butcher, the brewer, or the baker that we expect our dinner, but from their regard to their own interest. We address ourselves, not to their humanity but to their self-love, and never talk to them of our own necessities but of their advantages. Nobody but a beggar chooses to depend chiefly upon the benevolence of his fellow citizens.[1]

Smith continues, asserting that in transactions of the marketplace the individual

intends only his own gain, and he is *in this, as in many other cases, led by an invisible hand* to promote an end which was no part of his intention. Nor is it always the worse for the society that it was no part of it. By pursuing his own interest he frequently promotes that of the society more effectually than when he really intends to promote it.[2]

The notion of the synchronous workings of many individuals resulting in common welfare, as I've noted, gained credibility in the nineteenth century from its obvious affinity to Darwin's evolutionary theory. For Darwin, the progress of species was the result of randomly occurring mutations. Competition for food or other environmental pressures brought order out of this chaos of randomness by ensuring the "natural selection" of those mutations that provided an adaptive advantage. Those individuals inheriting the advantageous mutation would flourish, and eventually replace the less fit. The analogy with Smith's claim was an obvious one —

the environmental pressures that turned the chaos of primitive so-cial savagery into a benevolent economic process were contained in the institutions of the capitalist market economy, which auto-matically converted individual selfishness into general welfare.

Market theory, even today, amounts to a mechanization of the dynamics of ethical egoism and an elimination of the moral question of distributive justice — how wealth should be distrib-uted — through its complete absorption into a theory of natural, autonomous processes. It produces a *synthetic* morality, since be-havior determined in this way, by external influences or coer-cion, is not truly moral. The truly moral depends on the exercise of free choice, which in Smith's system is either restricted or pre-cluded altogether.

Throughout the history of economic theory, then, beginning with the writings of Adam Smith and right up to the present day, the "rational economic agent" — the individual in his or her inter-course with the market — is universally characterized as one whose only obligation is to procure the greatest possible balance of pleasure over pain.[3] This definition has been adopted by succes-sive generations of political economists, from Thomas Malthus, David Ricardo, and Stanley Jevons to the authors of today's text-books, for whom it has become simply an empirical description of "the economic way of thinking" supposedly native to each of us:

> It is, most fundamentally, an assumption about what guides human behavior. The theories of economics, with surprisingly few exceptions, are simply extensions of the assumption that individuals take those actions they think will yield them the largest net advantage. Everyone, it is assumed, acts in accor-dance with that rule.[4]

Another example, from the widely used McGraw-Hill text-book *Economics:*

GREED, INC.

> Capitalism presumes self-interest as the fundamental modus operandi for the various economic units as they express their free choices. The motive of self-interest gives direction and consistency to what might otherwise be an extremely chaotic economy.[5]

But a fundamental logical inconsistency is hidden here in what amounts to a statement of ideological dogma. While it assumes that it is (innate) self-interest that gives the market "direction and consistency," it is also quite possible that the converse is true — that it is the market that imposes the necessity of self-interest on individuals. And here we have the "Ptolemaic error" of Smith's system: it begins with the false premise of ethical egoism (Ptolemy's stationary Earth) and the assumption of a perfect order in nature (Ptolemy's circular orbits) and imposes on the economic intercourse of people an order that is not "natural" as claimed, but decidedly *un*natural.

Few social scientists have thought to challenge the by now commonsense "law" of psychological egoism as it relates to human economic behavior. But those who have, have discovered that it is a concept unsupported by the evidence. The political scientist C. B. Macpherson demonstrated in detail in his seminal book *The Political Theory of Possessive Individualism* that "it is only where capitalist relations of production prevail . . . that this is the necessary behavior of all men." In other words the behavior is generated by the system, rather than vice versa. People behave egoistically — they demand maximum income from minimum effort; they charge what the market will bear; they do not hesitate to gain advantage over their neighbors; they, in short, "look out for number one" — because that is the only way to survive within the institutional structure. In a market economy, it amounts to rational behavior.

The great economic historian Karl Polanyi has also written

54

that the notion of people's innate propensity to "truck, barter, and trade," in Adam Smith's phrase, and to always seek their own material advantage, is simply not justified by the historical record. In fact, he says, "Only in the nineteenth-century self-regulating market did economic self-interest become the dominant principle of social life," and then only because it was imposed upon people as the only way to survive in a market system. Polanyi is worth quoting at some length:

> Nineteenth-century thinkers assumed that in his economic activity man strove for profit, that his materialistic propensities would induce him to choose the lesser instead of the greater effort and to expect payment for his labor; in short that in his economic activity he would tend to abide by what they described as economic rationality, and that all contrary behavior was the result of outside interference. . . . Thus, nothing could be more normal than an economic system consisting of markets and under the sole control of market prices, and a human society based on such markets appeared, therefore, as the goal of all progress. Whatever the desirability or undesirability of such a society on moral grounds, its practicability — this was axiomatic — was grounded in the immutable characteristics of the race.

But historical and anthropological research conduced by Polanyi and his graduate students told another story:

> Actually, as we know, the behavior of man both in his primitive state and right through the course of history has been almost the opposite from that implied in this view. The tendency to barter, on which Adam Smith so confidently relied for his picture of primitive man, is not a common tendency of the human being in his economic activities, but a most infrequent one . . . [and] the market has been the outcome of a conscious and often violent intervention on the part of government which imposed the market organization on society for non-economic ends.[6]

Just to be clear, market capitalism is not a naturally occurring phenomenon, springing from certain features of "human nature." It is a human artifact, a deliberately and consciously constructed social system, like republicanism or parliamentary democracy or English jurisprudence or the public school system. Indeed (as I will suggest in the next chapter), if one *were* to design an economic system based on human nature it would have to take into account an innate concern for others that is at least as prominent a feature of our makeup as selfishness, and probably more profoundly emblematic.

Nor, it is worth noting, did the market economy arise out of the institutions of liberal democracy: it preceded them. It is a matter of historical record that liberal democratic society was erected in large measure as a means of protecting the power relationships already defined by the market.

While the assumption that economies must be organized around self-interest is open to serious challenge, few would want to argue with the Utilitarian principle that the purpose of an economic system is to provide the greatest happiness for the greatest number. But a moment's thought will show that this seemingly self-evident proposition raises a related problem. Which economic frameworks and policies best achieve the Utilitarian's optimally happy result? Do we make more people happy, more of the time, by concentrating on the private (and conflicting) happiness of the individual or by focusing on larger more inclusive social goals and programs? The second option can safely be ruled out if and only if we assume that individual self-interest (ethical egoism) is a law of nature, for in that case it would be folly to devise policy that ignored such an important, immutable, fact of life. If innate ethical egoism is *not* the case, however (and we have seen that it is at least a highly questionable proposition), then the second option is worthy of serious consideration.

\*     \*     \*

Over the past century and a half economics has consistently tried to erase any whiff of non-monetary, hard-to-quantify values from its language, a practice that is aimed at allowing economic precepts to be expressed in numbers and universalized, so that they can be made to apply across the board in the social sciences. This is a convention that reflects not just the economist's long-standing envy of that most respectable and "objective" science, physics, but also the ongoing academic turf war in which economics seeks to be foremost among the social sciences. But the fundamental moral issues raised by capitalist market theory and its institutions as they have come down to us refuse to go away. There simply is no plausible way in which a coherent economic theory can be constructed without reference to objective values.

A case in point: the assumption that avarice can and does lead to human well-being suggests that what is morally unacceptable is economically okay. This conclusion is supported throughout modern economic discourse, including its discussions of how "rational economic agents" make economic choices — in other words, decide what to buy. Here the connection between the exercise of personal preferences — called by economists "the maximization of personal expected utility" — and objective states of welfare, whether one is truly better off, has vanished. In economist-speak nothing is said of the *content* of the preferences to be maximized; no assumptions are made about what constitutes human well-being. It is assumed that well-being is a purely subjective state, that what is good for someone is determined solely by what he or she desires.

Only in the context of this peculiar use of language can it be accepted that avarice can be a good thing, that in Gordon Gekko's phrase, "Greed is good." There is no moral sense in which this can be true, because morality sees avarice as a principal source of unhappiness. A good social order constructed in the unavoidable presence of avarice will succeed not because of it, but *despite* it. The way economists use language allows them to *seem* to be talking about everyday life and its challenges without really doing so, because no such discussion can possibly take place in the absence of values. Economic policies that are sold as addressing those challenges may be doing something else entirely, such as addressing vested corporate interests. Economists do not speak the same language as ordinary people.

For the ordinary person, the concept of "interests" or "preferences" in economic theory means nothing without some idea of what the actual, objective components of self-interest are. Without some idea, in other words, of what we *ought* to desire. To say, as economists do, that self-interest is what interests the self is a content-empty, circular statement. Neutrality on moral questions is not objectivity, as so many modern economists suppose it to be. Neutrality is a political position, while objectivity is an epistemological concept, indicating a nearness to Truth. Thus, while value-cleansed discourse may be neutral, it is likely to be anything *but* objective. What it leaves out is likely to take it far from the truth of the matter, which, where economics is concerned, surely ought to include an account of *morally justifiable* human needs and desires — that is, what is objectively Good.[7] After all, if economics is not engaged in the promotion of genuine or objective human welfare goals, what purpose, ultimately, does it serve?

But perhaps the most obvious moral and ethical problem with both Utilitarianism and ethical egoism, and by extension with Smith's automated system for ethical behavior — and by further extension, with today's economic theory — is that *ethics and morality are not about reciprocity.* In other words, a truly ethical act is blind to its probable impact on the actor.

Ethics is not about evolutionary gain, or personal salvation, or the wealth of nations, but about simply and unconditionally being for the Other — doing the right thing, looking out for one's neighbor, caring for the needy. Acts that are calculated to redound to the benefit of the actor are not ethical, but, at best, prudent.

This fact of course presents serious if not insuperable problems for the Rationalist approach to morality, since the Rationalist conception of society is fundamentally rooted in the contract. In the world as it was imagined by Hobbes and Spinoza, moral behavior was the result not of any inherent moral impulse but of a combination of self-interest and social contract. The social contract, a mutual agreement among presocial groups to delegate ruling power to a monarch or governing body in return for peace and security, served to channel the pursuit of individual self-interest into communal welfare — organized society and its benefits. In Smith and his successors, the process remains essentially the same, though it takes on a more modern, biological mien and the role performed by the appointed ruler is assumed by natural processes, Smith's "institutional direction of the passions."

The Rationalists' approach to ethical behavior, in other words, was to uncover the ways in which morality *made sense* (was of benefit to the actor) — that is, to discover the "true" selfish motivation behind seemingly selfless acts — and then to incorporate those motivations into societal institutions. Moral acts, in the Rationalist world, are means to an end, and it is the end that counts. The "morality" of the market and by extension the morality of its agent, the business corporation, is *all about* reciprocity. It has to be, because it is based on contracts, and contracts are by definition instruments for guaranteeing reciprocity between their signatories. A contract is considered to have been broken when one of the parties fails to fulfill his or her reciprocal obligation to the other. In other words, whether one is obliged to comply with its terms depends on the other side's behavior. Genuinely ethical people are entitled to look beyond the formal agreement to ask, "Despite the contract, is the action right or wrong?"

When engaged in a contract, my actions are in fact remotely controlled by law and regulation, and their enforcement agencies. It is this behavior by remote control that, as we'll see shortly, chiefly distinguishes corporations from genuine ethical agents. There is no such thing as a "good corporate citizen," if by that we mean an ethical citizen and not merely one who is careful not to get caught breaking the law. Because their behavior is strictly determined by the web of law and regulation within which they act, corporations are incapable of purposeful ethical action, even though their nominal managers may be ethical people. As creatures of contracts, the best corporations are capable of is synthetic morality.

But just before getting to that, I must devote one more chapter to the important question of what it really means to be an authentic moral agent.

# 6

## What It Means to Be Moral

In television news writing, a craft to which I devoted too many years, there is a common stylistic error called "backing in to the story." It means taking a roundabout route to getting to the news content, which ought to be delivered right up front. In TV news there is no time to waste on the niceties of easing the audience into a topic: it's all wham-bam-thank-you-ma'am. Books are a different thing, thank goodness. Thus, I begin the last of these chapters in which I have been establishing the indispensable moral context with a story that may initially seem remote but turns out to be poignantly illustrative of the confusions of postmodern ethical life.

The Walters Life Sciences Building at the University of Tennessee is typical of up-to-date research facilities that house the laboratories of the worldwide community of research biologists. It was built more than two decades ago, at a time of rising public indignation over issues of cruelty to animals used in medical and industrial research. Animal rights activists were on the warpath, liberating lab rats, dogs, monkeys, and other doomed creatures and vandalizing research facilities, and philosopher Peter Singer's *Animal Liberation*, a groundbreaking plea for the moral rights of animals, was widely discussed.

The building's facility for housing research animals was therefore designed to be a model of ethical responsibility: clean, compassionate, and well managed. The American Association for the Accreditation of Laboratory Animal Care granted its seal of approval and a vet was always on call. United States Department of Agriculture inspectors paid regular visits. Before a scientist or graduate student was permitted to undertake research involving animal subjects, the project had to meet the university's ethical research standards and be approved by an animal care committee. In short, the university made, and presumably continues to make, a serious effort to address the issue of the moral status of its research animals, which are mainly mice.

The moral status of mice in the Walters Life Sciences Building was the subject of an article in the academic journal *American Psychologist* that was intended to make the point that what we consider to be ethical behavior depends on circumstances. In this case, it was dependant on the roles played by the lab animals under consideration. As the story unfolds, however, it also serves admirably to illustrate the kinds of dilemmas that can arise when a purely Rationalist approach is taken to setting ethical standards. As the article's author, psychologist Harold Herzog, says, "Although the university has demonstrated a sincere concern for the welfare of animal subjects, it has not escaped the paradoxes that emerge in the attempt to legislate ethics."[1]

The Life Sciences Building housed about 15,000 mice in a given year, the vast majority of them being "good" mice, the kinds used in laboratory experiments. "These are animals that are called upon to sacrifice their lives for what researchers hope will be the betterment of the human condition. . . . Their very existence depends on their utility; they would not exist if they were not lab animals." In this respect, Herzog points out, the "good" mice are no different than livestock or other domestic animals. Their moral status entitles them to the protection of

USDA inspectors and the animal experiment committee and to clean and comfortable quarters.

Also making their home in the building were a small but unknown number of pest mice. These are "bad" mice, "free-ranging animals that can be glimpsed occasionally scurrying along the corridors." They posed a threat to the integrity of lab experiments by threatening room-to-room contamination, and therefore had to be eliminated. Animal caretakers were reluctant to set poison baits, fearing that "good" mice might somehow come into contact with them, and ordinary household snap traps proved ineffective. "Sticky traps" became the preferred method of capture, set out each night and checked in the morning. These are pieces of cardboard about a foot square that have been impregnated with a mouse attractant and coated with a very sticky contact adhesive. When a mouse sets foot on one of them it becomes stuck, and the more it tries to escape the more its body touches the trap and the more inextricably it is trapped.

Though the traps contained no poison, Herzog reports that about half the animals were dead when they were found. "Mice that are still alive when discovered are immediately gassed," he reports, adding parenthetically that "each trap is used only once. Mice are not peeled from the traps."

Clearly, "bad" mice suffered excruciating deaths at the hands of Walters Life Sciences staff, and the author makes the obvious observation that "most animal care committees would have reservations about approving an experiment in which mice were glued to pieces of cardboard." Thus we have moral paradox number one: what is deemed ethically unacceptable for "good mice" is permitted in the case of other animals of the same species. The paradox deepens when it is noted that, as a relatively new building, the Life Sciences Center is not normally infested with wild rodents — the "bad" mice are almost invariably "good" mice who have escaped from their cages, a so-called leakage that is inevitable when dealing with such large numbers of animals. As soon as they hit the floor running, research mice change their moral status from "good" to "bad."

There is more to the story. A third category of mice inhabit the building. These are the animals that are kept as food for other animals, carnivores that are used in research. "Each week a number of these animals are offered to snakes, lizards, and even large toads. Feeders may be adult mice, juveniles, or pinkies (hairless newborns)." The moral status of these feeder mice is ambiguous, says the author, somewhere between "good" and "bad" mice. While a researcher did not need the permission of the animal care committee to routinely feed mice to carnivores that required them for food, he or she had to seek permission if the feeding process was to be recorded or otherwise observed for research on animal ethology. In other words, permission was needed to release a live mouse into the cage of a carnivore and videotape the results for research. As Herzog observes, in such an experiment the mouse is the *subject* of research, and thus worthy of protection: "The moral (and legal) standing of the mouse depends on whether it is labeled *subject* or *food*."

What are we to conclude from this touching and irresistibly comic tale? Simply that most attempts to codify ethical behavior, however well intentioned, are doomed to failure because laws and regulation are social constructs, whereas authentic morality *transcends* society and its institutions. No sane non-psychologist reading this report from the pages of a scholarly journal would seriously accept that the mice differ in their intrinsic moral status, even though they may well bear varying legal standing. Surely, morality dictates that all sentient creatures deserve our respect and ought to be treated as humanely as possible.

The moral status of mice was never at issue — what proved

bafflingly complex was their legal and regulatory status. For the Rationalist, the two categories are identical — law and regulation being *that which produces* "moral" behavior according to its prescriptions for action. But for the moral realist, one who believes that objective, universal moral values have real existence, law and morality are separate and frequently quite distinct categories. In fact, one of the purposes of moral inquiry is to examine law and regulation to see whether it is just and can be morally justified.

In a broader sense, the story illustrates how it is futile to expect moral behavior to arise out of social institutions and their conventions and regulations. Following the rules may occasionally, or even regularly, coincide with doing the right thing in a moral sense, but when it does it is coincidence. Moral behavior and compliance with regulations (as will become crystal clear in the context of the corporation, below) are not the same thing.

This will come as a surprise to some readers of relatively late vintage. Nowadays we live, it is alleged, in a grown-up postmodern world in which we have risen above juvenile belief in the sureties of so-called foundational narratives, the stories we once told each other of honor, genius, duty, patriotism, love, beauty, sacrifice, justice, morality — stories that are the glue that binds us together as societies and civilizations. In the postmodern world we are too savvy for all of that, believing now, as one observer says, "There is no such thing as truth; everything is a matter of rhetoric and power; all viewpoints are relative; talk of 'fact' or 'objectivity' is merely a specious front for the promotion of specific interests."[2] It is a world in which, above all, moral truths are relative and not absolute — where good and bad are entirely dependent on the context provided by history, culture, and circumstance, and where moral indignation is politically incorrect, a symptom of closet authoritarianism. "Tolerance" is the watchword, the universal moral solvent and the prescription for getting along, even though it implies tolerance of intolerance itself.

This is an essentially ideological position, whose seeds can clearly be seen in Rationalism's belief that social institutions with their scientifically based rules and regulations precede, and are the source of, moral behavior. If morality is the product of society, different societies (or different life science laboratories!) are likely to have different ethical standards, each of which will be valid for that society. The grand narratives of the past, especially those that spoke of moral certainties, are thus little more than myths we agree on, or not, depending on circumstances.

So we are told. And yet . . . most of us would confess to hearing from time to time the small nagging voice of conscience, which, try as we might to dismiss it, will not be denied. This voice frequently seems to be giving us ethical advice that is in contradiction to what moral relativism teaches, telling us, for example, that regardless of cultural practices or other considerations, such-and-such an action is just plain wrong. It seems to specialize in creating pesky paradoxes.

And while it is undeniable that dominant views of what is moral and what is not do change over time, this seems to be related to social teachings (one might say propaganda) that reinforce power structures and privilege rather than to any mutability, elasticity, or relativity of moral truths. In other words, differing historical positions on moral issues are attributable to social conditioning, rather than to the absence of durable moral standards. Moral relativity exists in spite of, rather than in the absence of, authentic moral values.

There was a time, not long ago, when few would think twice about the moral status of most domestic animals, let alone mice, and before that there were periods in which human slaves were only grudgingly accorded the legal protections of livestock. But these ideas were always resisted, even in the blackest times, by a morally sensitive few, whose ideas eventually prevailed. It is those enlightened few whose views reflect and represent to the world the constant current of moral truth. The rest of us are more susceptible to the rationalizations of authority and convenience, the ideologies that urge us to repress or deny our deepest sensibilities and play along with the game.

It would seem that for people in many different social and cultural milieus, and in different historical eras, the small voice we call conscience speaks a common language with respect to a handful of what appear to be universally shared values. It seems to speak *truth*. How can this be? How do we account for the consistency of so many well-known moral injunctions, including the following:

*Christianity:* "All things whatsoever ye would that men should do to you, do you even so to them: for this is the Law and the Prophets." (Matthew 7:12)

*Judaism:* "What is hateful to you, do not to your fellow men. This is the entire law: all the rest is commentary." (Talmud, Shabbat 31a)

*Hinduism:* "This is the sum of duty: Do naught unto others which would cause you pain if done to you." (Mahabharata 5:1517)

*Buddhism:* "Hurt not others in ways that you yourself find hurtful." (Udana-Varga, 5:18)

*Islam:* "No one of you is a believer until he desires for his brother that which he desires for himself." (Sunnah)

*Confucianism:* "Surely it is a maxim of loving kindness: Do not unto others that you would not have them do unto you." (Analects, 15:23)

*Taoism:* "Regard your neighbor's gain as your own gain and your neighbor's loss as your own loss." (T'ai Shang Kan Ying P'ien)

*Zoroastrianism:* "That nature alone is good which refrains from doing unto another whatsoever is not good for itself." (Dadistan-I-dinik, 94:5)

In one of the earliest modern attempts to define the moral consciousness, the British philosopher the Earl of Shaftesbury (Anthony Ashley Cooper, 1671–1713) introduced what is known as "moral sense theory," which proposes that each of us has a moral sensibility similar to our aesthetic sense, which causes us to react with pleasure or displeasure to events or other persons.[3] Human beings, because they are able to think about their feelings, develop a sense of right and wrong out of these pleasant and unpleasant experiences.

Shaftesbury says that we naturally find pleasure — feel approval — in observing or thinking about events or personalities that exhibit benevolence, which he describes as a fundamental virtue. Benevolence in turn can be described as awareness of or action on behalf of the public good, which, for Shaftesbury, is a manifestation of the "universal system" of nature. In other words, he assumed nature to be a providential or beneficent system, as had the classical Greeks and most later thinkers right through to the seventeenth-century scientific revolution. Human benevolence or virtue he took to be the species' way of fitting in to that universal system of beneficence. (Or, one could say, the environment's imprint on our species.) Shaftesbury's virtuous person is one who maintains a balance between self-interest and benevolence.

The idea of a moral consciousness that prompts us to react in certain ways to actions, events, and people was widely accepted up until the early twentieth century and the triumph of Behaviorist science, a fact verified in the classic eleventh edition of the *Encyclopedia Britannica*, most of which was written by nineteenth-century savants, and which defines ethics (at the beginning of a thirty-two-page entry) simply as "the process of reflection upon the nature of the moral consciousness." Moral consciousness is a given, an innate human attribute: it precedes moral philosophy, and provides it with its subject matter.

Some of the strongest recent support for the existence of a moral instinct has come from the American linguist, social critic, and philosopher Noam Chomsky. Chomsky established the existence of an innate grammar in humans that permits them to learn language, and in doing so he effectively discredited earlier Behaviorist theory across a wide spectrum of interests. In a famous review of the leading behaviorist thinker B. F. Skinner's *Verbal Behavior,* he pointed out that much of Behaviorist "science" was meaningless at its core. Rather than explaining phenomena it examines, as it claims to do, it merely names them. To describe a painting, for example, as a "controlling stimulus" that evokes an individual's "verbal response" tells us nothing useful, since the individual might respond in an almost infinite number of ways, his or her reaction being determined as much by internal factors as external stimulation.

It was similarly absurd to claim that Pavlovian stimulus-response training, rather than native endowment, or what might be called an innate gift, was the key to language development.

Around the world, children of varying intelligence and cultures acquire language at much the same rate, Chomsky observed, despite the fact that few of them are systematically taught or rewarded. Furthermore, children use grammar in ways that suggest they are following rules, rather than merely imitating what they hear. Virtually all English-speaking children, for example, initially make the mistake of generalizing the grammatical rule that to form a plural one adds *s*. They say "foots" and "sheeps" instead of "feet" and "sheep." Nor could even the richest learning environment account for the apparently unlimited variety of wholly novel sentences small children are able to devise on their own, and understand.

His linguistic theory well established as the gold standard in the field, Chomsky went on to speculate that, if it is the case that the human mind is in a sense hardwired with basic grammatical information, it is likely that it is also equipped, at birth, with other fundamental structures of thought through which it interprets the world. Among these, he believes, may be a moral sense. When faced with ethical problems, people are able to call on a basic ethical grammar within which to find and articulate solutions:

> The acquisition of a specific moral and ethical system, wide ranging and often precise in its consequences, cannot simply be the result of "shaping" and "control" by the social environment. As in the case of language, the environment is far too impoverished and indeterminate to provide this system to the child, in its full richness and applicability. Knowing little about the matter, we are compelled to speculate; but it certainly seems reasonable to speculate that the moral and ethical system acquired by the child owes much to some innate human faculty. The environment is relevant, as in the case of language, vision, and so on; thus we can find individual and cultural divergence. But there is surely a common basis, rooted in our nature.[4]

Unethical actions are thus performed against the grain of individual moral insight, usually for institutional reasons: human instincts favor moral behavior, but social institutions and structures sometimes compel antihuman behavior. If we change the institutions, we can permit basic human moral instincts to prevail.

Where the moral sense comes from, Chomsky confesses, remains a mystery. But that does not make it any less real. Could its origins be evolutionary? Chomsky has alluded, without much enthusiasm, to Richard Lewontin and Stephen Jay Gould's theory of "spandrels," spin-offs of evolution that are not selected for but arise spontaneously as emergent properties of complex systems. But he prefers, for the moment, to see language, and moral understanding, as innate aptitudes whose origins remain obscure.[5]

Chomsky's speculations are emblematic of a long-overdue revival of moral sense theory in contemporary social science. A leading proponent is sociologist Zygmunt Bauman:

> We suspect that the truth of the matter is opposite to the one we have been told. It is society, its continuing existence and its well-being, that is made possible by the moral competence of its members — not the other way round. . . . Rather than reiterating that there would be no moral individuals if not for the training/drilling job performed by society, we move toward the understanding that it must be the moral capacity of human beings that makes them so conspicuously capable to form societies and against all odds secure their — happy or less happy — survival.[6]

The moral impulse is "the first reality of the self; a starting point rather than a product of society." Its existence is simply a "brute fact. . . . There is no self before the moral self, morality being the ultimate, nondetermined presence, indeed an act of creation *ex nihilo* if ever there was one." It took "centuries of power-assisted legal drill and philosophical indoctrination," Bauman says, "to make the opposite [that is, that society spawned morality] seem evidently true."[7]

The source of moral knowledge remains enigmatic. "The mystery of morality inside me," as Immanuel Kant described it, seems impossible to explain, and impossible to explain away. It must, for the moment at least, be taken on faith. If this seems a discouraging conclusion, we should not forget that science, too, is ultimately based on faith — faith that the universe is accessible to human reason and that what we discover using the scientific method is an accurate depiction of reality.[8]

As physicist and philosopher John Polkinghorne observes, "There is a middle way between certainty and relativism, which corresponds to the critical adherence to rationally motivated belief, held with conviction but open to the possibility of correction."[9] This is, in essence, the definition of a scientific fact, and it is no less useful as a touchstone for moral inquiry.

However impressive our intellectual capacities as human beings may be, they are undeniably finite. *All* human knowledge ultimately must be anchored in "rationally motivated belief" because we have no direct, empirical access to ultimate truths. Descartes's program of firmly rooting knowledge in clear and certain ideas has turned out to be an unattainable ideal, as testified to in the indeterminacy, the unavoidable uncertainty, discovered in the last century to be among the built-in features of our most advanced theoretical physics and mathematics.

Nevertheless, in the end, as Socrates noted (in the *Meno*), if you want to go to Larissa, a true belief about the road to take will get you there as well as knowledge. Perhaps, then, there is no need to define the moral impulse — we all know what it is because we've all experienced it. We sometimes act upon it and we sometimes ignore it, but in ignoring it we do not eliminate it — we merely repress it, and that leads to feelings of uneasiness or guilt. Among healthy people, the difference between the ethical and the unethical is not the presence or absence of moral sense, but the ability in a consistent way to act contrary to its ever-present demands, which is something that must be learned. (As I will demonstrate in subsequent chapters, modern corporate-capitalist society offers ample opportunity for such learning.)

The moral impulse is simply the desire we all feel at some level to come to the assistance of those who need help or comfort — to be *for* the Other. It extends beyond fellow humans, to include all animate life, and perhaps even beyond that. It is the flip side of the inhumanity we see portrayed on the news every day — it is what motivates the people we see rushing to the site of a bombing to assist the wounded, who are pictured comforting the bereaved, or who are merely sickened and paralyzed by what they see. For lack of a better word, we can call it an instinct.

There are other approaches to discovering the existence of objective moral values. We can, for example, think of absolute values as a form of *objective worth*. The philosopher Robert Kane has proposed a mind experiment in which we are asked to imagine a painter who has been ill and depressed because his work is not selling. A wealthy friend and benefactor plots a scheme to have people purchase several paintings from the gallery at high prices in the name of knowledgeable and respected collectors. The painter mistakenly believes that his paintings have been recognized for their worth and his spirits rise.

We are now asked to imagine another world in which circumstances are similar, including the painter's depression and the fact that he considers himself to be a great talent. In this world, legitimate collectors actually do recognize the merit of his work and purchase his paintings at high prices.

Finally, we are to imagine that in both worlds, the painter dies a happy man, in the belief that his talent has been recognized and acknowledged. But only in the second world is his belief correct: in the first, he was deceived. The notion of objective worth begins to come into focus, Kane says,

> when we ask whether it would make any difference to [the painter] which of these two worlds he lives in, given that he believes he is a great artist in both and does not feel less happy subjectively in one world than in the other. To say that there is an important difference in value in the two worlds for [the painter] *even though he would not know it and would feel equally happy in both*, is to endorse the notion of *objective* worth.[10]

Kane suggests, correctly, I think, that the painter, if asked, would certainly prefer the world in which he is not deceived. The reason is because there is objective worth or value to genuine artistic merit, which he is able to recognize. One could also argue that the objective worth resides in truth versus falsity. In any case, the painter's judgment does not rely solely on his subjective impressions, but takes into account objective values that must, therefore, have real existence.

Again, however, we are left with the unanswered question: What is it that enables him to recognize these absolutes?

Some readers will want to point to Kosovo, or Colombia, or Rwanda or any number of other datelines in the news as evidence that Hobbes was right and the idea of a moral impulse is fantasy, but it seems to me that these examples merely demonstrate the existence of moral absolutes. We know about these events, they are news, because they are aberrations. Normal behavior does not create headlines. The vast majority of people on the planet behave "normally" most of the time. As a sometime teacher of ethics, I consider it my task not to list rules but to offer advice in how to listen to the dictates of the moral impulse. This can be harder than it may sound, because it frequently involves a difficult process of challenging the lessons taught from infancy onward by consumer society and its supporting media voices.

It seems to me that the moral impulse is both a necessary and a sufficient condition for proving the existence of moral absolutes, that is, moral precepts that are applicable in all cases, at all times, in all places. The very fact of its existence certainly denies the validity of moral relativism as a coherent philosophy. The knowledge that we all possess a moral consciousness, and that, in its authentic voice, it speaks to each of us in much the same way, can only mean that there must be some acts that are universally "good" and others that are universally "bad."[11] The taking of an innocent life is one such universal; others deal with respect for human dignity. Even terrorists, who make a career of killing the innocent, consistently justify their actions with the argument that their victims only *appear* to be innocent, and are actually complicit at some level in objectionable policies of the offending group or state. Alternatively, or sometimes in the same breath, they claim that the taking of innocent life was necessary to advance some greater good. These are of course moral arguments that implicitly recognize the sanctity of innocent life.

The American philosopher Thomas Nagel has this suggestion regarding the so-called reductionist thought that backstops relativist ethics: "I think the right way to react to the cruder suggestions of the sociobiological [Behaviorist] outlook is to consider the alleged biological causes of this or that motivational disposition, and then go on to ask whether, if those are the facts, we are justified in continuing to act on them."[12] For example, it might be suggested that there exists an innate, biological disposition toward racism among humans. Or scientific research might be undertaken to show that one race is intellectually superior to another. Nagel asks, *Should racism thus be exempt from moral criticism?* Of course not, is the only possible answer.

But where does this "of course not" idea come from? It is not determined by biology — that would be contradictory. And if it is suggested that this attitude is in turn determined by some other evolutionary condition, we can ask the same sorts of questions and come to the same conclusion — that moral thought appears to be separate and distinct from evolutionary tendencies. Moral thought cannot be escaped in the evolutionary fundamentalism called reductionism. No doubt it is in some fashion a product of evolution — what isn't? — but it has a real relationship to real referents nonetheless.

Moral absolutes — moral realities — do exist. Once we have acknowledged this fact, it seems to me our clear obligation is to try to discover what they are and to live by them as best we can. That may be the most important consequence of making such a discovery — the moral relativist, it must be noted, is under no such obligation.

Tolerance of cultural difference, thought by some to be a hallmark of relativism, is certainly important, but it is by no means the exclusive purview of the relativist. It has often been noted that the relativist must deal with the paradox that her beliefs oblige her to tolerate intolerance in societies where it is encouraged, as, for example, in Nazi Germany. In the absolutist's world, tolerance as a virtue exists in the humility with which one approaches the morally inescapable project of identifying absolute values that everyone can share. In other words, we can know for certain that there is such a thing as moral absolutes, and at the same time admit that we do not know for certain what they are, and this admission obliges us to listen to the views of others, to acknowledge that even when it comes to understanding conscience and the implications of its admonitions, two heads are better than one. But it does not oblige us to accept that all ethical viewpoints are equally valid.

The search for moral realities is carried on much as it would be in science: by forming hypotheses, examining them in the light of authority, testing them against real-world experience, and adopting, provisionally, those that best fit our inner moral nature. Slavery was once justified on the "moral" grounds that the slaveholder is apt to treat his possessions better than the entrepreneur who merely "rents" his labor. This view was challenged in light of new ideas of human rights and older ideas of human equality and worth, and found wanting. A new ethical position, which fits more closely with our innate moral nature, was adopted. The twentieth-century successes of the feminist movement provide a similar example of the kind of moral progress that arises out of the realist (or better, "critical realist") agenda. This seems to be genuine progress — we do not expect to fall back. It is spurred onward by conscience, the admonishing voice of the moral impulse, the interior faculty to which we turn for practical advice when faced with the apparently universal ethical prescription that we do unto others as we would have them do unto us, that we be unconditionally *for* the Other, that we do the right thing.

Moral realism, as I have been describing it, seems to me from every perspective to be the correct approach to understanding ethics and morality. It is my experience that most people, in most places in the world, will, if pressed, turn out to be moral realists, and to acknowledge the existence of at least some moral values that are universally valid. I suspect that most readers share this experience. Certainly, the Rationalist alternative of radical relativism or cultural contingency of values, having had more than three centuries to prove itself, has been found wanting.

The paradox facing us in the context of this book, then, is that given that good and bad and right and wrong have real existence and are not just semantic distinctions, empty words, and that humans are endowed with a moral drive or impulse that not only enables us to distinguish between these oppositions but impels us toward the Good, we nevertheless consent to be governed in our daily lives by institutions that reflect the view that morality is relative and that humans are innately selfish. Despite the certain knowledge of our moral essence, we acquiesce in an ideology of the market and the corporation that denies it.

Understanding this will, I think, take us a long way in clearing up the confusion that clouds so much of our thinking about corporations and their role in our lives.

# Part II

## The Strange One-Dimensional Life of the Corporation and How It Shapes Us All

*The outcry against the concentration of capital was furious. Men believed that it threatened society with a form of tyranny more abhorrent than it had ever endured. They believed that the great corporations were preparing for them the yoke of a baser servitude than had ever been imposed on the race, servitude not to men but to soulless machines incapable of any motive but insatiable greed.*

— Edward Bellamy, *Looking Backward from 2000 to 1887* (1887)

# 7

# The Rise of the Modern
# Business Corporation

THERE ARE MANY BOOKS THAT LOOK AT THE CORPORATION from conventional perspectives: historical, sociological, economic, even anthropological. As I said in the introduction to this volume, my own unorthodox approach has been to deal with the corporation from the point of view of morality, which necessitated what I hope has been an entertaining as well as helpful excursion into the realm of moral philosophy in the preceding pages.

The moral perspective seems to me to make sense because while nothing looms larger in the current economic landscape than the modern corporation, economics, as the study of the distribution of scarce goods, is (or ought to be) a moral science. More to the point, both the corporation and the market were invented as tools for generating moral value in society. The moral perspective is, moreover, a fruitful one, because it raises questions economists and most other social scientists are unlikely to ask, and opens up whole new vistas of inquiry. These lead, I think, to a deeper understanding of the problem, and that in turn can only be helpful in framing solutions. And the moral perspective has the additional, not inconsiderable, advantage that, while relatively few of us are trained in economics or sociology or anthropology, we can all claim expertise in morality.

Corporations being the litigious creatures they are, it seems appropriate to begin this exploration of their fascinating, though poorly understood provenance with a couple of recent court cases that illustrate some of the more startling aspects of the law as it relates to them today. These cases, which would have astounded the likes of Adam Smith and James Mill, show that the large business corporation of today is a far cry from its ancestors of even half a century ago and a different species altogether from its earliest progenitors.

In July 2002 the U.S. Supreme Court was asked to rule on a question of law that had been raised in an earlier decision by the supreme court of California. The case involved Nike, the sportswear maker, and Marc Kasky, a California citizen. Some background: in the 1990s labor unions, human rights groups, and others began raising complaints about the exploitative labor practices of Nike and other large corporations that had outsourced their manufacturing to Third World countries where wages were low and health and safety, environmental, and other regulations minimal. The campaign was eventually joined by editorialists at the *New York Times* and elsewhere, and by the producers of TV current affairs programs like CBS's *48 Hours*. By 1996 Nike had become a prime target of protesters, and its response was to unleash its PR department, which reacted with press releases, letters to the editor, and letters to university presidents and athletic directors around the country. In 1998 Kasky sued Nike for unfair and misleading business practices under a provision of California law that permits private citizens to take such action, acting as a "private attorney general." He claimed that, in its letters and press releases, Nike had lied about and misrepresented its labor practices abroad. In effect, he accused Nike of false advertising.

The case quickly resolved itself into a question of whether

Nike's denials of abuse constituted "commercial speech" or advertising, or amounted to contributing to a debate on an issue of public importance. If the former, Kasky had the right to sue Nike for lying in its letter-writing campaign, since the lies would amount to false advertising. If, however, it was decided that Nike was merely acting as a participant in a public debate, then its lies would be protected by the Constitution's First Amendment right of free speech. Kasky's lawsuit would then not be allowed to stand. Thus the claim made by Nike was a bizarre one: whether it had lied in its letters was immaterial, because its right to participate in public debate was guaranteed absolute protection under the Bill of Rights, in which the right to free speech is primary.

The Supreme Court was asked to rule on two key issues: whether a company writing to customers and communicating with them through the media is engaging in "commercial speech" regardless of surrounding circumstances, and, more broadly, whether commercial speech is protected under the First Amendment. (It received more than thirty *amicus* or friend-of-the-court briefs from labor and human rights organizations, other corporations, and corporate lobby groups.) In the end it decided not to offer an opinion on the case and handed it back to the California courts, citing long-standing policy against deciding on constitutional matters before they had been fully explored in lower courts. The First Amendment issues, it said, were wide-ranging: on the one hand, it was reasonably well established in law that false statements of fact are not protected under the Constitution; on the other hand, it was constitutionally important that "knowledgeable *persons* should be free to participate in such debate without fear of unfair reprisal." I have emphasized the word *persons* here because it encapsulates an even more important underlying issue that the court would in all likelihood have had to face, and that is whether the law is correct in treating corporations as persons, and giving them access to constitutional human rights codes.[1]

The world's largest retailer, Wal-Mart Corporation, was in court in Canada in 2004 in a case that raises the same fundamental issue of corporate personhood. As part of its long-standing battle against in-store unions, Wal-Mart Canada asked the Saskatchewan superior court to quash demands from the province's Labor Board for documents relating to a campaign to unionize a company outlet in the city of Weyburn. The documents had been requested in connection with Saskatchewan Labor Act provisions forbidding coercion of employees by companies during union organizing drives. Wal-Mart challenged both the legislation and the Labor Board orders as "unconstitutional, for infringing on Wal-Mart's right to freedom of thought, belief, expression, and communication," all of which are protected under the Canadian constitution's Charter of Rights and Freedoms. In the Charter, these rights are granted to "everyone," which, for most of us, would reasonably translate to "all people."

These are only two prominent examples of a myriad of similar cases pressed by corporations in North America, Europe, and throughout the industrialized world, as they continue their push for rights and privileges and powers that were never imagined in the wildest dreams of the framers of our economic institutions, and are being granted to them in the complete absence of democratic process. How did this come about?


The earliest corporations date from Roman times and were created as a means of ensuring continuity in the operations of important institutions. By the Middle Ages, corporate charters were being granted to cities, universities, holy orders, and craft guilds.

A form of immortality was bestowed on these groups by the process of incorporation, which amounted to the granting of a legal identity to the association separate and distinct from that of its human members. Officers of the corporation might come and go, performing various roles and then leaving to be replaced by others, and the corporation itself would carry on, unperturbed.

By the fifteenth century the idea of limited liability had become attached to the corporation, with corporate law evolving to ensure that individual corporate officers, such as city councilors or guild officials, could not be held liable for corporate debts or infractions of law. This further enhanced the stability of the institution.

The corporation began to change in the sixteenth and seventeenth centuries, when monopoly trading and colonizing enterprises like the Hudson's Bay and East India companies and the syndicates holding rights to settle Virginia and Massachusetts were venturing, at enormous expense, into newly discovered or little-known parts of the planet. As a means of minimizing the risks faced by investors in what were in many cases enterprises of strategic importance to the state, these companies sought and were granted corporate charters by European monarchies. Chartered for business purposes, they were radically unlike their predecessors, in that they were associations of capital rather than people. Where a city corporation represented the citizens and their government, the new business corporation represented the money placed in its hands by speculators. Investors pooled their money and shared in the profits, encouraged by the benefits of limited liability for losses to accept the often enormous risks involved in those swashbuckling ventures.

These early business corporations, as both reflections and tools of national foreign policy, retained their charters only as long as their activities reflected national goals. Governments saw them as instruments created for special purposes, with a life span to be determined by their usefulness in carrying out that purpose. By the mid-nineteenth century, however, the institution had undergone another metamorphosis. In most jurisdictions the laws of incorporation no longer required business ventures to fulfill any public purpose in return for the protection and privileges conferred on investors by their corporate charters. As we've seen, it was assumed by this time that public purpose could be safely left in the hands of the market mechanism itself. Business corporations had come to be seen not simply as useful vehicles for the undertaking of financially risky but socially beneficial enterprises but also as a good thing in themselves, a helpful adjunct to the Rationalist model of the self-governing market mechanism. According to the laissez-faire ideology in vogue at the time, the less governments interfered with their workings, the more likely it was that social good would result.

The infancy of the business corporation in its present multipurpose form can be dated to 1811, when the state of New York enacted a law of incorporation that required only a very general description of the type of business being undertaken. The other American states followed suit during the 1840s and 1850s. In Britain, the Joint Stock Companies Act of 1844 allowed corporations to be created by a simple act of registration with a summary description of the nature of the enterprise.[2] The corporation had transformed itself from a creature of the state or some monopoly interest in society with clearly defined public purpose, into an all-purpose legal mechanism for facilitating the carrying-on of business within a market economy, its charter no longer subject to any meaningful review.

The nineteenth century was characterized by mammoth engineering undertakings, including the building of railroads, transcontinental telephone networks, and world-girdling telegraph cables, and the opening up of vast new regions to farming. Enterprises on this scale called for infusions of manufactured goods such as steel rails, copper wire and glass insulators, farm machinery and grain ships, locomotives and rolling stock, and huge quantities of coal and petroleum fuels. The engineering projects themselves would typically be undertaken by corporations, many of which had been formed with the active encouragement of governments and whose stock was widely held.

This was the case, for example, with the great, continent-spanning railways and telegraph lines of the era. But their capital-goods requirements were still frequently filled by older-style business ventures — partnerships and sole proprietorships. These increasingly obsolescent business entities were stubbornly maintained because they were safe from the public disclosure of financial records that the state demanded of the corporations it chartered. Many of these companies were nevertheless enormous. For example, Andrew Carnegie's Carnegie Steel was a partnership, and several of John D. Rockefeller's Standard Oil affiliates were not incorporated. But the penalty for that privacy, the inability to raise capital by selling shares to the public, became increasingly onerous as economies grew and capital requirements soared.

The Panic of 1873 touched off a long depression that was marked by a frenzy of business mergers in the United States. Undertaken primarily to control overproduction and stabilize markets, these "combinations" or "combines" — monopolies and oligopolies — led to a restructuring of major portions of American industry. The number of partnerships and proprietorships among major business enterprises declined dramatically, and at the same time a great many new and powerful public corporations were spawned, their shares trading on stock markets. The era of the robber baron was ending, and the era of the modern business corporation had begun. Between 1899 and 1904, United States Steel, International Harvester, American Can, and 2,500 other corporate mergers changed the face of American business. By 1904 one in ten American workers was employed by a corporation.

As the old business patriarchs died off or were replaced, corporate management was increasingly placed in the hands of university-trained functionaries who saw all corporations as essentially alike in terms of the skills required to run them efficiently and profitably. A generalized set of professional management techniques stressed not the product or the customer, but the manipulation of corporate capital to maximize the rate of return on shareholder investment. And capital was no longer raised primarily through internal financing but by the sale of shares on the stock market, which meant that ownership, once closely held, was now widely dispersed. These developments had the enormously significant effect of divorcing management from ownership.[3]

Where the business corporation had once been an extension of the personality of its owner, *it had now become the embodiment of pure market theory*, as taught in the business schools of the industrial world. It had, in other words, undergone another metamorphosis, recast this time into the exemplary "rational economic agent" as imagined by the classical economic theorists, an autonomous creature of pure and unswerving self-interest and of unlimited material desire.

While it is usual to speak of corporations as a capitalist innovation designed to promote the accumulation of capital and its investment in enterprise, an ethical perspective will see this somewhat differently. From an ethical perspective the corporation can be seen to have been designed for the specific purpose of *representing in the market the collective acquisitiveness or self-interest of its shareholders*. Individual shareholders pool their capital, placing it under control of corporate managers, who are expected as a condition of their employment to maximize the value of those assets and thus the return on investment.

From an economic perspective, the advantage to this arrangement lies in the fact that individual human persons do not, to the distress of generations of economic theorists, behave well in their role as rational economic agents. They all too frequently act in unselfish or altruistic or "irrational" ways, denying their "natural" instinct for self-interest and material gain. They are not the thoroughgoing ethical egoists they need to be for the market economy to function at maximum efficiency.

The corporation, however, *is* perfectly egoistic or selfish, and what is even better, there are no moral or cultural limits to its acquisitiveness (though there may be legal constraints). Corporations are, in a word, indifferent to right and wrong, good and bad, except insofar as these can be expressed in terms of the corporate equivalents of pleasure and pain — which are profit and loss. The corporation is the ideal Rationalist, Utilitarian instrument, the perfect embodiment of economic Reason.

As an evolving piece of socio-legal technology, the corporation, as it emerged from the nineteenth century, was ideally adapted to its environment, the elegantly machine-like market economy as theorized by the great liberal economists of the Victorian era. National and world markets had become, in the eyes of economic theorists, an integrated, self-regulating, mechanistic system capable of autonomous operation as long as it was carefully shielded from human interference.

The modern business corporation, as it reached its full maturity in the mid-twentieth century, would become a kind of servomechanism attached to the market. Essentially robot-like, it also exhibited an unexpected, parasitic tendency to take over the host mechanism *in toto*, subverting it to the service of corporate, as opposed to human or even national, needs.

Today the burgeoning global economy is the playing field of the large multinational corporation, which ensures that the inconveniences of national boundaries are minimized through its powerful advocacy of comprehensive regional and global trade agreements. With the establishment of the World Trade Organization in 1993, corporate influence over the regulation of international trade and investment gained great power. Industry ministers and cabinet secretaries who represent the member states are closely aligned with national corporate interests, regularly seeking their advice, and corporate lobby groups are in constant attendance.

The WTO might be thought of as a corporate nation, more powerful by far than many countries of the world. Since its inception it has repeatedly required member countries to modify or withdraw laws aimed at protecting the environment or workers' or consumers' rights or other fields of public interest. Populist response has been to turn WTO meetings, wherever they are held in the world, into something resembling sieges of medieval cities. Predictably, these anti-corporate, anti-globalization demonstrators are characterized by corporate interests as irrational.

Perhaps the most surprising thing about the modern business corporation is the fact that, despite its origin as a piece of social technology, as deliberately purpose-designed as any machine tool, it is treated in law as a *person*.

To understand how corporations gained their personhood, we need to backtrack a little and recall that the original intent and genius of the corporation had been to provide a means of continuing the life of an institution across generations of human officers. Owners and other principals could come and go, but the corporation itself carried on eternally, without having to reorganize itself with each death or departure. The corporation could be sued, fined, and taxed as an entity, and for these reasons it always seemed to have a life, even a personhood, of its own. But in English jurisprudence of the seventeenth and eighteenth centuries, lawyers acting on behalf of corporations were at pains to insist before the courts that their clients were fictitious or *artificial* persons, creations of the state that granted their charter. As artificial persons, they were, of course, not subject to laws directed at real human people, even though those laws were typically framed in language such as, "No person shall. . . ." The laws clearly referred to natural persons, to human beings.

Toward the end of the nineteenth century, however, and particularly in the United States, corporations and their lawyers changed their age-old tactics as they attempted to minimize regulation by those state governments in which the rising chorus of corporate critics and reformers were able to exercise power.[4] They began to pressure the courts for formal recognition of corporate personhood, and now the plea was that corporations were not artificial, but *natural* persons.

The distinction is one of great significance. If corporations are artificial persons, creatures of the state, then the state has the clear right to exercise unlimited control over their activities. If, on the other hand, they are natural persons, then, like that other race of natural persons — humans — they and their basic rights pre-exist the state. As natural persons, corporations would thus become heirs to primordial "natural rights" — human rights — intended to protect individuals from government interference beyond what is strictly necessary to maintain civil and social order.

After years of pressure and lobbying, the remarkable boon of natural personhood was peremptorily granted to American corporations by the U.S. Supreme Court in 1886, in the case of *Santa Clara County v. the Southern Pacific Railroad.* The legal context was provided by the Fourteenth Amendment of the U.S. Constitution (written to protect freed slaves from abuse and exploitation), which declares that all state citizens are also American citizens, and that no state government shall "deprive any person of life, liberty, or property, without due process of law; nor deny to any person within its jurisdiction the equal protection of the laws." By granting the railroad personhood in this context, the court effectively made it impossible for state governments to regulate railroad tariffs on the movement of agricultural and other products. As persons, corporations now had the same rights as human individuals to charge what they liked for their services. Though the court did not explicitly state whether it was natural or artificial personhood it had accepted, it was evidently the former, since it had given the railroad corporation access to the protection of legislation that had clearly been designed for human, that is, natural, persons.

Ignoring some lingering ambiguity on this issue owing to the absence of supporting legal reasoning in the court judgment and to a handful of contradictory judgments in subsequent years, corporations immediately mounted a concerted legal campaign to gain access to the full panoply of protection offered to human persons under the Bill of Rights. These vigorous efforts began bearing fruit in a significant way in the mid-twentieth century, in a series of Supreme Court decisions that successively granted corporations the same protections as humans under the First, Fourth, Fifth, Sixth, and Seventh Amendments. These cover rights to free speech; freedom from unreasonable searches and searches without warrants; freedom from double jeopardy; and trial by jury in both criminal and civil cases.

The effect has been significantly to reduce state and federal government's ability to regulate, inspect, and generally exercise control over the operations of corporations. For example, Fourth Amendment protection from regulatory searches without warrants was established in *Marshall v. Barlow's Inc.* (1978), in which the Supreme Court struck down federal Occupational Safety and Health Administration regulations mandating unannounced safety inspections of corporate premises — in this case, the premises of an Idaho electrical and plumbing corporation.[5] Many inspection provisions in federal laws were rendered presumptively invalid by the decision. The court found that corporations enjoy privacy rights equivalent to those of human persons and that commercial buildings should be treated in the same way as private homes under the amendment's protections. A corporation's factory is its castle.

In the same year as the *Marshall v. Barlow's* case in another watershed ruling the Supreme Court abruptly abandoned the undeniably strange and legally troublesome notion that corporations are somehow natural persons. But it did so in a way that strengthened rather than weakened corporate access to constitutional rights. The case was *First National Bank of Boston v. Bellotti*, a dispute over First Amendment rights to free speech. The 1978 trial centered on corporations' right to spend money to influence the outcome of a referendum on instituting a graduated personal income tax in the state of Massachusetts. It had been brought by a consortium of Boston corporations seeking the right to campaign against the tax: First National Bank, New England Merchants National Bank, Gillette Co., Digital Equipment Corp., and Wyman-Gordon Corporation.

In its judgment, the court chose to sidestep the whole natural/artificial personhood controversy and instead relied on its interpretation of the intent of the amendment. The question was no longer whether the corporation, as either natural or artificial person, was entitled to free speech rights originally intended for human persons, but whether conferring of those rights on corporations furthered the amendment's goal of encouraging free and open debate. The Massachusetts Supreme Court had employed the artificial entity theory to rule that humans enjoy broader First Amendment protections than corporations, which were entitled only to the long-standing Fourteenth Amendment property protections under the Bill of Rights. On appeal, the majority of the Supreme Court dismissed this reasoning as "an artificial mode of analysis." Its judgment stated:

> The Court below framed the principal question in this case as whether and to what extent corporations have First Amendment rights. We believe that the Court posed the wrong question. The Constitution often protects interests broader than those of the party seeking their vindication. The First Amendment, in particular, serves significant societal interests. The proper question therefore is not whether corporations "have" First Amendment rights, and if so, whether they are coextensive with those of natural persons. Instead, the question must be whether [the statute] abridges expression that the First Amendment was meant to protect. We hold that it does.[6]

In its ruling in *Bellotti*, the Supreme Court granted to corporations virtually the same First Amendment rights under the Constitution as are enjoyed by human beings, granting them, it has been argued, "precisely what the Bill of Rights was intended to prevent: domination of public thought and discourse."[7]

A series of cases argued on this premise of "intent" quickly extended to corporations' explicit rights under the Fourth, Fifth, and Seventh Amendments as well. The process is continuing. In June 2001 the Supreme Court preempted state laws that would have protected children from tobacco advertising by banning such ads within a thousand feet of schools and playgrounds. The Court agreed with tobacco industry lawyers, who had argued that the laws were in violation of First Amendment free speech protections. Such rulings have become routine.[8]

And so we have, in 2004, the strange case of Wal-Mart Corporation exercising its *Bellotti* free speech rights to usurp the legislative authority of the city council of Inglewood, California. When the council rejected the giant retailer's plan to build a 130,000-square-foot superstore in the city, Wal-Mart charged that the councilors were dupes of organized labor and other special interest groups. The corporation hired a team of election specialists and collected the 6,500 signatures needed under California law to sponsor a referendum to reverse the decision. As the *New York Times* reported, "In the ensuing referendum campaign the company spent more than $1 million to convey the idea that it would create hundreds of jobs and pump up the local tax base." While opponents emphasized the company's legacy of deserted downtowns and falling wages, it was a more disturbing issue that ultimately defeated the initiative. Under the proposed new regulation, Wal-Mart would have been exempted from Inglewood's zoning, planning, and environmental protection laws, including provisions for public hearings. And the new deal would be subject to amendment by only a two-thirds majority vote in another referendum. "By the time voters rejected the initiative at the ballot box [by a surprisingly modest 60.6 to 39.3 percent majority]," the *Times* reported, "the strategy had acquired a name: Wal-Mart sovereignty."[9]

The extension of human rights protections to corporations quickly spread beyond the United States to most major industrial democracies. The Supreme Court of Canada made a ruling similar to that of *Marshall v. Barlow* in the case of *Hunter v. Southam*, in 1984. The case involved alleged collusion between two major newspaper chains in closing down a series of big-city dailies in a scheme that limited competition. The Crown was unsuccessful in its prosecution of the chains due to crippling court challenges to search provisions of federal anti-combines legislation. A succession of rulings made under the Canadian Charter of Rights and Freedoms made the gathering of documentary evidence impossible.[10]

Corporate rights to freedom of speech was the issue when in 1986 the Quebec Court of Appeals struck down provincial legislation banning all TV ads aimed "at persons under thirteen years of age," as an infringement of the corporation's Charter rights.[11] In the subsequent appeal, the Supreme Court of Canada accepted the notion that corporate advertising, as a form of corporate speech, is protected by the Canadian Charter of Rights free speech provision. It nevertheless held (by a 3–2 vote) that the Quebec law was a "reasonable limit" on freedom of speech (an escape clause provided for under the terms of the Charter) because a "particularly vulnerable group" was being protected by the law.[12] On the other hand, Canadian corporations have been granted the right to prohibit the free expression of political opinion anywhere on their private property.[13]

What these Canadian Supreme Court rulings are saying, York University law professor Michael Mandel has concluded, is that if a corporate "person" is to be charged with a serious crime, it must be granted the full panoply of human rights protections that were originally put in place to protect human citizens from the arbitrary and excessive use of state power.[14] That is, the Supreme Court of Canada has established that when corporate crime involves criminal behavior as opposed to simple breaches of regulations, the corporation must be granted the same Charter protections as a human defendant:

> The Supreme court took us by a circuitous route involving many windfalls to corporate criminals to the position . . . of two alternatives equally guaranteed to satisfy business and to leave the regulatory state in a much-weakened position: either we go easy on business crime, in which case the courts will dispense with some, but not all, Charter guarantees, or we take it seriously, in which case the courts will arm business to the teeth with Charter defenses that make it invincible.[15]

It's not as if we hadn't been warned. Long before human rights were much of an issue even for humans, Thomas Hobbes worried about the potential for mischief posed by the corporations of his day. Adam Smith thought they needed to be kept on a very short leash. And as early as the mid-nineteenth century, influential Americans had begun to voice their alarm at the growth of corporate power and influence. President Abraham Lincoln wrote in 1864, as the American Civil War was winding down:

> We may congratulate ourselves that this cruel war is nearing its end. It has cost a vast mount of treasure and blood. . . . It has indeed been a trying hour for the Republic; but I see in the near future a crisis approaching that unnerves me and causes me to tremble for the safety of my country. As a result of the war, corporations have been enthroned and an era of corruption in high places will follow, and the money power of the country will endeavor to prolong its reign by working upon the prejudices of the people until all wealth is aggregated in a few hands and the Republic is destroyed. I feel at this moment more anxiety for the safety of my country than ever before, even in the midst of war.[16]

President Rutherford B. Hayes (elected 1877) admonished, "This is a government of the people, by the people and for the people no longer. It is a government of corporations, by corporations, and for corporations."[17] On the eve of his becoming chief justice of Wisconsin's supreme court in 1873, Edward G. Ryan warned:

> [There] is looming up a new and dark power . . . the enterprises of the country are aggregating vast corporate combinations of unexampled capital, boldly marching, not for economical conquests only, but for political power. . . . The question will arise and arise in your day, though perhaps not fully in mine, which shall rule — wealth or man; which shall lead — money or intellect; who shall fill public stations — educated and patriotic freemen or the feudal serfs of corporate capital.[18]

In 1888 President Grover Cleveland expressed similar concerns: "Corporations, which should be the carefully restrained creatures of the law and the servants of the people, are fast becoming the people's masters."[19] Half a century later U.S. Supreme Court Justice Louis D. Brandeis referred to corporations as "the Frankenstein monster which States have created by their corporation laws."[20]

Beyond the legal fact of personhood and the consequent access to human rights codes, two further characteristics that help define the modern business corporation are its enormous size, and what in human terms would be referred to as its stinginess.

The tendency to gigantism is explained by the fact that profits are highest in markets that are under the control of monopolies and oligopolies, which, in the absence of effective competition, are in a position to set prices as they see fit. The profit imperative thus draws corporations implacably in that direction, as opposed to the direction of increased competition and lower prices. The corporate mantra is grow, grow, grow, in both size and market share. Growth, both absolute and relative to the competition, is achieved in many ways — through mergers and acquisitions, through legal harassment of competitors over patents and copyrights, through vertical integration of production processes, and so on. There is no ultimate limit to corporate size, no ideal number, though it is often in the corporation's interest to stop short of achieving full monopoly powers in order to maintain the fiction of market competitiveness. This is done for both ideological and regulatory reasons. As long as the company can argue that its market remains free, it can credibly fend off public indignation and regulatory backlash, each of which has the potential to damage profits.

Corporations are stingy because they are designed to be that way, both in law and in economic theory. They are simply not expected to be responsible for social welfare because it is assumed that if they maintain their focus on profit, social good will flow automatically, via the automated processes of the market. This piece of Rationalist ideology was firmly entrenched in law as early as 1916, in the case of *Dodge v. Ford*. As Canadian legal scholar Joel Bakan tells the story, in 1906, John and Horace Dodge had invested more than $10,000 in Henry Ford's new automobile company and had an exclusive contract to make Ford parts in their Chicago machine shop. Ten years later the two decided to begin making cars on their own, and they planned to finance the new venture with quarterly dividends from their Ford shares. Their plan hit a stumbling block when Henry Ford, ever the visionary, decided that the profit he was making on his Model T cars was unconscionably high, and that both his company and society at large would stand to gain if he reduced the price. His plan, in effect, was to divert corporate profit to his customers, in the form of lower prices.

The Dodge brothers took him to court, claiming that Ford

had no right to give away company profits, however magnanimous his motives. The judge agreed. He reinstated the dividend and rebuked Ford for saying in open court that "business is a service, not a bonanza" and that corporations should be run only "incidentally to make money." Ford had erred, the judge said, in forgetting that "a business corporation is organized and carried on primarily for the profit of the stockholders"; it could not be run "for the merely incidental benefit of shareholders and for the primary purpose of benefiting others." As Bakan observes, "*Dodge v. Ford* still stands for the legal principle that managers and directors have a legal duty to put shareholders' interests above all others and no legal authority to serve any other interests — what has become known as 'the best interests of the corporation' principle." Bakan concludes, "Corporate social responsibility is thus illegal — at least when it is genuine."[21]

Corporate philanthropy exists, of course, but it must be undertaken, according to the "best interests" principle, in the clear and calculable interest of company shareholders — it must ultimately redound to the bottom line. It must not, in other words, be true altruism. Only the Utilitarian brand of pseudo-morality is permitted — only actions undertaken in self-interest that incidentally assist others. Lord Bowen, an English Chancery Court judge with a penchant for metaphor, had expressed a similar view in a precedent-setting 1883 case: "Charity has no business to sit at boards of directors *qua* charity. There is, however, a kind of charitable dealing which is for the interest of those who practice it, and to that extent and in that garb (I admit not a very philanthropic garb) charity may sit at the board, but for no other purpose."[22] The law severely restricts philanthropic activities of corporations, regardless of the views or sentiments of their "managers," and in fact most publicly traded corporations cautiously limit their charity to about 1 percent of revenues.

Thus, when Wal-Mart announced it was donating $17 million to disaster relief following hurricane Katrina in 2005 (a minuscule proportion of its earnings, even in the Gulf states), it did so on CNN's *Larry King Live,* a large company logo glowing ethereally behind the company's CEO as he read a prepared statement congratulating his own company on its generosity.

Influential economic theorists such as Milton Friedman and Theodore Leavitt continue to insist that the role of the corporation ought to be strictly limited to making a profit. In a famous article, Friedman asserts: "I call [social responsibility] a 'fundamentally subversive doctrine' in a free society, and say that there is one and only one social responsibility of business to use its resources and engage in activities designed to increase its profits."[23] Leavett says that "welfare and society are not the corporation's business. Its business is making money. . . . Government's job is not business, and business's job is not government. And unless these functions are resolutely separated in all respects, they are eventually combined in every respect. . . . Altruism, self-denial, charity . . . are vital in certain walks of our life. . . . But for the most part those virtues are alien to competitive economics."[24] One is entitled to ask, If human persons are not exempt from social responsibility, why are corporate persons so absolved, when they enjoy so many human rights?

In light of this history, we can pause here to regroup, and note that the "modern business corporation," as I use the term, has several distinctive features. It is typically very large in terms of revenues and numbers of employees; owned by large numbers of individual and/or institutional shareholders; and run by highly trained cadres of professional managers. Significantly, it has achieved the legal status of personhood, and thus can (and frequently does) claim protection from the state under human rights codes. Finally, whereas early corporations were formed for the achievement of specific goals detailed in their charters (typically, overseas trade or large, onetime engineering projects), the modern business corporation has a single purpose — to make money. It is this definition that should be understood whenever I use the word *corporation* in the following pages.

I do *not* include in this discussion companies that are privately held or majority owned by an individual or family. While these companies often behave in ways indistinguishable from publicly owned and professionally managed corporations (as in the case of Microsoft), they don't always. They sometimes, for example, exhibit genuine altruism, distributing largesse in ways that would cause a shareholder revolt or legal action in a public corporation. Controlling ownership gives individuals the freedom to express their humanity, for better or worse, with the company's money.

Thus, when I speak of a split between ownership and management in the modern business corporation (discussed in chapter 8), I mean ownership in this proprietary sense. Modern management theory has recognized this distinction by propounding something called "founders syndrome." This is a corporate pathology characterized by a (founding) manager's focus on product and customer, at the expense of profit. The prescribed cure is to get rid of the founder and let professionals take over.

In the summer of 2004, as the world awaited the search engine giant Google's IPO (initial public offering), business pundits were all but unanimous in predicting that once the company had gone public its famous mission of "Making the world a better place" and its "Do no evil" motto would go by the boards.

"How much of this culture will survive Google's new life as a publicly traded company?" one such writer asked. "In the medium to long term, not much, I expect."[25] The skepticism is rooted in the experience of such famous, principled company founders as Apple Computer's Steve Jobs and Body Shop's Anita Roddick, who found themselves and their ideals banished from their corporate boardrooms after their companies went public.[26] And, indeed, within a year Google was being criticized for overaggressive business tactics and for its apparently insatiable appetite for market share in each new field it entered.[27] ⌐

It needs to be noted here that the question of how corporations are governed has spawned a number of explanatory models. The earliest of these proposed that corporations were controlled by their owner/shareholders, through democratic processes involving annual shareholder meetings. By the turn of the twentieth century, these meetings, to the extent that they had any impact on management, had devolved into proxy battles in which individual shareholders had negligible input, and control was maintained within management circles.[28] At the time, critics raised concerns over the degree of management control, suggesting that managers would not be sufficiently anxious to maximize profit, but would have other priorities revolving around their own financial security and working conditions.[29]

In a variation on this manager-control theme, Adolph Bearle and Gardiner Means in a famous work called *The Modern Corporation and Private Property* (1932, revised and reprinted in 1967) painted a picture of American business that saw virtually complete autonomy for management in the face of ineffectual or indifferent shareholder/owners. But Bearle and Means went on to suggest that the control could be used to further important social goals, such as the humane treatment of workers and attention to product quality, which otherwise would be sacrificed to profit maximization.

J. K. Galbraith, in *The New Industrial State* (1967), saw corporate management as a bureaucratic "technostructure," still firmly in control but focused on achieving "a secure minimum of earnings" as opposed to maximum profit. This provided optimal working conditions for the managers.[30] However, this style of comfort-seeking management, to the extent that it lost focus on maximizing profit and stock value, could not last for long, and it soon fell victim to corporate raiders, who specialized in taking over and reorganizing firms that underperformed in terms of stock market valuation. The result was the notorious leveraged buyout craze on Wall Street that peaked in the 1980s and eventually collapsed in a series of enormous legal and financial scandals.

Today, writers like Doug Henwood see a resurgence in shareholder activism, but of a novel kind.[31] Financial institutions such as pension plan funds, mutual funds, insurance funds, and so on, corporations in their own right, run by portfolio managers, play an aggressively active (and essentially parasitic) role in determining corporate goals. The interest of these so-called rentiers is in high stock valuation — no matter how achieved. As Henwood says (for example), "Public justifications for . . . downsizings have almost always pointed to technological change and global competition . . . but in fact the proximate cause has more often been pressure for high stock prices coming from Wall Street portfolio managers." It is a demand "that translates into layoffs and investment cutbacks." Where rentiers exert control, shareholder value is all:

> Just because Wall Street's short-termism is a cliché doesn't mean that it isn't true. In surveys, CEOs and corporate investor relations managers repeatedly complained of pressure

from money managers and Wall Street analysts to produce quick profit growth. . . . Money managers themselves confirm to survey-takers that their colleagues are too obsessed with quarter-to-quarter news, and take too little heed of long-term prospects. It can hardly be otherwise, since most big investment managers are graded on their quarterly performance.[32]

In the end, whether managers, shareholders, or rentiers exert dominant "control" over corporations, it remains true that the various schemes of governance are simply ways to determine who gets control of the profit generated by the corporation. All models begin with the premise, in other words, that corporations exist for the purpose of making money. Both rentiers and shareholders demand maximum profit, which is why Galbraith's lackadaisical managers couldn't survive. In all cases, the corporation is expected to maximize the value of the assets it controls — though the definition of "maximize," and to whose benefit, may differ in nuance.

In twenty-first-century America 90 percent of all corporate stock is held by 10 percent of shareholders; the top 1 percent of shareholders own half of all stock. Almost all of these large shareholders are other corporations, such as pension funds, mutual funds, and insurance companies. Only a very few are individuals. These institutional shareholders, the controlling factor in the stock market, will as corporations operate as "rational economic agents" as they were designed to do, and have no interest in their holdings beyond the returns they produce. To the extent that they choose to intervene in the management of the corporation whose stock they own, the sole purpose will be to maximize the value of that asset.

As I'll argue in more detail later on, no matter who claims to be in control, corporations are singularly impervious to interference with their primary goal and go about the business of producing profit (or attempting to) with machine-like single-mindedness. Theories of "control" are thus largely irrelevant to the realities of the market and the role played by the modern business corporation. Understanding this helps to explain much of the current confusion over issues of corporate responsibility. Corporate responsibility is the topic of much of the rest of this book, but a few initial observations can be made here in the context of defining the characteristics of the beast.

In their pursuit of profit, corporations, because they are moral cretins, tend to push their behavior to the extreme limits that define the border between what is merely socially unacceptable or unethical, and what is illegal. Most humans, even those with a clouded ethical sensibility, will curb themselves long before that borderline is reached, if only because human society prescribes painful reprisals for ethical misdeeds, punishments such as ostracism and public shaming. Corporations, too, can be susceptible to a kind of shaming and ostracism, in the form of boycotts. The "pain" is registered as financial loss.

Here, the etymology of the verb *ostracize* is both interesting and relevant. The word is derived from the Greek *ostrakon*, denoting a potsherd. In the ancient Athenian democracy, there was provision for voting (by dropping a potsherd in a marked vessel) for or against a motion to exile for several years any individual the populace deemed to have become too powerful within the community. The assembly was asked, "Is there any man among you whom you think vitally dangerous to the state? If so, whom?" The assembly could then choose to banish, for either five or ten years, one citizen, not excluding the mover of the motion. The ostracism involved no confiscation of property or even disgrace: it was simply the democracy's way of cutting off the "tallest ears of corn."[33]

Corporations certainly qualify in that respect in today's society: the biggest among them pose a danger to democratic institutions merely by virtue of their size and influence, and indifference to the public interest. But boycotts are only sporadically effective, and government antitrust laws and trust-busting actions, another generation's solution to the problem, have ceased to be effective in the face of immense corporate legal and political resources. The biggest of modern corporations can frequently bring more effective power to bear in such cases than government. Another form of ostracism will have to be found.

One author has asked, "If General Motors holds society responsible for providing the conditions of its existence, then for what does society hold General Motors responsible?" Answering his own question, he says society's minimum requirements ought to be that "productive organizations avoid deception or fraud, that they show respect for their workers as human beings, and that they avoid any practice that systematically worsens the situation of a given group in society." But don't our laws prescribe exactly that already?

Another writer suggests that criminal corporations be systematically subjected to "shame" through court orders forcing them to commit some portion of their advertising budget to publicizing their lawbreaking, and to do community service. It is an appealing idea, but it would not cover the many gray area cases in which unethical but not strictly illegal actions are involved.[34] In any event, it would immediately be challenged under First Amendment and similar human rights legislation. Furthermore, people can be shamed by the disapproval of a single, significant individual, or even by their own internal sense of right and wrong. In other words, humans can feel shamed even in committing an *undiscovered* unethical act. For a corporation to be "shamed," it is necessary that a significant number of its customers become aware of its actions and mobilize themselves to take action. Corporate shame is felt only when profits are threatened and is activated only by widely publicized acts.

All modern business corporations engage public relations staffs and consultants whose function is to supply a human mask for the corporate automaton and, when necessary, to minimize corporate "shame" by convincing the public that objectionable actions have been ethically defensible. This is a thoroughly synthetic process: truth and contrition are human concepts that are alien to corporations. They are sometimes simulated in the guise of public relations devices that may, on occasion, help to minimize the "shame" of sagging profits. But it is the *appearance* of virtue, rather than virtue itself, that interests corporations, virtue being a metaphysical concept not accessible to the corporation's machine mentality. Having a good reputation — having the appearance of virtue — is always a benefit and always, by definition, widely known, while *being* virtuous may not be known to others at all and it may not be particularly advantageous in the Rationalist framework within which corporations function.

The classic, paradigm-setting case, the action taken by the manufacturers of Tylenol when it was discovered that capsules of the painkiller had been contaminated with cyanide, is lauded in business texts as a study in corporate virtue, though it is, in reality, an exemplary case of the successful *simulation* of virtue. The first poisoned capsules were ingested by some of the seven victims on September 29, 1982. Johnson & Johnson made its first public statements on the story October 5, and on October 7 announced the national withdrawal of 31 million Tylenol capsule bottles (at a cost of about $100 million), until a new safety seal could be put into use. It had been recognized by the pharmaceutical industry some time earlier that gel capsules presented a product security threat, and Johnson & Johnson already had a safety-sealed bottle on the drawing board for that reason. Sales returned to normal levels shortly after the new package was introduced, less than two months following the poisonings.

In popular accounts of the events, Johnson & Johnson is typically praised for honesty, transparency, and doing the right thing regardless of cost. This perception differs significantly from the facts of the case, though it does coincide closely with the version of events constructed by corporate public relations initiatives following the incident.

Although it took about a week for Johnson & Johnson to order the withdrawal, two public relations textbooks, *Effective PR* and *PR Strategies & Tactics,* use the term "immediately" in referring to the Tylenol recall. (The latter textbook dropped mention of Tylenol altogether in its 2000 edition.)[35] In the movie *The Insider,* actor Russell Crowe perpetuates the myth of the immediate recall in conversation with actor Al Pacino: "James Burke, CEO of Johnson and Johnson, when he found out that some lunatic had put poison in Tylenol bottles, he didn't argue with the FDA, he didn't wait for the FDA to tell him, he just pulled Tylenol off the shelves in every store right across America instantly." As for transparency, Johnson & Johnson never did "go public" with the story in any normal sense of the phrase. It held no press conferences, choosing instead to deal with thousands of reporters' inquiries on an individual basis, over the telephone. Of course, there is no public record of what was said in those conversations. Public relations strategy in this case has served Johnson & Johnson well, preserving the appearance of virtue and maintaining its good reputation.

This virtuous reputation was stained, however, when in 2000 Johnson & Johnson's LifeScan division pleaded guilty to criminal charges in a U.S. court and anted up a $60 million fine. The offense? Selling faulty glucose monitoring devices to diabetics, failing to notify them of defects, failing to notify the Food and Drug Administration of the defects, and then providing the agency with false information. A class-action suit filed in the case alleged that at least three diabetics had died because of the false readings on their SureStep monitoring devices.

More recently, threatened class-action suits against manufacturers of fast foods have provoked an outburst of "virtuous" behavior on the part of corporations painfully aware of the success of similar suits against cigarette makers. Frito-Lay, Inc., a division of PepsiCo and a major manufacturer of potato chips, announced it is developing chips "flecked with bits of broccoli" and lowering the fat content in several of its other snack foods. Al Bru, president and CEO of Frito-Lay North America, told a newspaper reporter that the "company is working to be part of the solution to the obesity problem." But the same newspaper report quoted dietician Elisabeth Pearson, author of a book called *When in Doubt, Eat Broccoli,* as saying, "It's a marketing ploy. It wouldn't provide anything of nutritional value. We need to get back to real basics like [unprocessed] fruits, vegetables, whole grains, and nuts." The Texas-based company also announced, in September 2002, that it is switching from hydrogenated oils to trans-fat-free corn oil in production of its fried snacks. Dietician Pearson told the newspaper that it is new labeling laws being introduced in 2006 in Canada, forcing manufacturers to include information about trans fats, that has motivated the shift toward corn oil. "They got away with it as long as they could," she said.[36]

The first company to switch, marketers know, has the advantage of being able to claim leadership in taking the moral high road. With that in mind, another industry giant, Kraft Foods, surprised the $1 trillion U.S. processed-food industry with the announcement that it will reduce portion sizes, develop healthier products, and discontinue its Wienermobiles and other fast-food in-school promotions across America. Kraft, a $29 billion business with such brands as Oreo cookies, Velveeta and Cheez Whiz processed-cheese products, Oscar Meyer meats, Jet-Puffed marshmallows, and Ritz crackers, is owned by Altria Group, formerly called Philip Morris International, a major tobacco manufacturer and defendant in the enormously costly tobacco class-action suits. A Kraft spokesman seemed to concede the company's financial motives for the changes to its product line, saying that if the company's initiative "also discourage a plaintiff's attorney or unfair litigation, that's just fine with us."[37] The company faced a flood of obesity-related lawsuits, led by one filed by a California lawyer on behalf of Oreo cookie eaters who, according to Kraft, have consumed 450 billion of the chocolate creme sandwiches since they were introduced in 1911. The suit alleged that Kraft continued to use trans fats in its product despite decades of research showing that these low-cost hydrogenated oils are a major cause of heart disease.[38] It was dropped by the plaintiff when the company announced it had plans to reduce or eliminate trans fats in Oreos and other snack products.

Kraft's new policies are another case of a corporation's choosing to act unethically until forced to do otherwise. A leading Canadian food scientist noted, "We've been urging the industry to get progressive for years. . . . I had an executive from a U.S. food company in my office talking about trans fats and he said, 'If the government isn't going to force labels on us, it's not worth our while to change it.'"[39]

The patent inability of modern business corporations to behave morally in any authentic sense of that term is, for me, the best evidence of the essentially inhuman, machine-like nature that defines them. For corporations, the concept of doing the right thing is unintelligible, because the very notion draws on a well of human experience that is inaccessible to machine entities. For a machine, even a decision to obey the law must be an abstract calculation rather than a moral instinct, and obedience will only be forthcoming when penalties are severe enough to affect profitability.

# 8

# Who's in Charge Here?

WHEN I BEGAN SERIOUSLY TO STUDY THE HISTORY and nature of the modern business corporation I found myself, by slow degrees, beginning to look at it in a new and somewhat unnerving way. The more I learned, the more the corporation took on the appearance and attributes of an alien life-form — one of our own invention, that had adapted so successfully to its environment that it was squeezing out all its competitors and taking over our world.[1] That sent me to the literature of artificial intelligence (AI) and artificial life (AL), where I was able to conclude that corporations in their modern guise fit the criteria for life-form in these emerging so-called sciences of the artificial. Corporations may not be living creatures, but they behave as if they are, and that's what counts in AL: what is being sought by AL researchers is behavior that we would ordinarily describe as "alive" or "living," if we didn't know we'd made it ourselves.

Researchers have begun to study artificial life — one might say *simulated* life — because of a problem unique to the science of biology: it has only one example to study, and that is life on Earth. It is the only life we know of, and all of our current conclusions about the nature of life have been drawn from this sample of one. By constructing a selection of (artificial) life-forms, biologists hope to create a wider context for their inquiries into life, one that will provide a new viewpoint from which we will be able to look back on and better understand life as we currently know it.

The insight that makes this possible is that life is not an object or a material or a condition, as is supposed, for example, in the old idea of an *élan vital*, but rather what we call life is a complex relationship generated among non-living materials. This does not bring us any closer to understanding what life itself actually *is*, but it does present a possible approach to making serious inquiries. The idea being pursued in AL is to set up a system of relationships among simple entities, usually strings of computer code, meant to represent basic biological components such as molecules. The relationships are governed by a small set of simple rules provided by the programmer, governing the conditions, for example, of reproduction and death. (Note that these computer algorithms, should they produce a convincing artificial life-form, can in principle be translated into some form of robot or other mechanical representation that can act within and upon the real world around us.)

What interests researchers most is the unexpected properties or behaviors that emerge spontaneously out of complexity as the components interact over time, evolving into more and more complicated systems. To date, artificial life-forms consist entirely of programs running on computers. It seems to me that the corporation is at least as interesting as these, and I wish somebody would take it up as a serious AL inquiry.

At one point, I idly considered writing this book as a work of science fiction, taking a cue from stories like John Wyndam's *The Midwich Cukoos* and Ray Bradbury's "The Meteor," and movies like *Invasion of the Body Snatchers* and *Invaders from Mars*. On the surface, these stories are about the arrival on Earth of alien species and the frantic struggle of humanity to resist ultimate conquest. But their underlying theme, and the reason for their enduring popularity, is not so much invasion and resistance as our own alienation from basic human impulses right here on Earth: the "invaders" have been recognized by critics alternately as the threat posed by a faceless Communist uniformity (the movies flourished with the Cold War), or the moral emptiness of consumer society (as in the 1978 remake of *Body Snatchers*). The alien enemy in the movies is us.

I'm no novelist, though, and after toying with the idea for a few days I reverted to plan A: I leave the sci-fi novel to someone more capable. Nevertheless it is a fact that corporations do meet the most commonly accepted criteria for "life." Here, for example, is a list of properties associated with life as presented in a current survey of AL theory:[2]

- *Life is a pattern in space-time rather than a specific material object.* Life, in other words, is to be found inherent in dynamic relationships, rather than in material objects. That is why disassembling a living entity, destroying the pattern of relationships, kills it. There is an obvious match here, because corporations are not physical objects so much as webs of association and cooperation. Corporations are comprised of these relationships rather than physical objects, such as their headquarters buildings.

- *Self-reproduction, in itself or in a related organism.* Corporations routinely spawn subsidiaries and frequently divide in a cellular way into new corporate entities, either by choice, or in response to government litigation as in the case of AT&T becoming several "Baby Bells," each of which has since grown and further subdivided. More recently, Canadian Pacific voluntarily split itself into several independent corporations responsible for various aspects of the transportation giant's business.

- *Information storage of a self-representation.* That is, some DNA-like mechanism for storing the data necessary for replication. This, too, applies to corporations, which archive electronically and on paper the data necessary to replicate themselves.

- *A metabolism that converts matter/energy.* This involves an organism's taking in matter or energy from its environment and using it for its own purposes. Corporations clearly do this: one might even include in this category their use of human energy.

- *Functional interactions with the environment.* Once again, corporations clearly interact with their environment in ways that alter it.

- *Interdependence of parts.* Here the case is not quite so obvious. One of the things that defines living organisms is that they cannot be arbitrarily divided up without destroying them. Corporations would appear to be extraordinarily robust in this sense, and it is not clear how much radical surgery it takes to cause extinction.

- *Stability under perturbations of the environment.* The robustness of the corporation has been steadily improved through centuries of corporate-initiated jurisprudence and regulation aimed at achieving economic stability. Bankruptcy protection laws are a case in point.

- *The ability to evolve.* Another obvious match. Whereas early corporations were limited in their activities and form to the specifications of their charters, modern corporations have no such limitations and do routinely evolve, some-times dramatically adapting themselves to environmental (market) conditions.

- *Growth or expansion.* Enough said.

The 1991 Nobel Prize-winning economist Ronald H. Coase claimed that "the economy runs itself," and that beyond the personal planning of individual agents or participants, no other coordinating institution is needed. Within that autonomous and automatic system, Coase said (quoting a colleague), corporations are "islands of conscious power in this ocean of unconscious co-operation, like lumps of butter coagulating in a pail of butter-milk."[3] Though he did not mean to suggest that corporations are autonomous life-forms, his imagery is suggestive of conscious-ness appearing spontaneously as an emergent property of the complexity of the market, just as life is thought to be an emer-gent property of the complexity of the planetary biosystem.

Some readers will want to object at this point that corpo-rations are not autonomous at all, that they are *run* by humans. But there is good evidence to suggest that corporations, as they had evolved by the mid-twentieth century, manage their hu-man "managers." We can certainly make the empirical observation that corporations often do not *appear* to be managed by humans, since they so consistently act in contradiction of human interests.

Examples abound: the corporate lobby against measures to reduce the impact of global warming; corporate practices that are environmentally destructive; corporate dislocation of em-ployee's lives through "rationalization" measures; corporate ex-ploitation of Third World workers; corporate participation in the worldwide illegal arms traffic; corporate resistance to regulation of the production of toxic chemicals; corporate concealment of harmful side effects of widely used pharmaceuticals; systematic corporate tax evasion (impoverishing the public sector); corporate suborning of information media; corporate incitement of the excesses of consumerism, etc.

For a more specific example, the recent case of the use of a lead substitute called MTBE by oil companies to boost gasoline octane ratings can be taken as exemplary. A coalition of groups that can legitimately claim to represent the human interest in the issue — the National League of Cities, the U.S. Conference of Mayors, the National Association of Counties, the American Public Works Association, the American Water Works Association, the Association of Metropolitan Water Agencies, the Association of California Water Agencies — has protested new federal regulations that permit continued use of the cancer-causing chemical despite evidence that it has infiltrated groundwater in dangerous amounts. Congress responded to an aggressive and well-documented corporate lobby in framing the legislation, and in so doing clearly favored the corporate interest over the human interest.[4]

The phrase "corporate crime" is so loosely defined in media reports that it leads to serious confusion. I want to make it clear that the kind of behavior we are concerned with here is the crimes (or moral lapses) *of* corporations, and not crimes *against* corporations. The first is far more socially significant, and interesting, than the second.

Crimes *against* corporations — theft, fraud, embezzlement, and the like, are committed for the personal financial gain of the perpetrators. They represent garden-variety criminality of the kind that has always been with us and no doubt always will be. They are committed by people most of us would have no difficulty in identifying as crooks, and the perpetrators almost always act in the knowledge that what they are doing is wrong.

Crimes (or moral lapses) committed *by* corporations, on the other hand, are committed in the name of profit, on behalf of the corporation and its shareholders. They are committed, ostensibly, by people who believe themselves to be operating in good faith within an ethical framework that is widely recognized and respected. The people involved in the commission of these crimes more often than not do not think of them as such.

The victims of crimes *against* corporations are corporations and their shareholders. The victims of crimes *of* corporations are individuals, groups, nations — in some cases, all of humanity. Environmentalists will want to further widen the class to include wildlife and ecosystems. We recognize the human motivations for crimes *against* corporations; the explanation for crimes *by* corporations is less obvious.

This once-clear distinction between the two categories of crime has been muddied in recent years with the practice of providing corporate stock as part of the compensation package of senior managers. As shareholders, these managers often find it in their personal interest to take corporate risks that result in short-term increases in stock values, and thus of the manager's net worth. I would classify these cases as crimes against the corporation, because they involve actions that were taken with personal, and not corporate, interests as the primary motivation. Unfortunately, there is frequent overlap in motivation, as appears to have been the case with the Enron and WorldCom debacles, in which senior managers were pursuing on behalf of the corporation a strategy that was concurrently making them very rich as individuals. Nevertheless, it is important to maintain the distinction if only because it places in proper context the frequently heard argument that the problem presented by the modern business corporation would be solved if only we could weed out the few "bad apples" that are behind "corporate crime." It is, indeed, bad apples who commit crimes *against* corporations. But putting them in jail will do little or nothing to solve the problem of crime committed *by* corporations. Thus, the vaunted Sarbanes-Oxley Act enacted by Congress in 2002 in the wake of Enron, World-Com, and a raft of other corporate scandals, designed to toughen corporate accountability and accounting practices, cannot be seen in any way as offering a solution to the problem of the corporation as I have been discussing it here. It is aimed overtly at curbing what I have defined as crimes against the corporation, and, not incidentally, increasing public confidence in both the corporation and the stock market.

I recently ran across this news story on a Web archive, and I can reproduce it here in full confidence that few readers will be aware of the details — this kind of tale has become so common-place as to receive scant coverage in popular media:

> LONDON — The cigarette industry, including leading executives of Philip Morris Co., has waged a long campaign to discredit the World Health Organization and deflect the United Nations unit from curbing smoking around the world, according to published reports Wednesday.
>
> Articles citing a draft of a WHO report said investigators from the UN's public health agency found cigarette companies attempted to discredit scientific studies by the WHO, and sought to have its budgets lowered.
>
> "The attempted subversion has been elaborate, well financed, sophisticated and usually invisible," said a WHO report on its probe into formerly secret tobacco industry documents. The papers were released after lawsuits against the firms in the United States.
>
> According to the *Washington Post*, the report says the industry's attempts to combat the influence of the WHO included a plan

in 1988, headed by Geoffrey C. Bible, Philip Morris's current chief executive. The plan reportedly aimed to attack WHO anti-smoking measures worldwide. The draft report says some aspects of the scheme remain in place today, the *Washington Post* wrote.

## Not guilty, says Morris

Philip Morris denied seeking to undermine WHO's anti-smoking campaigns and attacked the agency's report as based on selective use of old documents. "Public health messages on smoking by WHO and other organizations have not been altered by Philip Morris, nor were any WHO initiatives prevented or obstructed by any conduct on the part of Philip Morris," the U.S. company said in a statement from its European headquarters in Lausanne, Switzerland.

The WHO report says the tobacco industry placed allegedly independent consultants at the Geneva headquarters of the WHO, concealing the fact that these people had financial ties to the industry. The report also maintains the tobacco firms attempted to turn other UN agencies against the WHO, in part by highlighting the economic wealth developing countries generated by growing tobacco.[5]

Judging from this example, the kind of people who run tobacco companies do not appear to resemble any of the people that most of us know, unless we happen to work in a clinic for the treatment of the mentally ill. The crime being committed seems vastly out of proportion to any benefit likely to be received by any individual manager in terms of increased remuneration. The corporate managers responsible seem to be devoid of the moral sensitivity that is a hallmark of the healthy human individual. I would suggest, in view of this fact and in light of the distinction between crimes against and by corporations, that this is a case of a crime or moral offense committed *by* the corporation.

Another example: for many years, asbestos was the insulator of choice in many electrical and thermal applications. Millions of homes and public buildings contained asbestos, used in one of the estimated three thousand products that incorporated the mineral. As early as 1928, when the Prudential Insurance Company stopped insuring asbestos worker's lives, the Johns Manville Company, a major producer, knew of the adverse health effects of the product. Although court records show that even at that time some executives were concerned about the product's potential for harm, warning labels were not placed on asbestos packaging until 1964. The documents also show that company doctors lied to asbestos workers about the cause of their health problems. Company executives systematically hid scientific data from workers, the public, and government inspectors. Thousands, perhaps tens of thousands, of preventable deaths were the result.

During court proceedings a lawyer testified about a confrontation he'd had with a Johns Manville attorney about failure to share X-ray results with workers: "You mean to tell me you would let them work until they dropped dead?" The corporate counsel replied: "Yes. We save a lot of money that way." The company had determined that it was cheaper to pay workers compensation than to clean up the work environment. By 1982 there were more than 17,000 active lawsuits against the company, and with thousands more from World War Two shipbuilders in the offing (asbestos was used extensively in naval construction) the company filed for Chapter 11 bankruptcy. It now operates under the name Manville Corporation.

Again, this clearly falls into the category of crime committed by the corporation, but beyond that, how is one to account for this kind of behavior? Are we to assume that corporate managers are, as a class, morally deficient?

There is some evidence that students who enter business schools are less ethically adept than their campus cohorts. In U.S. research, they rank lower in moral reasoning than students in philosophy, political science, law, medicine, and dentistry.[6] They are also more likely to cheat on tests, commit plagiarism, and engage in other kinds of academic skullduggery than students with majors heading for other careers.[7] But nothing in this research suggests that these students are afflicted by anything comparable to the level of moral obtuseness routinely displayed by the corporations that will eventually employ them.

The hypothesis that humans aren't really "in charge" seems to me to be the only reasonable way to explain the fact that so many corporations commit acts of economic injustice, environmental degradation, and outright criminality — acts that their alleged managers would never consider doing in their lives as private individuals.

The paradigm-setting case is that of the Ford Pinto, of interest here not because of its exceptional nature, but precisely because it is so unexceptional, despite its appalling details. By all accounts, Lee Iacocca is not in his private life a person inclined to kill in return for money. And yet as president of the Ford Motor Company, he and his fellow Ford executives (including CEO Henry Ford II) permitted many deaths and injuries to occur when he could have prevented them by spending a relatively small amount of corporate money ($11 per vehicle) to relocate the compact Pinto's gas tank and thereby reduce the likelihood of explosions in low-speed, rear-end collisions — a flaw that had shown up in the company's own preproduction testing in 1970. Ford executives commissioned a cost-benefit analysis that was based on a U.S. National Highway Traffic Safety Administration estimate of the economic cost of auto fatalities. Each death, the

NHTSA data said, cost the economy $200,725. This was taken at Ford to be the approximate amount that would have to be paid out in each successful lawsuit for wrongful death in its exploding vehicles.

In a memo entitled "Fatalities Associated with Crash-Induced Fuel Leakage and Fires," Ford executives estimated that the cost of fixing the gas tank problem would be almost three times greater than the estimated cost of the 180 fatalities and 180 serious burn injuries in 2,100 burned vehicles that could be expected without gas tank improvements. Ford chose not to fix the problem. Pintos were produced and sold (and caught fire) for eight years, until an outraged jury awarded a victim $125 million in mostly punitive damages (reduced on appeal to $6 million) and media attention to the exploding gas tank problem caused sales of the car to drop off dramatically, at which time Ford initiated a recall. What had prevented Iacocca and other executives from obeying their human instincts in the Pinto case?[8]

A new generation of Ford Motor Company executives in 2000 decided against recalling several models of light trucks and SUVs that had substandard door latches that caused occupants to be ejected in collisions. The recall had been recommended by Ford's own safety engineers, who found the latches did not meet U.S. safety standards. Several deaths had been reported and about sixteen product liability lawsuits had been filed. Ford's approach to the problem was to turn to its lawyers, who found a rarely used alternative compliance test that the latches, Ford claimed, can pass. The problem is clearly intergenerational.[9]

General Motors was recently successfully sued for $4.9 million (reduced on appeal) by six passengers in a Chevrolet Malibu that exploded in a collision. The case closely paralleled that of the Ford Pinto in that the company knew from its own testing that the placement of the gasoline tank exposed occupants to danger of being burned to death in minor collisions, but after a cost-benefit analysis, GM decided not to alter the car.[10] A number of GM executives were involved in making this decision, and none of them, so far as we know, was a psychopath. How could any of them have possibly justified it in terms of the morality they profess in their private lives?

The same question might be asked of the managers of Nestlé or ExxonMobil or Shell or Dow Chemical or Monsanto or Nike or any number of other corporations that have been involved in deliberate actions that are clearly and obviously immoral. The answer, it seems to me, can only be found in the fact that these crimes are committed not by the individual corporate officers but by the corporation itself, which in a very real sense manages its "managers." I find it impossible to believe that all of these corporations (and many more that could have been mentioned) are managed by psychopaths. As Sherlock Holmes famously observed, when you have excluded the impossible, whatever remains, however implausible, must be the truth.


While corporations can be and frequently are called to account in court for the damage done by dangerous or poorly made products, as has happened in the examples above, another aspect of the harm they can do is less obvious and harder to pin down. Until very recently, it was routinely dismissed as one of the unavoidable costs of "progress." In a broad sense it can be said that corporations specialize in the creation of what economists call "externalities," which are the materially, socially, and morally harmful side effects of the production of profit. They are called externalities because they are made external to the corporation's interests and concern, and are instead dumped on the wider public to deal with. Air and water pollution are obvious cases in point, as are the social dislocations caused by the closing of factories, and the harm done to children by violent television programming. Externalities are a way of privatizing profit while socializing costs.[11]

But corporate "externalities" can be much more subtle than these, and at the same time more broadly significant. Sociologist Zygmunt Bauman has traced the rise and fall of the welfare state over the past sixty years and concluded, with compelling logic, that universal welfare measures (the so-called social safety net) were accepted without serious political opposition in Britain, continental Europe, and in North America following World War Two because they served the interests of business, which would otherwise have fought to block their implementation. The amenities provided by the welfare state underwrote the development of a strong, healthy, and well-educated workforce that was willing to take risks in employment and was ready and able to be retrained in periods of joblessness. These same universal measures are currently under attack across the industrialized world by proponents of "workfare" (mandatory work in return for welfare) and "focused spending" (means tests required of recipients), "two-tier Medicare" (public health care for the poor and indigent only), tax breaks for private schools, higher university tuition fees, and so on, because business no longer has a need for the same quality in its workforce or in the reserve labor pool provided by the unemployed.

The need is no longer there because domestic jobs are increasingly of the McJob burger-flipping variety, and those that require serious assembly line or piecework drudgery are being shipped offshore to destitute Third World nations. Increasingly, high-skilled technical jobs are being filled by relatively low-paid, but well-educated, workers in emerging economic powers like Singapore, India, and China. Social welfare measures no longer obviously serve the interests of Western business, so business now throws its weight behind proposals to slash spending on health, education, and welfare, and instead hand out tax cuts. What these "flag of convenience" decisions in exporting jobs involve is the "promise of opportunity without responsibility, and when such 'making economic sense' opportunities come by, few sound-minded businessmen, hard-pressed by the stern demands of competitiveness, would insist on their responsibilities."[12]

As an analysis of the current resurgence of classical liberal or laissez-faire ideology, Bauman's argument makes sense. But it is flawed, it seems to me, in one important way. Like the Pinto case and other examples given above, it demands of us that we accept that the people who are responsible for business decisions of this kind are a species of monster, with no regard for human welfare. Or, what is equally difficult to accept, that they actually believe that in refusing to recall exploding vehicles, or in continuing to market cancer-causing products, or in concealing adverse drug reactions from industry regulators, or in lobbying to kill public health regulations — that in all of these actions they are actually serving in some magical way a larger public good.

It seems to me altogether more reasonable to suggest once again that the "inhuman" decisions are being made not by humans, but by their master, the corporation. What is missing in Bauman's analysis is an acknowledgment that *no* "sound-minded" corporate manager in a position of authority would ever, all things being equal, choose responsibility over profit. To do so would be to behave irrationally in the context established by the market.

One can of course imagine scenarios in which a choice in favor of responsibility could be contrived to result in profit, or at least the avoidance of loss. This would be the case, for example, where "responsible" action is dictated by government regulations backed by effective enforcement and heavy fines. Most business school ethics texts argue that ethical behavior need not impinge on profit maximization, that ethical behavior is actually profitable.[13] However, what is being promoted in the textbooks is not really ethical behavior, but mere prudence. Authentic ethical behavior takes place outside any consideration of benefit, and may frequently involve a sacrifice. In any case the routine behavior of large business corporations suggests that they do not perceive the textbook advice as holding true in real-life market conditions. It can be stated as a general rule of corporate life that to place moral responsibility ahead of profit is to fatally imperil one's executive career. Corporate employees, as a condition of employment, place responsibility to the corporation (the responsibility to maximize profit) ahead of everything else, including responsibility to humanity.

Is this too harsh?

Consider the consumer electronics industry. For many years it has been known that materials widely used in the manufacture of electronic gadgets of all kinds, from computers to cell phones to clock radios, present a range of hazards to human health ranging from various cancers to nerve damage and mental retardation. Materials such as lead, cadmium, mercury, hexavalent chromium, and flame retardants such as PBE and PBDE are extremely toxic even in small quantities, and can and do contaminate groundwater when disposed of in landfill dumps. Despite this knowledge, and despite explosive sales and enormous profits in the industry, no action was taken by any of the corporations involved to eliminate these dangerous materials. It was not until the European Union, China, and Japan all passed legislation prohibiting manufacture or import of electronic products containing these materials that the industry finally took action, initially to meet Europe's July 2006 deadline for compliance.

Why hadn't any of these enormously wealthy corporations — giants like Sony, Philips, GE, and Westinghouse — acted on their own? Why had no courageous corporate leader taken the initiative? After all, a serious, well-documented, and widespread risk to human health and welfare was at stake, and the families and loved ones of corporate executives were in no way immune.

A fascinating insight into the internal processes of a corporation faced with a straightforward choice between profit and morality is provided by the classic case of the Ford Pinto and the recent revelations of one of the corporate participants. During the 1978 civil suit arising out of the Pinto fires and deaths, Ford executives insisted that cost-benefit analyses of the kind the company used in deciding not to fix the gas tank problem are *a normal and essential part of doing business.* What had happened, in plain language, was that the corporation had decided that if the cost of repairing a known defect exceeded a certain dollar value, then it was permissible to take human lives. But it presented its case in court quite differently. Its lawyers argued that everybody knows that making cars safe makes them more expensive, but buyers want low prices. Therefore, people knowingly accept risks when they buy cars — they make a conscious and deliberate trade-off between price and safety. Ford's lawyers concluded from this that it was okay for Ford to make unsafe cars — that the company in fact had no choice — because consumers demanded it! There is no reason to believe that this kind of twisted logic has gone out of fashion.

When it comes to "doing the right thing," corporations take a radically different view from humans. From the corporation's point of view, any act is right that improves shareholder return on investment. An act is wrong only if it poses a risk of legal penalty serious enough to more than offset the projected gains. Intelligent, healthy humans can ordinarily be expected to experience ethical qualms long before the threshold of lawbreaking is reached. Nevertheless, humans employed by corporations at all levels generally conform to the corporate ethical model while on the job. Most feel they have no alternative, because they voluntarily submit to contracts, both tacit and written, that limit their actions to the narrowly defined parameters that serve corporate interests.

The constraint may be either internal or external. Corporate managers may be coerced by law, regulation, and corporate policy into "behaving responsibly" — adopting corporate behavior while in the job. For example, labor law in many jurisdictions explicitly states that employers are entitled to the expectation that employees will exhibit corporate loyalty and not work against their employer's goals and interests. Or they may adopt corporate behavior of their own volition, in accordance with internalized or indoctrinated beliefs. In either case — by coercion or by persuasion — the corporation is imposing its will on its human functionaries. The corporate ethical system must be imposed (or learned) because it is essentially inhuman, that is to say, unnatural in a human context.

Dennis A. Gioia is a case in point. Currently a management scholar and a specialist in "social cognition in corporations," he has the kind of real-world experience that lends a special piquancy to his views, and further illuminates the exemplary Ford Pinto case.[14] He graduated with an M.B.A. in 1972, got a job at Ford, and within two years was the company's field recall coordinator. Although he and his colleagues were aware of the Pinto explosion problem from the earliest reported incidents, and he actually inspected a car in which people had burned to death, he consistently voted against recall when the question was raised. He did this, he says, knowing nothing of the preproduction testing that exposed the flaw in gas tank placement, and never having seen the notorious cost-benefit analysis that had been done by his superiors.

Gioio says he failed to act on his native ethical impulses because, as a corporate functionary or appliance, he was conditioned to acting within the framework of a "cognitive script" that enabled him to cope with what would otherwise have been overwhelming amounts of information and responsibility. We all use such scripts in our lives: they are simply established patterns of behavior that enable us to perform routine tasks such as driving to work or using proper table manners at a dinner party without giving our actions much conscious thought. Scripts are especially useful in dealing with the routines of work, and help to make employees interchangeable by providing a set of routines that can be adopted with relative ease. As psychological phenomena, they are manufactured in the first instance by human workers and managers, but they are produced within the template provided by corporate exigencies and rules of conduct, and they therefore embody corporate values along with workers' and managers' shorthand techniques for operating within those values.

Gioia explains that he "looked right past" the evolving Pinto tragedy because his on-the-job "script" did not identify the pattern of cases he was receiving as a crisis *for the company*. More important, the script had no ethical content. His description of his moral and psychological position as a corporate manager is revealing in that it demonstrates how, even in such an extreme case, the corporation, in shaping the script, controls managers' behavior:

> The recall coordinator's job was serious business. *The scripts associated with it influenced me more than I influenced* [*them*]. Before I went to Ford I would have argued strongly that Ford had an ethical obligation to recall. After I left Ford, I now argue and teach that Ford had an ethical obligation to recall. But, while I

was there, I perceived no obligation to recall and I remember no strong ethical overtones to the case whatsoever. It was a very straightforward decision, driven by dominant scripts for the time, place, and context. [Emphasis added]

Sociologists have provided a variety of explanations of the phenomenon of aberrant ethical behavior exhibited in the corporate setting by otherwise "normal" people. Some point out that people employed within corporations act not as individual decision makers but as agents of others — ultimately, of the corporate entity — and in this way avoid feelings of personal responsibility. Managers make decisions and give orders in the name of the corporation and not in keeping with their personal standards and values.[15] Others point to the "psychological realities" of corporations that lead to increased risk taking on the one hand and failure to acknowledge moral and legal responsibility for harm on the other. These include diffusion of responsibility; role specialization; incomplete information; organizational culture; and management's ability to punish nonconformity and disobedience.[16] David Luban sees three distinct ways in which corporate structure clouds culpability:

> Psychologically, role players in such organizations lack the emotional sense that they are morally responsible for the consequences of organizational behavior. . . . Politically, responsibility cannot be localized on the organizational chart, and thus in some real . . . way no one — *no one* — ever is responsible. Morally, role players have insufficient information to be confident that they are in a position to deliberate effectively, because bureaucratic organizations parcel out information along functional lines.[17]

These sociological analyses, like Gioia's script analysis, merely raise in a different way the central question I have been asking: Do managers in any real sense manage corporations, or does the corporate entity actually manage its "managers"? The latter proposition seems, on the evidence, to be clearly the case. The corporate structure, with its rigidly defined goals and its state-sanctioned and reinforced power to discipline, constrains managers to act in ways most would find ethically abhorrent in their private lives. That is, it forces (or seduces) them to consistently act so as to enhance corporate profit even at the expense of human welfare, from the individual to the entire species.

The case of the electronics industry and its reluctance to remove hazardous materials from its products demonstrates the point. Corporate executives were prevented from taking action, doing the right thing, because they were and are bound by contracts, formal and informal, that constrain them to act always in accordance with the corporation's paramount goal of maximizing profit. To be the first in an industry to take any action that might raise costs, however little and whatever the moral benefit, is to risk losing market share and thus profit. So, not one of these prodigiously wealthy and resourceful corporations would act unless all were forced to act in concert. And what forced them to act was the credible threat of financial penalties that would outweigh the benefits of noncompliance. Many an industry CEO was no doubt mightily relieved when the new laws were passed, but the fact remains that they did not — could not — do the morally right thing until that happened. They were being controlled and prevented from acting in the interest of human health and welfare by the corporations they ostensibly managed.[18]

# 9

# The Corporate Worker's Dilemma

I HAVE BEEN FOCUSING, SO FAR, on the ethical problems of corporate managers, but non-management corporate workers have significant moral dilemmas of their own. Those dilemmas are rooted in the axiom of classical market economics, which says that workers can be treated as more or less interchangeable factors of production, or "human resources." Land, labor, and capital is the classic triad of economic theory, and each is ideally reducible to homogeneous units of measurement. In the classical economic tracts of the nineteenth century, and in the government policies they so deeply influenced, society was reduced "to a mere reservoir of factors of production for enterprise: not only the land and the trees were . . . commodities, but people too, all to be used and disposed of as economic expediency required, as judged by the cold calculus of accumulation."[1]

In the twentieth century this Rationalist bias was triumphant in the work of Frederick Taylor and the scientific management movement he inspired. Historian David Noble makes the important observation that most of the early professional business managers were, like Taylor himself, drawn from the ranks of professional engineers who put the stamp of their trade's results-oriented worldview on management theory. "The scientific management of labor followed directly in the minds of [engineer-managers] from the standardization of materials and machinery.

While standardization was the 'elimination of waste in materials' . . . scientific management was 'the elimination of waste in people.'"[2] A leading American engineer and educator of the 1920s, Dexter Kimball, observed that "the extension of the principles of standardization to the human element in production is a most important and growing field of activity."[3] To achieve this end, leading American manufacturing corporations set up in-house training programs, which were linked through an organization known as the National Association of Corporation Schools, founded in 1913. The NACS and its members would ultimately play an important role in the development of university engineering schools throughout America following World War One. David Noble supplies some representative views from NACS educators:

> "Man-stuff," in the view of Elmo Lewis [of the Burroughs Adding Machine Company], was the "most important thing" with which the companies had to deal. It was the substance "out of which they make their business." E. A. Deeds of the National Cash Register Company agreed: "I am most interested," he said, "in increasing the efficiency of the human machine." In addition to technical proficiency, these educators all stressed the need for training for management. "Electrical engineers," Arthur Williams [of New York Edison, President of NACS] observed, "are from the practical standpoint . . . men without peer in running machines, in running plants, but not men trained, necessarily, in running human machines."[4]

In Taylor's vision, "science would serve to remove the irrational and the emotional dimension of the human element from organizational life, replacing it with formal, Rationalistic structures that would ensure maximum efficiency and minimal conflict."[5] In his classic *Shop Management* (1911) he wrote: "All possible brain work should be removed from the shop and centered in the planning or laying-out department, leaving for the foremen and gang bosses work strictly executive in nature. Their duties should be to see that the operations planned and directed from the planning room are promptly carried out in the shop."[6]

Managers, too, fell victim to the drive to shape individuals to corporate requirements. The successful manager, even today, "dispassionately takes stock of himself, treating himself as an object, as a commodity. . . . He analyzes his strengths and weaknesses and . . . then he systematically undertakes a program to reconstruct his image, his publicly avowed attitudes or ideas."[7]

Fordism, named of course for that great industrial innovator, Henry Ford, combined Taylor's scientific management ideas with assembly-line production techniques, giving concrete form to the long-standing Rationalist dream of humans working in perfect harmony with the machinery of production. The ultimate Fordist corporate worker would be a close approximation of an intelligent robot, which would behave perfectly rationally in the context of its mechanical environment. In other words, it would do its job according to instructions, consistently, tirelessly, and without complaint. Another twentieth-century innovation, workplace automation, seeks to fulfill that dream, replacing human workers with machines. The role of humans in corporate capitalist enterprise is succinctly summarized by economic historian Noah Kennedy:

> Humans fill the roles in productive processes that are uneconomical to mechanize. This should not be a shocking statement, for if any of our jobs could be done at a lower cost by a machine there is no doubt that this would come to pass. Similarly, there is no doubt that each day technology closes in on new intellectual tasks that previously required human intelligence, which is just another way of saying that the task is being rationalized to the point that it can be reduced to formal description and performed by an algorithm. If there is not at

this very moment someone formulating a plan for displacing all or part of your labor with machinery, then the sad fact is that you make too little money to make it worthwhile.[8]

The successes of scientific management and automation led to a rapid expansion of industrial output that, as we saw in the history of the corporation (chapter 7), created pressure for corporate mergers and acquisitions on an unprecedented scale in the late nineteenth and early twentieth centuries. But while the new management techniques undoubtedly increased worker productivity, they also created a work environment that was suited more to machines than humans, and this led to widespread worker unrest.

The seething worker dissatisfaction that marked the early decades of the twentieth century was only partly assuaged by such "humanizing" initiatives as pioneering social theorist Meyer Bloomfield's "social capitalism." The science of handling workers must move beyond the factory to their communities, Bloomfield asserted in a 1915 article in the *Annals* of the American Society of Political and Social Science. "Wise business management recognizes the good sense of organizing the *source* of labor supply."[9] This meant instilling desirable physical and mental traits in workers and their children (future workers) at the community level. Corporations established schools and recreation facilities within factories and in adjacent workers' communities. Teaching curricula focused on literacy, fluency in English, and proper work habits. Eventually, the social capitalism idea would motivate corporate complicity, or at least acquiescence, in the construction of the welfare state following World War Two, as noted in chapter 8.

The late-twentieth-century advent of neoliberalism, Thatcherism, Reaganism, and the trend toward corporate "rationalization" saw a jettisoning of the long-standing social contract between worker and corporate employer that had been implicit in Fordist organizational technique. It was a contract baby boomers can remember their fathers (and occasionally mothers) signing on to, the one that guaranteed the security of employment that brought with it "economic freedom" and the "democracy of (consumer) choice" for workers, in exchange for their voluntary submission to what was often called wage-slavery. One kind of freedom was sacrificed at the altar of another.

But under the 1980s neoliberal management ethic, workers were laid off en masse, often for cosmetic reasons designed to boost share valuation; factories were shut down and relocated to low-wage regions of the world; pension funds were raided to inflate corporate earnings; workers found themselves expected to be on the job or on call for most of their waking hours.

Albert J. Dunlap, a celebrity CEO and financial-page poster boy, was seen as a role model by many ambitious managers of the era. Dunlap took over the profitable though unfashionably conservative Scott Paper Company in 1994 and immediately sold $2 billion of nonessential business divisions. He then fired a third of the corporation's employees — more than 11,000 workers in all. He moved the company headquarters from the Philadelphia area, where it had been founded 116 years earlier and where it had been a pillar of the community, to the more salubrious Boca Raton, Florida, where he happened to live. The company's share value leaped by 146 percent in fourteen months and profits doubled. Dunlap walked away in less than a year and a half with $100 million in salary, stock profits, and other perks, celebrated as a managerial genius. The self-styled "Rambo in pinstripes" went on to become CEO of Sunbeam in 1996 and promptly fired half the company's 12,000 employees and shut down two-thirds of its factories. Sunbeam stock soared and Wall Street once again hailed him as a hero.[10]

The "anything goes" attitudes of neoliberal business practices, typified by Dunlap, severely damaged the traditional relationship of trust between employer and employee and produced a deep and abiding skepticism among workers of all ranks. At the same time, the promise of material prosperity that was part of the consumer culture born in the 1920s was meaningless to the worker who had been laid off in late middle age, or was finding it increasingly difficult to find full-time employment at a living wage.

Corporations were able to be cavalier in their treatment of employees in this period because they were involved primarily in shedding personnel. However, one class of employee was retained because its members were of such high value that it was important to ensure their loyalty and continuity. Simply stated, they were very expensive to replace. Organizational theorists were called upon once again to find new ways of ensuring adequate supplies of docile, productive labor, this time of elite status.

One response has been the Human Relations Movement in organizational theory. It claims to be critical of Fordist policies, and has sought to "humanize" workplace relations.[11] The HR Movement emphasizes the social character of work and the importance of "interpersonal dynamics" on the job as a means of improving morale and productivity. A highly visible manifestation of HRM theory is the so-called enterprise culture introduced in Thatcher's Britain and taken up in Reagan's America and subsequently (though with less enthusiasm) in much of the rest of Europe and North America. An enterprise culture is one in which entrepreneurial values — the values of business and the corporation — are promoted as values to be encouraged in the individual as well.

Employers and managers equipped with HRM visions of work have thus claimed that there is no conflict between the pursuits of productivity, efficiency, and competitiveness on the one hand, and the humanizing of work on the other. On the contrary, they claim, the path to business success lies in engaging the employee with the goals of the company *at the level of his or her subjective identity*, aligning the wishes, needs, and aspirations of each individual who works for the corporation with the successful pursuit of corporate objectives. Through striving to fulfill their own needs and wishes, goals and aspirations, at work, each employee will at the same time be working for the advancement of the enterprise; the more the individual fulfills himself or herself, the greater the benefit to the corporation.

The idea is to capture the hearts and minds of employees — their very identity as persons — and then to define their goals and purposes, managing what they think and feel and not just how they behave on the job.[12] One could be forgiven for mistaking the Human Relations Movement in management theory for fascism, which is defined this way: "According to communitarians [of whom fascists are an extreme manifestation], individuals are constituted by the institutions and practices of which they are a part, and their rights and obligations derive from those same institutions and practices."[13]

In its attempt to extend the rationalization of labor to the very soul of the worker, enterprise culture is the ultimate expression of Rationalist economic and moral thought. It seeks to mold people at the level of their personal identity in ways that make them a better fit for the economic institutions we've inherited from the Rationalists. By virtue of being transportable from the corporate world to everyday life, HRM technique seeks to close the chasm between corporate and personal morality. It has become "an approach capable, in principle, of addressing the totality of human behavior."[14] Individuality becomes an enterprise; the individual becomes "an entrepreneur of the self."[15]

Fordism, too, had operated beyond the workplace, through

the invention and promotion of consumerism as a virtuous lifestyle. But the virtues of the ideal consumer and those of the ideal worker were not closely aligned, as they are in enterprise culture. Fordism saw two distinct, though structurally related, realms of life for the employee. The Fordist trade-off involved the worker sacrificing aspects of his humanity while on the job (behaving, ideally, like an automaton) in return for steady employment, high wages, and the consumer products these could buy. There is no such trade-off necessary in the enterprise culture, which assumes high wages (given corporate success) but not security of employment, and which also imposes ever-increasing workloads and ever-longer working days on employees. In enterprise culture, work is a virtue in itself — one no longer works to live, but lives to work. The Fordist dilemma of security versus freedom is erased. The HRM worker has neither.

Managers, especially senior managers, are not exempt from the blandishments of enterprise technique. Even if they do not personally buy into the corporate culture they have imposed (almost always with the help of outside HRM consultants), in their position as role models and leaders they are in a real sense held captive to it, with less opportunity to deviate and faced with more severe penalties for resistance than the ordinary worker or lower-echelon manager. This is most obviously true in union shops, where workers have some institutionalized protection from discipline.

Indeed, so-called post-Fordist management cultures foster a climate in which distinctions between workers and managers are systematically minimized. In such facilities, workers and managers park their cars in the same lot, wear the same overalls, share lunch facilities and toilets, and are described as "team members." To the extent that enterprise culture succeeds as a strategy, then to that extent both workers and managers alike become extensions of the corporation and its values, and to that extent they become cyborg appliances: they begin to take on machine-like characteristics in their behavior, jettisoning those purely human moral attributes that may have survived Fordist conditioning but conflict with corporate values and goals.

Information technologies have the potential to greatly accelerate this robotizing process. Enterprise Resource Planning (ERP) software has become big business in recent years for companies like Germany's SAP and America's Oracle. Its appeal lies in its ability to automate the management structures of large corporations, making them conform to strict efficiency guidelines and criteria embedded within the computer programs. At ERP-friendly corporations, managers spend most of their time in front of computer displays that monitor the activities of subordinate workers, for example, call-center employees.

But now ERP software is making it possible for the activities of the manager himself to be monitored (since almost all of his managerial actions are mediated by his computer). As one researcher has noted: "Senior managers can set targets for the speed and efficiency of the supply chain, and then at any time activate the system to find out whether the supply chain manager is meeting his goals."[16] More complex still, some advanced ERP systems can gather and analyze information from every level of corporate activity, in real time. The computer, programmed according to optimal corporate goals, begins to behave like a primitive corporate brain, and the old distinctions between managers and the managed vanish. The corporation itself, idealized and abstracted into software commands and responses, manages.

The celebrated French philosopher, sociologist, and historian Michel Foucault wrote about the ERP system before it had been invented, in his *Discipline and Punish* (1979). Foucault was interested in early prisons, especially one conceived and worked out in detail by Jeremy Bentham (whom we met previously as a pioneering Utilitarian thinker). Bentham's "panoptic" prison was based on an ingenious idea. It was a twelve-sided polygon formed in iron and sheathed in glass, creating what Bentham called "universal transparency." A single guard in the hub of the wheel-like structure would be able to see into each of the cells radiating like spokes from the center — prisoners would have no privacy, ever. "The major effect of the panopticon," writes Foucault, was "to induce on the inmate a state of conscious and permanent visibility that assured the autonomic functioning of power."

The really clever part of this is that for the power of authority (management) to be exercised effectively, it is not necessary that the inmates (workers) be under constant surveillance, only that the *possibility* of being under surveillance is constantly present. In Foucault's words, "He who is subject to a field of visibility and who knows it, assumes responsibility for the constraints of power; he makes them play spontaneously upon himself; he inscribes in himself the power relation in which he simultaneously plays both sides; he becomes the principle of his own subjugation." The effect of this, in turn, is that authority (management) can evade the appearance of coercion. "It is a perceptual victory that avoids any physical confrontation and which is always decided in advance."[17]

For workers in ERP-enabled corporations, "the empowered computer that confronts the employee at the beginning of every working day is nothing less than Foucault's 'tall outline of the central tower from which he [the employee/prisoner] is being spied upon.'"[18]

The call center and telemarketing industries of today admirably fulfill the dream of eighteenth- and early-nineteenth-century management theorists of applying time-and-motion study to the service industries (currently 80 percent of the workforce in North America). Like few other businesses they exemplify the vision of the "white-collar workforce marching to the drumbeat of scientific management." In the acres of cubicles of the call center and other information-centered workplaces we find "digital assembly lines in which standardization, measurement, and control come together to create a workplace of relentless discipline and pressure."[19] In ERP we have

> the outlines of a project truly Orwellian in its ambitions. The project is to develop technologies that are essentially human-proof in their operation, technologies whose control over employee behavior is so powerful that, no matter how ill-trained, alienated, or transient a workforce may be, technology can still be relied upon to deliver strong and improving levels of employee productivity.[20]

Lest the reader think this is of no particular importance to his or her personal life ("I don't work in a call center"), it needs to be pointed out that ERP is making major inroads into (among other areas) so-called managed care in U.S. medicine. As in other areas of ERP involvement, the role of the skilled worker, in this case the physician, is drastically devalued. In managed care medicine sold to corporations and offered by them to their employees, physicians are reduced to the role of sorting patients into subgroups. Patient care is provided according to the appropriate "protocol plan," described in detail in cost-efficiency-optimizing computer databases and closely monitored by "case managers" who typically have little or no medical training. "The great ambition of the managed care industry is to incorporate the physician within a regime of process whose rigor and discipline resembles those governing the activities of machinists and call center agents."[21]

ERP systems claim to radically increase worker productivity, and the assumption of standard economic theory is that when that happens, some of the benefits will be passed along to the workers in the form of better compensation. In other words, one would expect that in an economy increasingly dominated by ERP techniques, the growth of labor productivity would be closely matched by growth in real wages and benefits. In the United States, however, between 1989 and 2002, productivity of non-farm workers rose by an average annual rate of 2.07 percent, while workers' total compensation grew at an average rate of just 0.43 percent. In other words, productivity gains outstripped compensation rewards by 481 percent. Where had the economic gains gone? They were distributed mainly to shareholders, managers, and CEOs. According to research done by Simon Head, "The link between higher productivity and higher real wages and benefits breaks down when technology is used in ways that de-skill most workers, undermine their security in the workplace, and leave them vulnerable to employers possessed of overwhelming power."[22]

In their textbook *The Virtual Corporation: Structuring and Revitalizing the Corporation for the 21st Century*, William Davidow and Michael Malone speak glowingly of the new corporate model in which "traditional offices, departments, and operating divisions are constantly reforming according to need. Job responsibilities will regularly shift, as will lines of authority." All of this will be made possible with the help of ERP systems. "It is better to talk of the virtual corporation in terms of patterns of information and relationships."[23]

The authors describe what appears to be a revival of the

145

"social capitalism" ideas of the 1920s, detailing corporate educational schemes such as Motorola University, the giant electronics manufacturer's in-house teaching facility that employs more than one hundred full-time faculty and three hundred part-time teachers: "The university specializes in the teaching of interpersonal skills, and in recent years has worked with local community colleges and technical schools. . . . The program also stresses team-building skills and the inculcation of the Motorola corporate culture."[24] In Silicon Valley, the pioneering Intel Corporation "spends more than $2,000 per employee each year on skill development and inculcating both workers and mangers in the company's basic values regarding work ethics, risk taking, and customer orientation."[25] The emphasis on values training is universal in such corporate training schemes and is a reflection of the goals of enterprise culture.

The Marriott Corporation of hotel fame, another prime example of the well-managed twenty-first-century corporation, has addressed the problem of chronically high turnover in its employee ranks (more than 100 percent annually — i.e., every employee is replaced more than once per year) by turning to what are termed "nontraditional workers." In plain language, these are the physically and mentally handicapped, and they "often show dedication, loyalty, and even special skills not typically found in traditional employee groups." Although the program has its costs — "special social and job training courses, as well as teaming the new hires with company managers" — Marriott reports that "the turnover rate of this group is just 8 percent."[26]

No one would deny that it is a fine thing to have the handicapped gainfully employed, should they wish to have a job. But what does Marriott's program say about the working conditions they offer "normal" workers? The turnover rate suggests something far from satisfying. Should we expect the handicapped to put up with workplace conditions that ordinary workers spurn? What does this say about the status we assign to them? The question remains unasked in Davidow and Malone's glowing account. In a way, "the Marriott solution" epitomizes the goals and values of ERP and enterprise culture generally. Were we all as vulnerable and needy as the physically and mentally challenged among us, the goals of enterprise culture and ERP would be much more readily attainable.


Whether the productivity gains claimed by the corporate advocates of enterprise culture are real, the human and social impact of this ideology is plainly enormous. The human products of enterprise culture, valued as they are solely for their ability to produce and to consume, are in a kind of moral limbo when they can do neither. The unemployed and destitute in such a culture have a unique status — they have no value. Society thus has no responsibility to assist them in any way, though it will want to protect itself from them, especially when their numbers grow large enough for them to become a potential threat. This helps to explain the otherwise inexplicable and unconscionable tendency of neoliberal governments everywhere to mimic the Rationalist eighteenth-century Poor Law "reformers" by slashing welfare support and other social safety net provisions, while increasing police budgets.[27]

Whether it is even possible to construct a personal identity based on entrepreneurial values, as the Human Relations Movement envisages, is highly questionable. According to the philosopher Charles Taylor: "I can define my identity only against the background of things that matter. . . . Only if I exist in a world in which history, or the demands of nature, or the needs of my fellow human beings, or the duties of citizenship, or the call of God, or something else of this order *matters* crucially, can I define an identity for myself that is not trivial. . . . Not to have a [such a] framework is to fall into a life which is spiritually senseless."[28]

But it is difficult, if not impossible, to see how a meaningful spiritual life can be constructed on the entrepreneurial values of the modern business corporation, as HRM theory advocates. If "to know who I am is a species of knowing where I stand," as Taylor suggests, who am I if my fundamental moral precepts are drawn from the cyborg-like business corporation?

Moral realism, discussed in chapter 6, proposes in a similar vein that personal identity emerges from the innate moral impulse to be for the Other. One might say, in other words, that authentic identity is that which is created by acting on one's moral obligations.

If these ideas are correct, the only self that can be constructed within the framework of enterprise culture is one that is synthetic rather than authentic, spiritually barren, and dependent for its sustained existence on its usefulness to the corporation. Such a self is similar in that respect to the ant or bee or other social insect that can survive only within the relationships of the hive, which is necessary to make it in some sense "whole." This might be the definition of an ideal "human resource."

For the psychoanalyst Erich Fromm, the "entrepreneur of the self" who has bought into the notion of the enterprise culture, the "adjusted" person, "is one who has made himself into a commodity, with nothing stable or definitive except his need to please and his readiness to change roles."[29] Philosopher François Perroux has made the following observation relative to humans as commodities or things: "Slavery is determined neither by obedience nor the hardness of labor but by the status of being a mere instrument, and the reduction of man to the state of a thing."[30] For Herbert Marcuse, "This is the pure form of servitude: to exist as an instrument, as a thing. And this mode of existence is not abrogated [even] if the thing is animated and chooses its material and intellectual food, if it does not feel its being-a-thing, if it is a pretty, clean, mobile thing."[31]

If we can think of the corporation as an autonomous, artificial life-form, as I am proposing, then it seems to me that the ways in which it shapes and programs the humans it recruits to animate it are as nightmarish as anything in the realm of science fiction. What we have here is truly an invasion of the body snatchers. At least, that's one way of looking at it. The uncanny thing about reality is that it turns out to be pretty much whatever we imagine it to be. For two or three hundred years, we have imagined that Rationalist institutions, including the corporation, shape otherwise unruly and selfish individuals into a constructive force that produces continuous improvements in human welfare — in other words, something we call "progress." But if we pause in our increasingly frantic daily lives to look around at what we have created, in ourselves and in the world at large, we might well wonder if we have been caught up in the wrong dream, and if science fiction didn't get it right after all.

A generation after *Invasion of the Body Snatchers*, the cult film *Terminator* and its sequels portrayed a man/machine that is made invincible by its lack of human emotions. The special effects are superior, but the theme has changed little — the *Terminator* cyborg "acts as a symbol of the fear that humanity itself is in danger of becoming entirely absorbed into a wholly technological future within which the machine becomes a paradigm by which the organic itself functions."[32] Not communism, not consumerism, but the machinery through which they operate has become the object of fear.

The modern business corporation might well be the machine in question. The corporate cyborg, half human, half (bureaucratic) machine, a Rationalist social technology *par excellence*, has subsumed and provided synthetic counterparts for important aspects of authentic human experience. It has become the model by which, in important respects, the organic human sphere we call consumer culture — or perhaps even more broadly, Western culture — now organizes itself.

# 10

# Artificial Ethics for Artificial People

ONE OF THE ACCOMPLISHMENTS I TOOK SOME PRIDE in as a corporate television executive was the writing of a set of rules governing acceptable behavior for employees of the network's news division. After a flowery introduction outlining the conventional notions of the importance to democracy of a free and fair press, the document went on to list a number of prohibitions that were designed to ensure both the fact and the appearance of impartiality on the part of everyone involved in news production, and in particular those who appeared on camera.

Employees were, for example, prohibited from participating in political campaigns, or getting involved in "controversial issues" that might be the subject of news coverage. The rules required them to get the approval of the vice-president of news before "publishing books, magazine articles, or other literary works which concern a controversial issue." Another rule prohibited news employees from "performing services for any government or agency of government, foreign or domestic, whether or not payment is involved."

A much longer list of "editorial standards" set out rules designed to ensure the fairness and accuracy of news coverage. Twenty admonitions covered everything from the need for sensitive treatment of traumatized interview subjects at the scenes of disaster or accidents to the use of music (prohibited), to reenactments (prohibited, except in extraordinary circumstances), to payment for information (prohibited), to avoiding the use of stereotyping pictures or language.

If I were to take on the job of writing a set of standards for journalists — or any other professionals — in light of what I have learned since then, I would approach it quite differently. I would begin with an affirmation of the reality of moral values — the real existence and validity of Good and its opposite — and the fact of our ability to distinguish between the two, thanks to the moral impulse, or moral sense, or simply conscience. I would also point out that the moral impulse demands that one be unconditionally for the Other, that this demand defines morality. In these two fundamental precepts, it seems to me to be possible to securely establish the basic condition for the ethical conduct of journalism or any other profession.

In the case of the journalist, the Other is clearly not her publisher or editor, or the advertisers who ultimately pay her salary. The Other consists of those who are excluded from power, the voiceless and the powerless — hence the hoary admonition to young journalists to "comfort the afflicted and afflict the comfortable." This places a responsibility on the journalist that goes beyond the classical notion of "news gathering, fact finding, reporting . . . to find out what is going on and transmit that information to others, together with a proper explanation of its significance."[1] It is not enough to carry out these tasks according to standard journalistic ethical admonitions to fairness, impartiality, balance, and comprehensiveness. The authentic moral responsibility is to act in such a way as to alleviate pain and give a voice to those victims of the system discovered in the line of duty. In other words, the ethical journalist has a responsibility not just to seek out and expose injustice, but to be an advocate on behalf of its victims.

In fact, a balanced and "impartial" report will frequently fly in the face of that responsibility. "Fairness," that other watchword, cannot be reduced to equality in seconds or column inches of coverage, nor can "balance." The only morally legitimate role for fairness and balance as they are conventionally defined is to give voice to opposing positions in circumstances where the Other is difficult to identify — where the moral issues are too obscure to allow confident judgment. This will frequently, but by no means always, be the case. All of this was perhaps understood in the newspaper business as it existed prior to the so-called penny press revolution of the late nineteenth century, before advertising displaced subscriptions and street sales as publishing's main revenue source, and publishers sought ways to broaden their subscriber bases in order to make their papers more attractive to advertisers. Such is the commercial provenance of the supposedly "ethical" precepts of objectivity and balance.[2]

It is often argued, however, that even in the routine processes of news production, journalists are living up to their moral responsibilities in that, by identifying and publicizing the plight of Others, they are at the same time empowering them. It's certainly what I believed for many years in the business. But it is an essentially Rationalist idea, reminiscent of laissez-faire market theory and its processes for automating ethical behavior. The notion that journalism has fulfilled its duty simply by presenting "facts," which are then by institutional alchemy turned into the gold of moral response, must be deemed suspect if only by association. Neither the reporter who witnesses an injustice, nor the editor who presents the reporter's work to the public, nor the publisher who owns the outlet that makes publication possible, have exhausted their moral responsibilities to the Other through their actions.

Despite their purported devotion to objectivity, balance, and fairness, journalists today find themselves down at the bottom of pollsters' lists of trusted individuals, along with used car dealers and snake oil salesmen. People simply don't buy the rhetoric — they recognize that, as employees of media corporations, journalists are not independent moral agents, but rather represent the commercial and political interests of their employers. Journalists, for their part, find this to be a scurrilous accusation and will deny it indignantly when offered the chance. "We are professionals," they will say. Which is the problem. The ethical position of professionals and agents of all kinds is a thorny question, made all the more prickly these days by the fact that so many professionals are employed by corporations.

In contemporary society we are far more likely than ever before to find ourselves in the position of *actors*, performing work at the behest of others we can call *authors*. The words and the distinction belong to our friend Hobbes, who was the first philosopher to think seriously about the moral position of the artificial person, more than two hundred years before corporations were granted personhood by the U.S. Supreme Court.

Hobbes's interest was in another kind of artificial person, the individual who carries out tasks on behalf of someone else. The terms he used were chosen deliberately to reflect the relationship between the stage actor and the playwright or author, one he thought might provide a fruitful analogy. Hobbes points out that the actor portraying a character on stage is in no way responsible for the character's moral or immoral actions in the play: he or she is simply performing a role. He was curious to know whether the "actors" in real life — the lawyer, for example, or the soldier, who act at the behest of others — can claim immunity from moral culpability with the assertion that they were only following orders. What is the ethical relationship between actors (or agents) and the people who employ them — the presumed "authors" of their deeds?

We all frequently employ actors to perform duties we do not have the time or the inclination to do for ourselves. We also sometimes use their services where they have knowledge or abilities that we, as authors, do not possess, and they therefore make it possible for us to do something we could not accomplish on our own. Hiring a surgeon or an architect is a case in point: the client is the author and the professional becomes an actor.

This is seldom a straightforward relationship. There are cases, for example, in which actors are required to suppress their knowledge and abilities, as a job requirement. This is the case, for instance, for the engineer who must overlook design criteria important to reliability and safety in order to satisfy the demands of the marketers (as occurs frequently in the automotive industry), or the architect who must accept his client's poor aesthetic judgment and lack of concern for context, and build to his specifications (as happens in many large real estate developments). Lawyers, the classic case, frequently have to set aside their personal judgment and ideals in order to serve their clients well in an adversarial environment. "The adversarial procedure forces lawyers to lower their sights . . . [and] withdraw their vision from the higher aims of justice . . . [focusing instead on] the humbler good ends of a client's triumph and an opponent's defeat."[3] Public relations consultants and speech writers frequently must stifle their own knowledge and instincts in order to satisfy their clients. In each of these examples, the actor is required to suppress not only talent, knowledge, and judgment but ethical sensibility as well, in order to be useful to the author on whose behalf he works.

In general, it can be said that, to the extent that actors are reliable instruments of an author's intentions, they sacrifice their own freedom of action or autonomy. And to the degree that they shed autonomy, they are less credible as moral agents. This is because moral agency (the ability to respond to the moral impulse) requires freedom of choice: it is of no use to say someone *ought* to do something if she *cannot*. In some cases, of course, an actor's ability to "think on her feet" and improvise are assets highly valued by an author. But this autonomy of action must not extend beyond the boundaries of the assignment being carried out: although there may be some flexibility in the means, the end is seldom negotiable.

Clearly, as Hobbes noticed, the position of both the actor and the author is morally ambiguous. To what degree is the author to blame when the actor does something ethically wrong in pursuit of his assignment? To what degree is the actor morally culpable for carrying out unethical instructions from an author? What is the status of their contract in such cases? The questions are so difficult to answer that they are too often simply ignored.

Professionals are frequently engaged as actors; in fact, that is their principal role in life. And just as the stage actor is not responsible for the actions of her character, the professional may be tempted to believe that she is not ethically responsible for her actions on behalf of a client. Think of the lawyer who evicts a penniless family in the dead of winter on behalf of the landlord, her client. She may return home in the evening and complain to her spouse about having had a hard day at the office dealing with obnoxious clients, but she is unlikely to feel the full weight of moral culpability. Or take the military pilot who bombs a densely populated city in the course of his duties. Few would think of him as being morally responsible for the death and destruction he causes. He is merely an actor, an agent of his government, and thus not accountable. So-called rules of war of various descriptions extend further absolution. Or consider the journalist who produces newscasts that feature violence and mayhem without context, and spurns "boring" but significant stories. He will simply be following a format laid down by his bosses, whom he may well think are irresponsible. He does it nonetheless.

But Hobbes's theatrical actor-author analogy is dangerously inappropriate, for this reason: the stage actor is not morally culpable for the things he says and does on stage because his actions are fictitious — they have no result in real life. If that were not the case — if when he fired a stage pistol somebody died — moral (and of course legal) responsibility would need to be assigned in the ordinary way.

Despite this, it is probably fair to say that most professionals — indeed, most employees who bear any significant on-the-job responsibility — think of themselves as assuming a role when they are at work, one that affects their moral status. Frequently, the role played on the job incorporates ethical standards that differ from those they hold personally. The advertising copywriter or PR professional who, as it were, makes up lies for a living may well be no less mendacious than the rest of us when not at work.

The presumption is that the actor's role can be shed at quitting time, or in other words, that there is a core person, a "real" or authentic being, behind the mask. That authentic person takes on roles, sometimes several at a time (mother, wife, real estate agent, volunteer, stock market investor, etc.) and sheds them or changes the blend according to circumstances. Thus it is possible for the authentic person to hold on to one "true" or core set of ethical values even while acting in an ethically compromised professional context. We tell ourselves that the actor carrying out deeds on behalf of some author is "not really me."

But this argument rests on two dubious assumptions. The first is that the actor is not morally responsible when carrying out an author's instructions. We've seen that this is only the case in the world of fiction, where actions have no real-life results. In real life, "I was only following orders" is no defense.

The second assumption is that the person is distinct from the roles he or she assumes, and can shed the role at will. Enron's Kenneth Lay provides an example. According to *Newsweek*, Lay grew up a poor preacher's son and pulled himself up by the bootstraps in true Horatio Alger style — he actually won something called the Horatio Alger Award for entrepreneurship. At the university, he led a dry fraternity and earned a Ph.D. in economics. He created Enron not long after graduation, and by 2000 it had grown to be the seventh-largest company in the United States. Despite his newfound wealth, he lived modestly and devoted time to civic charities and causes.

But in his role as Enron chairman, Lay was an arrogant gambler whose only interest was in the company's stock price. He fired one accounting firm and hired another that would be more amenable to the kind of freebooting practices for which the company would become notorious. He created a "cut-throat" corporate culture in which those who didn't meet quotas were summarily fired, and the large company security force became an object of fear. He hired bright unprincipled managers like Jeff Skilling (CEO) and Arthur Fastow (CFO) to run the show for him. He gave large donations to political candidates and in return received exemptions from state and local regulations. When things unraveled for Enron in 2001, Lay told employees that the company's finances were in good shape, and that they should hold on to their stock, though he had been unloading his own Enron shares for years. Those who listened lost their life savings in the oncoming collapse. According to *Newsweek* and other observers, Lay had to have known about Enron's "elaborate schemes to hide losses and debt."[4]

Is Lay two people, like Jekyll and Hyde, or one? Only he can say for sure, but experienced stage actors know that the process of continually taking on roles alters the authentic self, and common sense tells us that personal identity is to some degree an amalgam of the roles the individual assumes. Over time, people tend to absorb the values inherent in or attached to the roles they perform, if only to avoid the stresses of cognitive dissonance. To some degree — and this varies with the extent to which we identify with our work — we are what we do.

Certainly, the person who behaves unethically at work (even though, perhaps, complying with the corporate or professional "code of ethics"), *is* that unethical person and not some "core" person playing a role. Sociologist Zygmunt Bauman, as we've seen, asserts that "moral responsibility is precisely the act of self-constitution."[5] Philosopher Charles Taylor agrees: "To know who I am is a species of knowing where I stand."[6] In other words, to know where I stand, ethically, is in large measure to know who I am as an individual. The Good that is important to me, the values I adhere to, constitute "me." Each time I compromise that Good, I alter my self, I change who I am.

Psychotherapist and philosopher Viktor Frankl, a Nazi death camp survivor, took this line of thought one step further to argue that the choices we make in dealing with life's constant calls to action — whether we choose good or bad, right or wrong — are how we achieve meaning in our lives. The "meaning of life" is not something to be *found* by searching, he believed — it is actively *created* by each of us in our day-to-day choices. In his book

*Man's Search for Meaning*, Frankl recalls a passage from Dostoevsky: "There is only one thing that I dread; not to be worthy of my sufferings," and then continues in his own words:

> The way in which a man accepts his fate and all the suffering it entails, the way in which he takes up his cross, gives him ample opportunity — even under the most difficult circumstances — to add a deeper meaning to his life. It may remain brave dignified and unselfish. Or in the bitter fight for self-preservation he may forget his human dignity and become no more than an animal. Here lies the chance for a man either to make use of or to forgo the opportunities of attaining the moral values that a difficult situation may afford him. And this decides whether he is worthy of his sufferings or not.[7]

In a world in which men and women are forced, on pain of losing their livelihood, to live at least part of the time by alien values, the never-ending enterprise of formation of self and the concurrent construction of a meaningful life are made difficult. Yet each of us seeks both identity and meaning. If we can't have the authentic, we will accept the ersatz, because anything is better than nothing. In today's consumer society, individuals are encouraged by ubiquitous media to adopt the synthetic values offered by the ideology of consumerism. Or, they can buy into enterprise culture, the stepchild of the Human Relations Movement. The substitution, however, can never be satisfactory: for these individuals, a good life in the Socratic sense is not in the cards.

All of this brings us back to where we began this chapter, with the idea of professional codes of behavior or codes of ethics. I wrote my policy manual in part because, like most professionals, journalists frequently find themselves in ethically ambiguous positions vis-à-vis their corporate employers. Indeed, part of the intention was to erect a bulwark to defend the network news division's integrity from our new CEO. Some of the practices it prohibited could conceivably have helped boost ratings and therefore ad revenue. That's one reason for a code of ethics, but there are others, some of which are well publicized and others that are less frequently acknowledged.

The oldest professional organizations are those of lawyers and doctors, and both groups have been given wide jurisdiction in most countries to regulate their own affairs and discipline their own members. Each has an elaborate code of ethics. At the same time, each is a tightly held monopoly, and has fought sustained battles over the years to prevent encroachment on its territory by politicians, laypersons, and other professionals. Doctors, for example, have consistently resisted both attempts by the nursing profession to enlarge their area of recognized competence and authority, and the legalization of midwifery. Doctors and lawyers, through their associations, have also consistently fought state attempts to regulate fees in the public interest.

Underlying these obviously self-serving provisions of so-called codes of ethics is a desire to ensure competency on the part of practitioners and standardize the quality of their product at an acceptable level, and many trade and professional associations are heavily involved in educational programs for members and prospective members. Engineers, through their professional associations, played a major role in the early development of schools of engineering and management in American universities. Doctors and lawyers establish and run law and medical schools, often with state funding.

When a new professional group begins to organize itself — it may be an entirely new trade, such as Web site development — it usually does so for the initial reason of raising the status of the trade and improving its public image. Indeed, a code of ethics is

frequently the totem around which the early members gather and
organize themselves. Services and qualifications are standardized
within the group with a view to bringing predictability to the market, which is of benefit to both buyer and seller. But most codes
quickly turn their attention to protecting the interests of those
who are expected to operate under them.[8] For instance, they frequently prohibit the public criticism of association members by
their fellows, so as to protect individual and collective reputations.

A major priority is limiting the number of practitioners
(through professional certification rules) in order to create a partial monopoly of the skills involved, which in turn makes possible
the setting of higher prices than the market would otherwise determine. In this connection, the U.S. National Society of Professional Engineers included as part of its code of ethics a prohibition
on competitive bidding, until the provision was overthrown in a
Supreme Court ruling in 1978. Statutes of medical associations
that prohibit advertising have been challenged in courts in many
jurisdictions, with mixed results. Codes of ethics are also sometimes used as a means of preempting state regulation of a trade
or profession with a semblance of self-regulation, frequently at the
behest of the state itself.

Codes governing conduct within the various trades and professions differ widely, of course, but they have certain generic
features that make it possible to draw up a list of rules that covers many of the commonalities. Such a list might include the following:

- concern for public good

- concern for image, reputation

- confidentiality concerning clients, employers

- due diligence/concern for quality of product

- fidelity to professional responsibilities/respect for fellow professionals

- compliance with laws and regulations

In my view, the most important thing these touchstones have in common is that none necessarily has anything to do with ethics. A "code of ethics" based on this template could be adopted by Colombian death squads as easily as used car dealers or florists. With the obvious exception of the Hippocratic oath and its famous "First, do no harm" (a clear moral admonition), professional codes of ethics tend not to be what they claim to be. They are, rather, codes of professional or corporate conduct, which is an entirely different thing. They are generally, either implicitly or explicitly, formulas for legal and financial risk management, and many professional associations lump the topics of ethics and risk management together in their courses of professional instruction leading to certification.

A problem with corporate and professional codes of ethics is that rules they contain are generally far too specific to be considered true ethical precepts. Ethics is basically "an open-ended, reflective, and critical individual activity," and to assume that ethical standards can be settled by committee meetings and then codified and distributed is to confuse ethics with lawmaking, or policymaking, or rule making.[9] Ethical principles, as opposed to rules of conduct, cannot be established by organizations, or by a consensus of their members. Even if such a consensus could be reached on rules that could be set out in a code, "imposing the code on others in the guise of ethics contradicts the notion of ethics itself, which presumes that persons are autonomous moral agents." And attaching disciplinary procedures to such codes compounds the error.

To label such conventions, rules, and standards "ethical" is to succumb to a philosophical confusion about their status and function. Ethics clearly does have relevance for such lists of rules, but the connection is the same as it is between ethics and law. The proper role of ethics in relation to these lists is "to appraise, criticize, and perhaps even defend (or condemn) . . . the rules, regulations, and procedures they prescribe, and the social and political goals and institutions they represent."[10] Despite what we have been taught for many generations, ethics *precedes* community. It is not a product of social institutions and their rules and regulations; it is what makes them possible, and it provides the perspective from which we are able to pass judgment on them.

Philosopher Elizabeth Wolgast reports that U.S. Army General Maxwell Taylor in 1980 worried about the "absence of an explicit ethical code for the military and proposed that each officer should work one out on his own." She quotes Taylor as suggesting that the officer might

> begin with the idea that "an ideal officer is one who can be relied upon to carry out all assigned tasks and missions and, in doing so, get the most from his available resources with minimum loss and waste." Such an ideal person "would be deeply convinced of the importance of the military profession and its role . . . [and] view himself as a descendant of the warrior, who, in company with the king, the priest, and the judge, has helped civilization survive."[11]

The noteworthy thing about the general's musings is that he believes that "professional requirements must condition the moral ones and not the reverse."[12] Taylor's conclusion in this regard will be echoed in any professional code of conduct that seeks to skirt the tensions and ambiguities of the author-actor relationship. Any such code will have the principal purpose of adapting moral requirements to conform with professional or corporate ones. It will be an invitation to act without genuine moral accountability, to assume a cloak of moral invisibility.

Another, less noticed effect of the proliferation of professional "codes of ethics" is the ongoing professionalization of ethical criticism, taking it out of the purview of the ordinary worker or citizen and placing it in the hands of specialists. Medical ethicists, business ethicists, and bioethicists, to name just three of the new specialties, are expected to have extensive knowledge of — even postgraduate degrees in — the disciplines they monitor. This may seem merely sensible, but the danger is that it "captures" the ethicist to the discipline and its internal standards.

The sciences are a case in point. Given the prestige that science and medicine command, the argument that, with their specially trained ethicists, these fields of endeavor can regulate themselves is a potent one. Few ordinary citizens are likely to feel themselves competent to argue with someone bearing the imposing title of bioethicist and a list of degrees after her name. Moral debate is thus increasingly confined to the "experts," and carried on in technical language inaccessible to laypersons, including most journalists.

This is all good news to those professionals who would seek to escape interference in their work by the public or government. However, as I have argued throughout this book, in the last analysis there are no experts when it comes to ethics. Or rather, we are all more or less equally expert in the field. Any thoughtful, well-informed citizen is as capable of making ethical judgments concerning the outcomes of scientific and technological projects as anyone claiming special expertise. What the expert's training may allow her to do is ferret out and publicize issues of ethical import. Or she may be expert in her knowledge of the rules and procedures of her profession. But making authentic value judgments is better done by ordinary people exercising their ordinary moral sense. Plato pointed out long ago (in *Protagoras*) that knowledge of virtue is different from the specialized knowledge or expertise we call technical knowledge. Everyone, he said, has access to ethical knowledge and everyone can and should be an ethical teacher.

Prior to the mid-1980s, the corporate position of "ethics officer" didn't exist. Today there are so many executives who are formally assigned to oversight of corporate ethics that they have their own organization (the Ethics Officer Association) and hold large conventions.

A big part of the ethics officer's job is to create and then administer corporate ethical codes. Ninety percent of Fortune 500 corporations have "codes of ethics" or "codes of business conduct" that employees are expected to have read and understood.[13] These are even more problematic than the codes of professional associations, since the corporate view of ethics is, as might be expected, different from the human view. The practical implications of this are manifest in that many, if not most, corporate codes are called *codes of ethics and compliance*. As the word *compliance* indicates, a prime purpose of these codes is to ensure that employees do not break the law or government regulatory codes, because this might result in financial penalties.

Altria Corporation, to choose one of thousands of possible examples, posts its code of "compliance and integrity" on its Web site. It begins: "Each member of the Altria family of companies is committed to pursuing its business objectives with integrity and in full compliance with all laws." It lists four questions employees are expected to ask themselves before undertaking any questionable action: "Is it legal? Is it consistent with company policy? Is it the right thing to do? How would it look to those outside the enterprise?" Altria is the new name for the former Philip Morris group of companies that includes Philip Morris International, one of the world's biggest cigarette manufacturers, and Kraft Foods, one of the world's largest makers of snack foods. A group of American states were recently awarded $10.1 billion in damages in a suit that alleged Philip Morris knowingly sold cigarettes that were harmful to its customers. Kraft is currently facing lawsuits based on similar health claims relating to the harmful health effects of its food products. The UN's World Health Organization has accused the company of trying to undermine its efforts to combat smoking in Third World countries. (See chapter 8.) "Doing the right thing" clearly has a different meaning within Altria than in the wider world.

The international security firm Pinkerton makes a business out of "corporate ethics" with a program called AlertLine ethics and compliance hotlines. The company describes it this way in its promotional literature:

> Representing virtually every type of industry, AlertLine® ethics and compliance hotlines provide a trusted third-party resource available 24 hours a day, 7 days a week for reporting concerns on ethics, compliance, loss prevention, safety, human resources, workplace violence, and other critical workplace issues. This resource, a toll-free hotline, is the foundation of Pinkerton's effective compliance programs for more than 100,000 client locations worldwide.[14]

This "ethics and compliance" program is in fact a kind of snitch-line service that records and tabulates reports of violations and prepares periodic reports for corporate management.

It is remarkable, in reading through scores of corporate codes of ethics, how often (as in the case of Altria, above) the phrase "committed to" crops up. BAE Systems, a major manufacturers of guided missiles, is "committed to . . . ensuring that our CSR [Corporate Social Responsibility] activities are fully aligned with our efforts to deliver on key business objectives." The McDonald's Corporate People Promise reads: "We are committed to social responsibility. We are committed to doing the right thing. We want to make a positive difference in the world. This commitment began with our founder Ray Kroc. It continues today with our Board of Directors and executive leadership, is shared by our staff and franchises, and reaches across our front counters to our customers and their communities." McDonald's fast-food products have been identified as a major contributing factor to widespread obesity among Americans, which is blamed for epidemic levels of cardiovascular disease and diabetes. CACI, a U.S. defense contractor, assures customers: "At CACI we take pride in our commitment to: Quality service and the best value for our clients; individual opportunity, and respect for each other; integrity and excellence in our work; distinction and the competitive edge in our work." CACI was one of the contractors involved in running the notorious Abu Ghraib prison near Baghdad, exposed in 2005 as a hotbed of prisoner torture and abuse.[15]

Clearly, "committed to" in this context falls into the category of weasel words, and ought to provide a warning that what follows will be empty rhetoric signifying nothing in terms of genuine ethical performance or even intent.

What examples like these tell me is that compliance, as the Rationalist's synthetic substitute for authentic ethical behavior, in no way supplants or supersedes the real thing. We can leave the last word to Zygmunt Bauman, who has made a lifelong study of the matter and correctly observes, "There are no hard and fast principles which one can learn, memorize, and deploy in order to escape situations without a good outcome and to spare oneself the bitter aftertaste (call it scruples, guilty conscience, or sin) which comes unsolicited in the wake of the decisions taken and fulfilled. Human reality is messy and ambiguous — and so moral decisions, unlike abstract ethical principles, are ambivalent." We must ultimately, as he says, attend to our innate "moral impulses" to discover how to be good and kind to one another.[16]

# 11

# Consumerism and the Corporation

I PROPOSED EARLIER THAT CORPORATIONS can be likened to alien invaders bent on taking control of our lives. Pursuing that metaphor, I would add that the main area of contested authority has turned out to be ethics and morality. It is the moral impulse that has caused people to become aware of, and mount a stiffening resistance to, the corporate way of doing things. It is on the basis of the moral impulse and its prescriptions that we will ultimately find new and better ways of conducting our economic affairs. It seems to me to follow that the corporation ought to be placed in the same category as another institution that is frequently referred to as a machine — the military.

Both the corporation and the military provide useful services to the state and its people, and both employ people in doing so. But in the case of the military, we have for many centuries understood that the institution must be held on a short leash, that it needs to be kept scrupulously away from the political and economic systems. We know this because there have been many occasions in many countries on which these rules were broken, and the result has been military takeovers. The military has a job to do and we expect it to do that job well and to do no more.

The same ought to apply to the business corporation. In each case we are dealing with a tool to accomplish societal goals, and in neither case does society have any interest in having the tool take charge. When we consider that the corporation is simply an artifact designed to facilitate the complex processes of carrying on a business, it seems peculiar in the extreme that we should have granted it personhood and access to human rights charters, and that we seek the advice of its mouthpieces in formulation of political and economic policy, when we know that any advice we receive will be — must be — self-serving.

Societies reaching all the way back to Sparta and beyond, where the military has been allowed to usurp control, have had distinctive attitudes to ethics and what constitutes virtuous behavior. The same is true of societies in which corporations hold sway. These attitudes may at first be experienced as an overlay upon existing value structures, but as time passes they come to constitute mainstream perception. The military ethic suggested by General Taylor in the previous chapter proposed, for example, that an ideal officer "would be deeply convinced of the importance of the military profession and its role . . . [and] view himself as a descendant of the warrior, who, in company with the king, the priest, and the judge, has helped civilization survive."

The corporation has not just one such "ethic," but two, and both have been deeply implanted in our consciousness. The famous (or notorious) work ethic — essentially, the internalized motivations that impel people to work — has for a century and more been the focus of zealous research in the cause of boosting industrial productivity. There is a parallel ethic that, while well-known, is not generally understood in its historical relationship to the work ethic — it is the consumer ethic. Both are shams in that neither is an ethical concept. While a strong work ethic may be classed as a virtue, and may even assist one in leading a good life, it is not, in itself, a Good thing. One can work hard for bad causes. The phoniness is at the same time both more and less obvious in the case of the consumer ethic, which claims that consumption is Good, in a special historical sense.

The linkage between the two so-called ethics is that the work ethic, as we are familiar with it today, is justified by the promises of consumption, and consumption is the reward accorded to those who work. In earlier times, as it was embraced by Protestant teachings, the work ethic had served emerging industrial capitalism by instilling the communal virtues of punctuality, hard work, obedience, and frugality. While virtuous behavior was said to be its own reward, it was also a feature of Protestant theology to recognize, even celebrate, that these virtues could and often did bring with them wealth, which could thus be regarded as an outward sign of moral rectitude. Wealth, in other words, could be a sign that one was heaven-bound.

By the mid-twentieth century, the symbiotic coupling between the work ethic and the consumer ethic had evolved to better serve an era of entrepreneurship and individualism, as opposed to wage labor. Work hard and get rich sums up the relationship. Heaven on earth through consumption was the promise.

It was that promise that made work bearable in the world of the time-and-motion consultant and meaningless, repetitious, mindless tasks. For many the wealth accrued by a steady income was affluence enough: for others wages were a stepping-stone to starting a business of one's own, which was the route to true riches. In either case, work and consumption had been made into points on a continuum: one works in order to consume; consumption requires more work. This is a purely Rationalist ordering, a cybernetic system regulated by positive feedback without any reference to morality, and as such it is ideally suited to the Rationalist institutions of the market economy.

Thus was consumerism spawned in the early years of the

twentieth century — not born a "natural" birth, but created as a substitute for the intangible rewards of virtue that previous generations of workers had attached to work for its own sake.[1] It was made necessary by the fact that the tentative, early-twentieth-century forays by a handful of large corporations into capitalism with a human face — called social capitalism — and the best efforts of the early scientific management gurus of corporate capitalism had failed to quell the radical unionism and socialism that had swept the working classes both prior to and immediately following the war years of 1914–18. The alarming spectacle of the Bolshevik Revolution in Russia raised fears of similar upheavals in the West. And for once, the staunchest market capitalists agreed that factory working conditions were at the root of the problem. The purpose of consumerism was to assuage this worker alienation, by making the payoff for unsatisfying labor — for wage slavery — a handsome one.

It would have the added virtue of helping to solve another pressing problem facing market capitalism and the emergent modern business corporation — overproduction brought on by the very "efficiencies" that were responsible for labor dissatisfaction. The invention of the consumer ethic was to provide the global solution to both, and a comfortable mythology within which the century's various scientific management schemes could justify themselves.

Cultural historians have thoroughly documented how the rise of contemporary consumer culture was deliberately fostered by the emerging giants of corporate industry in the early twentieth century.[2] The family, always a necessary foundation of social stability, had been denied its historical role as a center of *production* with the emergence of the factory model of production and the wage economy. The ideology of consumerism remade the family as a center of *consumption*, in which each family member had a special role to play. The roles were defined by the advertisers of the 1910s and '20s: the father earned the money and purchased the food, clothing, and furnishings for himself and his home that advertisers told him were necessary for success; the mother was the household quartermaster and aide-de-camp, dependent for her continued employment on her ability to maintain her husband's sexual interest, and dependent in that on the products of the hygiene, beauty, and fashion industries; children, initially, were a market for commercially produced "healthy" foods, and would later become consumers in their own right. The new paternal voice of authority was provided by the corporation and its spokespersons, real and concocted.

American advertisers of the 1920s and '30s frequently spoke in parables, attempting to draw moral lessons from the everyday life of the consumer. With repetition, the parables became so familiar they could evoke a response with a few lines of copy and an illustration. Roland Marchand, who has catalogued hundreds of these calculating tableaus, points out that their purpose was to reinforce, and encourage conversion to, a "modern, secular 'logic of living.'"[3] There was, for example, the parable of the First Impression, which emphasized how first impressions can seal one's fate both at work and in social settings. Marchand paraphrases an illustrated department store advertisement of the period this way:

> In the "Open Door," [a young woman] and her husband faced the greatest social crisis of their five-year marriage: they had taken the bold step of inviting the vice president in charge of sales and his wife for dinner. For days, the eager young wife planned the dinner menu. Her husband researched and rehearsed several topics for appropriate conversation. But both completely forgot about their tasteless front doorway, with its lack of beautifully designed woodwork. And neither realized how dreary and out-of-date was the furniture they had purchased soon after their marriage. Thus, all of their efforts at preparation came to naught, for their guests formed an indelible

impression during "those few seconds" from "the touch of the bell" to their entrance into the living room. No feats of cooking or conversation could counteract that first impression of dowdy tastelessness and lack of modernity. It fatefully bespoke a deficiency in character and ambition. Twenty years later, with the husband still third assistant for sales at the small branch office, they anxiously passed on to their children a hard-won bit of wisdom: "Your Future may rest on what the Open Door reveals."

An ad for a cement manufacturer asked: "Would you willingly be judged by the looks of your basement walls?" The Kohler Company warned, "No room in the house is more expressive than the bathroom." Shaving cream, toothpaste, and even garter makers produced advertisements dramatizing the tragedy of lost opportunities for love and business advancement due to less than perfect grooming.

The advertising parable of the Democracy of Goods portrayed a world in which the humblest household could have the benefit of goods and services that were once the exclusive purview of the wealthy and powerful. A 1929 ad for Cream of Wheat featured the tricycle-riding scion of the fabulously wealthy Biddle family, and noted that his glowing good health was the result of a diet prescribed for him by "famous specialists." Though expense was no object, young Biddle was fed Cream of Wheat for breakfast and supper. And, thanks to consumer society's democracy of goods, the ad enthused, "every mother can give her youngsters the fun and benefits of a Cream of Wheat breakfast just as do the parents of these boys and girls who have the best that wealth can command."

"According to this parable," Marchand comments, "the wonders of modern mass production and distribution enabled every person to enjoy the society's most significant pleasure, convenience, or benefit." The C. F. Church Manufacturing Company advertised, "If you lived in one of those palatial apartments on Park Avenue, in New York City, where you have to pay $2,000 to $7,500 a year rent, you still couldn't have a better toilet seat in your bathroom than they have — the Church Sani-white Toilet Seat which you can afford to have right now." Still in the democratic vein, Lifebuoy Soap warned that "body odor plays no favorites." Paramount Pictures told Americans that they were "kings in cottages," and "No monarch in all history ever saw the day he could have half as much as you." Clearly, there was no need for socialism in America.

"Advertisers did not have to impose the parable of the Democracy of Goods on a contrary-minded public," Marchand comments. "Theirs was the easier task of subtly substituting this vision of equality, which was certainly satisfying *as a vision*, for broader and more traditional hopes and expectations of an equality of self-sufficiency, personal independence, and social interaction."

In the parable of Civilization Redeemed, the redeemer is modern technology and particular food-processing techniques and patent medicines. Even cigarettes were advertised as the solution to the stresses of modern life. The moral, Machand says, was that "civilization and nature were not antithetic. No brakes need be applied to the wheels of progress."

The notion of the technological fix was extended to family life in the parable of the Captivated Child, in which mothers are given advice on the care and feeding of their children. Old-fashioned coaxing or discipline was to be replaced by products so desirable (Campbell's vegetable soup) that no persuasion or coercion would be necessary to get children to do what is best for them. A 1920s Ex-Lax ad cajoled, "Don't make your children dislike you" by forcing them to take "hateful doses and bitter cathartics that so often cause tears and tantrums." Instead, mothers should tempt them with candy-like Ex-Lax: "They'll love it . . . and love you for giving it to them."

Ubiquitous ads like these "invited readers to a new 'logic of living' in which the older values of discipline, character-building, self-restraint, and production-oriented achievement were subordinated to the newer values of pleasure, external appearance, and achievement through consumption," concludes Marchand. This was the logic of consumerism. Later advertising, perhaps influenced by television, avoided voluminous copy and relied instead on subliminal iconic imagery and psychological subtlety in copywriting to convey messages similarly designed to exploit consumers' insecurities. We're all familiar with it.

In view of the ideology's corporate ancestry it should be no surprise that the values implicit in consumerism bear little resemblance to traditional values of family, community, thrift, piety, self-reliance, charity, modesty, love, and others that characterized the best aspirations of nineteenth-century and prewar twentieth-century society. As newly minted "consumers," members of the emerging middle and lower-middle classes were encouraged to spend to and beyond the limits of their incomes, and to use their acquisitions to gain advantage over their fellow workers and citizens. As soon as production capacity permitted, this new materialist ethic was promoted among the poor as well, through the mass propaganda of advertising. Writing in 1929, one enthusiast said, "Consumptionism is the name given to the new doctrine; and it is admitted today to be the greatest idea that America has to give to the world; the idea that workmen and masses be looked upon not simply as workers and producers, but as *consumers.* . . . Pay them more, sell them more, prosper more is the equation."[4]

Advertising encouraged people to seek new identities more in keeping with the corporate-age ethos of consumption. Consuming was pitched as a creative process: you are what you own; you are what you consume. In order to efficiently mop up the tremendous capacity of increasingly productive manufacturing processes, it was necessary to ensure that consumers' desires remained essentially insatiable and a concerted effort was made to achieve this goal with advertising that relied heavily on the technique of systematically undermining confidence in the self — a self increasingly dependent for its construction on commodities. It was a process analogous to creating a drug dependence, and then treating that addiction with more drugs.

The fledgling advertising industry of the early twentieth century was in the process of discovering the nascent human sciences of Behaviorism, psychoanalysis, and social psychology. Advertisers plundered research findings in the nature and origins of human longings and insecurities, capitalizing on them to create economic demand among consumers. Among those attracting their attention was the famous Russian behaviorist Pavlov, who experimented with "conditioned reflexes" in experiments involving electric shock and other forms of persuasion. In one, a dog was induced to salivate at the sound of a bell, by virtue of having been "conditioned" to associate the sound with food. As we have seen, Pavlov concluded that all human behavior could be so explained. Advertisers dreamed of making of consumerism a Pavlovian culture — jolt, salivate, and spend. And spending was becoming easier than ever with the arrival of the new concept of buying on time, the beginnings of a consumer credit industry that rapidly became a major source of corporate wealth.

The sciences of motivational research had come along just in time for advertisers, because the task of turning workers and citizens into consumers was discovered to be anything but simple.

Advertisers needed all the psychological sophistication they could muster because the materialist ethic was not yet a part of the cultural repertoire of most working-class people, who were stubbornly uncomfortable with the idea of living beyond their means or consuming beyond their needs. Nor is there any evidence that is it in the nature of people to wish to beggar their neighbors through economic competition. Consumer society, however, was all about creating identity and competing for status through consumption, and so ancient habits had to be overcome. People needed to be trained — often against their native instincts — for their new responsibilities as consumers of the fruits of the industrial cornucopia.

The behavioral and management sciences that had led to enormous increases in worker productivity were pressed into service in the molding of compliant, insatiable consumers. Scientific insights into human conduct became "equivalent to industrial discoveries, more valuable to manufacturing than the uses of electricity or steel."[5] As an article in a 1922 scholarly journal noted, advertising had developed into an essential instrument of social manipulation, whose purpose was "the nullification of the customs of ages; . . . [to] break down the barriers of individual habits." Advertising was "at once the destroyer and creator in the process of the ever-evolving new. Its constructive effort [is] . . . to superimpose new conceptions of individual attainment and community desire."[6]

And since it was large cyborg-like business corporations that were more often than not paying the bills for this program of reeducation, it was corporate needs and values that informed it throughout (and continue to do so). By 1990 corporations worldwide were spending more than $240 billion annually on advertising and another $300 billion on packaging, design, and other point-of-purchase promotion — $120 for every man, woman, and child on the planet. In 2001 the top 100 marketers alone spent $70.95 billion on media advertising — almost half of it, $34.17 billion, in the United States, followed by $24.09 billion in Europe, $9.19 billion in Asia, and $1.79 billion in Latin America. Half of the top 100 global marketers — and six of the top ten — are U.S. companies. Much of the direct advertising money is spent on television, which is watched by American adults for about twenty-eight hours a week. Such a viewer is exposed each week to more than nine hours of commercials. These numbers are only marginally lower in Europe and other parts of the industrialized world.

Increasingly, though, corporate advertising money is being spent directly in schools, because, as Mark Evans, senior vice president of Scholastic Inc., told *Advertising Age*: "More and more companies see educational marketing as the most compelling, memorable, and cost-effective way to build *share of mind* and market into the twenty-first century." (Emphasis added.) Agencies such as Learning Enhancement Corp. and Lifetime Learning Systems Inc. find ways for corporate clients to insert material into North American school curricula, as videotaped teaching aids and even textbooks. The U.S. National Council on Economic Education promotes the teaching of economics in elementary and high school with "curriculum enhancing" material slanted toward neoliberal market theory. Channel One TV donates satellite television equipment to schools that agree to show Channel One programming on at least 90 percent of school days to 90 percent of students. The current affairs-oriented programming, of dubious merit in itself, is interspersed with corporate commercials. By 2004, about 12,000 U.S. schools had subscribed.

\*   \*   \*

In the United States, perhaps more than elsewhere in the industrial world, the consumer ethic has been linked to democracy, the two in combination forming a powerful new ideology. The argument goes like this: since industrial peace and prosperity are said to rely on the rewards of consumption, and since industrial peace and prosperity have been the cornerstones of a successful industrial democracy, consumption is critical to the maintenance of democracy. A bad consumer is a bad democrat. The idea was vividly exemplified in President George W. Bush's post-9/11 admonition to Americans to "go out and shop" as a show of defiance to anti-democratic terrorists.

Edward Filne, founder of the Consumers Union and author of the 1931 barn-burner *Successful Living in the Machine Age*, believed that consumerism provided an effective alternative to politics as an arena for democratic participation: "It is within the structure of business . . . [that] the wisest and best leadership is actually being chosen by the people," Filne wrote. By buying the goods and services produced by large corporations and thus contributing to their prosperity, consumers were effectively electing a government that would be focused on fulfilling their material desires, he said.[7]

Edward Bernays, nephew of Sigmund Freud and leading light of the American public relations industry in the years leading up to World War Two, claimed approvingly (in his *Propaganda*) that "we have voluntarily agreed to let an invisible government sift the data and high-spot the outstanding issues so that our field of choice shall be narrowed to practical proportions." The "invisible government" was composed of large business corporations and their advertising and public relations mouthpieces.

Despite the democratic claim, it is clear that the ideology of consumerism is essentially authoritarian. If democracy resides in

consumer choice, those choices are limited to what suits the interests of business. That is to say, the limits of choice are determined
by corporations. Corporate needs sometimes coincide with human
interests, but when this happens, it happens by coincidence.
Democracy's "one person, one vote," is an entirely different thing
than consumerism's "one dollar, one vote." Moreover, to the
extent that they were electing Bernays's "business leadership"
to run their affairs, consumers were actually electing corporate
automata, for as we've seen corporations manage their "managers." It was to be rule by machine, then, the political actualiza-
tion of eighteenth-century Rationalism and the ultimate triumph
of seventeenth-century scientific determinism. A far cry from
democracy.

As a moral corollary, consumerism-as-democracy reduces
ethical choices to a market equation. Neoliberal political leaders
facing social inequities and human misery are heard to say: "We
cannot afford what we cannot afford," or, as Margaret Thatcher
said on accession to the office of prime minister of Great Britain,
"The Good Samaritan would not have been able to do what he
did if he did not have money."[8]

Here, in the imposition of the consumer ethic, the methodical subversion of human needs in favor of corporate imperatives
can be seen in high relief. The historical congruities are too
striking to attribute to mere coincidence: the creation of consumer culture exactly coincides with the rise of the modern business corporation, and as one gained momentum, so did the other.
Advertising, which was not a major element of the American
economy prior to about 1910 (there was no nineteenth-century
"advertising industry"), developed as a tool for social control under the sponsorship of corporations. While this was happening,
these same corporations were to an increasing extent falling un-

der the control of professional management and being operated according to strict profit-oriented rules.

There were many possible solutions to the problems of industrial society in the early twentieth century: it is no accident that the ones that shaped public policy, and particularly economic policy in America and the West, were the ones that closely matched corporate needs, and frequently ignored or sought to modify human needs.

The so-called consumer ethic is actually a corporate ideology, and the often bewildering social changes of the twentieth century that historians normally attribute to human authors ("the ruling classes," "captains of industry," or Stewart Ewan's "captains of consciousness") are better understood when it is realized that their source is in the mechanical operations of the modern business corporation. When Edward Bernays speaks of "the conscious and intelligent manipulation of the organized habits and opinions of the masses" as being "an important element in a democratic society," and goes on to assert approvingly that "we are governed, our minds are molded, our tastes formed, our ideas suggested, largely by men we have never heard of," he is speaking of "business leaders" who are in fact merely the appliances of corporate automata.[9]

The realization helps to solve a major puzzle: How was business — big or otherwise — able to coordinate its action over such a vast sphere of activity and over so many decades of history to effect the kind of basic changes in values we've witnessed in Western society? No human conspiracy (or political program) seems capable of such an achievement. But if by business we mean corporations, the scenario becomes much more plausible.

Unlike business leaders who come and go and whose behavior is scandalously unpredictable, corporations *are* capable of the kind of consistency in policy and action that was needed to convert Western society from one ethic to another during the four or five decades following the emergence of the business corporation in its mature form. Nor was it necessary for corporations to conspire by communicating their intentions to one another: the tactics of commodification and mass marketing were programmed into their DNA as the most expedient way to navigate the turn-of-the-century crisis of market capitalism. In its unswerving dedication to maximizing profit regardless of collateral human cost, the corporation and only the corporation was capable of fostering, with absolute and unswerving dedication, an ethic that equated democracy and the good life with selfish consumption and competitive ruthlessness — and do it in the face of competing moral values that had stood the test of the previous two millennia.

# 12

## Risky Business

THE TOWN OF PORT HOPE, ONTARIO, is home to an industry that was for a brief few years following World War Two seen as the salvation of humankind, the source of unlimited energy, the panacea for the world's material needs. The town itself (pop. 12,500) was founded sixteen years after the American War of Independence and was settled partly by United Empire Loyalists who had fled the American colonies, preferring British colonial rule to American republicanism.

The factory that dominates its historic waterfront belongs to a corporation that once gloried in the romantic name Eldorado Nuclear but now goes by the more discreet corporate moniker of Cameco Ltd. It produces refined uranium fuel for CANDU nuclear reactors, and was among the first uranium refineries in the world. During World War Two, it supplied uranium for the A-bomb that devastated Nagasaki.

In the latter half of the twentieth century, the town was discovered to have a number of radioactive hot spots where careless husbandry of irradiated landfill, scrap, and building materials had contaminated houses, building lots, even a school. Eventually these were cleaned up, at great expense to the Canadian taxpayer (nuclear energy is federally regulated), and the town is now known mostly for its wonderfully well-preserved Victorian streetscapes and magnificent nineteenth-century homes and gardens.

The Cameco factory inhabits the Port Hope harbor like an abscess, surrounded by chain-link fencing. It was on the list of ICBM targets maintained by the Kremlin during the Cold War, and since the events of September 11, 2001, it seems more vulnerable than ever. A serious accident at the plant could render the town and much of the surrounding countryside uninhabitable.

In 2004, Cameco announced that it had applied for regulatory permission to begin producing "slightly enriched uranium" as a fuel for an updated version of the Canadian heavy-water-moderated reactors. Were permission to be granted, the risk to the town would increase severalfold, because of the increased toxicity of the product being produced and the increased risk of catastrophic accident. This renewed an old, always simmering debate among residents over whether Cameco ought to be asked to leave town and relocate somewhere away from concentrated populations and vital water supplies (tens of millions of Canadians and Americans draw their water from Lake Ontario). In the past when accidents or discoveries of new contamination have caused the debate to flare, "expert" spokesmen for the corporation, its regulators, and the town's chamber of commerce have always managed to convince townsfolk that the risk posed by the factory is minuscule, while its economic contribution in the form of employment and taxes is large.

A great many towns and cities across North America and around the world face similar kinds of risks from corporate enterprises on their doorsteps. The concept of the "risk society" introduced by sociologist Ulrich Beck in his 1986 book of that name offers a useful perspective on a problem that can be linked directly to the corporation's lack of instinct for human welfare. In his groundbreaking study Beck points out that cutting-edge technologies (products of corporate R&D) tend to pose such colossal risks to society that they are uninsurable under conventional actuarial practice. More precisely, the risks are frequently completely unknown, because these technologies are too hazardous to be "crash-tested" the way automobiles are — there is no way of knowing with any certainty what the consequences of an accident are likely to be. Nuclear power plants, for example, are not fully insured for public liability in case of accident, because the worldwide private insurance industry refuses to write such policies. Though the probability of a catastrophic accident is low, the potential payout is incalculably high. In nations that use nuclear energy, governments have passed special legislation exempting them from normal liability coverage, externalizing (that is, socializing) the cost of accidental damage.

This is a historic change. In the past, society has hedged its bets with technology through liability law that establishes responsibility for damage done and private insurance that guarantees compensation for victims. *Facilities too dangerous to be insurable did not get built.* Beck calls the new approach to high-risk technologies "organized irresponsibility," a system in which risk producers are shielded from both responsibility and compensation, all at the expense of their potential victims.

It is a defining characteristic of our late-industrial era, Beck says, that our leading social institutions — business, law, politics — are all engaged in producing these risks, and at the same time refusing to acknowledge their existence. The outbreak of mad cow disease in Britain is often cited as the kind of result that can be expected. Government sanctioned the feeding of animal material that included sheep brains and spinal cords to cattle because it was a cheap form of protein (it made beef production more profitable), and the risk of cross-species disease being transmitted to humans was small. Small, but as we all now know, very real. Government and industry cooperated in the creation of the risk, then tried to cover it up. The price was paid by society at large, as it was, to cite another memorable example, in the case of the nuclear accident at Chernobyl.

The chemical, pharmaceutical, and biotechnology industries all pose risks as incalculable as those of the nuclear industry. One need only consider that the HIV-AIDS pandemic appears to have been caused by well-intentioned tests of polio vaccine in Africa.[1] If that hypothesis were ever proved, the liability costs for the companies responsible would be unimaginably vast. What would happen if experimentally altered human DNA capable of being transferred from generation to generation managed to escape a biotech research lab somewhere in the world? What will happen when the cloning of human embryos becomes widespread (as it undoubtedly will if profit potential is any gauge)? How long will it be before the next step is taken, in the (highly profitable) cause of "improving" the human race? What might be the consequences?

"Ultimately," Beck says, "there is no institution, neither concrete nor probably even conceivable, that would be prepared for the WIA, the 'worst imaginable accident,' and there is no social order that could guarantee its social and political [continuity] in this worst possible case." We have entered a new phase of civilization, in which our technologies give us godlike powers and, unlike Einstein's God, we seem all too willing to play dice with the universe.

Prominent among the social institutions involved in risk society is the modern business corporation, the font of most current technological innovation. The corporation has no threshold beyond which risk to human welfare becomes unacceptable, since the only risk it is designed to respond to is risk to profit. Its response to operating in a sphere of activity where risks to human well-being are high is predictable: it will continue to take risks so long as profitability appears to be secure. It will seek to minimize regulatory oversight wherever possible, because this adds to expenses and forecloses potential avenues of profitability. Of course, the willingness of governments to socialize the potential liability costs of accidents, as they do with nuclear power, plays into this strategy.

The age-old "precautionary principle" for dealing with risk calls on humans to be prudent about their well-being, and to avoid action where consequences are unknown or unpredictable — that is, where risk is high, according to the formula: risk = probability x consequence. But to corporations, prudence is merely a call to scrutiny of risk with respect to the bottom line. A legal strategy for the avoidance of liability lawsuits and regulatory penalties may well be more acceptable to a corporation than a costly engineering policy that would exhaustively analyze human and environmental impacts of products and develop fail-safe design criteria.[2]

The very concept of risk in the context of industrially produced health and environmental hazards is Utilitarian and Rationalist. "Risk" implies that one has done the math to calculate possible harm versus potential benefits, and that the result has been established. Depending on that result, one sometimes decides to take the risk; on other occasions, to avoid it. In recent decades, an entire scientific discipline of risk analysis has been spawned by this idea, and the outcome has been the professionalization of judgment about when and whether individuals and groups ought to be willing to accept the presence of industrially produced hazards. And the result of this, sadly, has been that action on existing dangers tends to be postponed indefinitely.

Langdon Winner has summarized the situation this way: "If we declare ourselves to be identifying, studying, and remedying hazards, our orientation to the problem is clear. . . . First, we can assume that given adequate evidence, the hazards to health and safety are fairly easily demonstrated. Second, when hazards of this kind are revealed, all reasonable people usually can readily agree on what to do about them." On the other hand, "if we declare that we are interested in assessing risks, complications . . . immediately enter in." These involve myriad scientific considerations of "safe" levels of exposure, precise causal relationships, comparative epidemiological studies, statistical analyses, and so on. The focus of attention shifts from the hazard to its precise nature and consequences, which are almost invariably matters of intense scientific controversy. The question of risk taking is moved from the moral domain, where ordinary citizens can legitimately claim expertise, to the scientific, where only Ph.D.s need apply. It is now the norms governing the acceptance or rejection of scientific research that are the focus of attention. The result is, to say the least, ironic: "Faced with uncertainty about what is known concerning a particular risk, prudence becomes not a matter of acting effectively to remedy a suspected source of injury, *but of waiting for better research findings.*"[3]

This result is entirely in keeping with scientific Rationalism's inveterate impulse to reduce morality to mathematics, and will quite naturally be one favored by that child of Rationalism, the business corporation. Risk analysis "makes sense," whereas the identification and removal of hazards is likely to be "tainted" by emotion and value judgments. In the Rationalist's world, the proper way to approach an environmental atrocity like Love Canal is not with an active conscience but a pocket calculator.

The question arises: Should society be able to say of corporate innovations — new chemicals, new genetically modified organisms, new gene therapies, new technologies of all kinds — that they should be considered guilty until proved innocent?

Guilty, that is, of presenting a hazard to human or environmental well-being, unless proved innocent of this beyond some agreed-upon standard of evidence? Or, put another way, should society *ever* have to take a risk with technology unless the probable benefit is something beyond increased profit for a corporation? The presumption of innocence is so deeply ingrained in the Western psyche that we have effectively granted even the corporate person this foundational right under human rights codes. Of course, it makes no sense. Corporations are not human. Corporations are tools.

It can be no accident that the advent of risk society in the middle of the twentieth century coincides with the emergence of the fully empowered modern business corporation as I have described it. Risk society is essentially a product of the modern corporation acting out its destiny within the framework of Rationalist science and Utilitarian morality. Only an entity that had no concept of human values and human interests could have produced the technologies that threaten the global environment, and then resisted attempts by governments to regulate the hazards. It is corporate and not human values that are at work in implementing such biotech innovations as the "terminator" seed, or human cloning, or bovine growth hormone, or factory farming, not to mention the industry's attempts to patent genetic sequences and life-forms. There are no human values at play in the chemical and pharmaceutical industries' constant, exhaustively documented pressure on state regulatory agencies to be less rigorous in testing of their products and to relax restrictions on their sale.

It takes the corporation's talent for spinning off externalities, and its native amorality, to risk human and environmental health on vast scales by producing and aggressively marketing chemicals and biological agents whose impacts are largely unknown. As I've already noted, with many modern technologies the impact cannot be fully predicted and assessed until the product is placed on the market, or the technology is built and operated. This is because the consequences of a failed accident test would be in themselves catastrophic.

To market products that pose a positive risk, however small, of calamitous damage to human or environmental health is ethical, it seems to me, under only one condition. And that is that the technology in question will, with a high degree of certainty, ameliorate or prevent an even greater calamity. A great many high-risk products and technologies currently in use and under development do not fit this criterion. A long list of examples might be headed by pharmaceuticals like female hormone replacement therapy and thalidomide, each of which were designed to medicalize and then (profitably) treat what are, in most cases, minor discomforts that are a part of normal life. Nor is there any evidence, to cite one more case, that genetically modified organisms being developed and produced by the agro-chemical industry are necessary or useful in preventing famine. World food production is more than adequate using conventional farming technologies. What *is* achieved is increasing dependence of worldwide agriculture on these commercial products. The risks genetically modified organisms pose, on the other hand, are extraordinarily high — in fact, incalculably high, given how little is known about their long-term impacts.

It was never intended that corporations become as powerful as they are, and consequently we have no ready-made institutional mechanisms with which to curb their influence and control and thereby respond to the hazards they present to human well-being. The only effective linkages between people and corporations are legal ones, and, as they exist today, these are clearly inadequate to the job of ensuring socially responsible corporate behavior. We have, in effect, two distinct communities in the heart of the nation — the corporate and the human — and their values are profoundly in conflict. Each has access to the same legal remedies when it feels the other is infringing on its rights.

Corporations, however, acting in concert as they do when there is a legal threat, present a formidable, enormously resourceful adversary before the courts. They employ the best legal counsel available and can afford to extend disputes interminably, exhausting their opponents' enthusiasm and bank accounts. Microsoft, for instance, has an in-house legal staff of six hundred, and hires armies of outside counsel. Even national governments are increasingly hesitant to confront this kind of corporate legal might. When it is combined with equally formidable public relations muscle, the political risks of opposition can be more daunting than the risks posed by the corporate practices and technologies themselves.

# 13

# Who Do We Blame?

A QUESTION THAT INVARIABLY ARISES in the public mind, but is seldom answered in cases of what I have called the crimes of corporations, is: Who should we blame?

Conventional wisdom tends to treat the corporation as a collection of people capable of independent action but involved in achieving a common goal, and if this were the case it would be a relatively simple matter to assign ethical culpability under Hobbes's or someone else's terms of reference.[1] When a crime was committed or an ethical boundary overstepped, guilt would be shared by the people making the decisions and those carrying them out.

But corporations are more than collections of people. As artificial persons they seem to be "authors" — Hobbes's term for the autonomous instigator of action — in their own right. The laws under which they are chartered and regulated grant them agency, or the ability to act in their own interest, and humans within the corporation are expected to carry on their duties within this confining, profit-focused, legal framework.

It might, then, appear as though the corporation as legal person is an author and its human functionaries are all actors — again, using Hobbes's analogy for the roles of playwright/authors and stage actors. This impression is reinforced by the fact that human functionaries who fail to act so as to fulfill the corporation's overriding purpose of producing profit are dismissed. There is little or no tolerance for human motivation or values that contradict those of the corporation: the actors are required to closely follow the author's script.

But are corporations really authors in an ethical, or even a legal, sense? Or should blame for wrongdoing be assigned elsewhere, with employees, or perhaps shareholders? We've already touched on this complicated issue, but it is important enough to be looked at in further detail. Are you or I morally responsible for the things we do in our roles as corporate minions, or is responsibility vested solely in the corporation? It's a bit of a riddle, and many of those who have tried to solve it have concluded that an important part of the function of the modern corporation is precisely to keep both moral and legal culpability permanently afloat, as a way of providing protection from prosecution.

As Hobbes noted, the guardian who is acting on behalf of an inanimate entity such as a bridge or a building (or an incapable one, such as an infant) — a class in which most people would include business corporations — may appear at first glance to be behaving as an agent of that entity, that is, as an "actor." But it is the very fact that inanimate things are not capable of looking after themselves that warrants the appointment of the guardian in the first place, so clearly, the guardian must be something other than an actor. The guardian in these cases seems to be an *author*, making autonomous decisions on behalf of his ward and carrying them out. But he cannot be an author, either, because even though he is not operating under direction from the entity he represents (which is inanimate and incapable of giving direction), he undertakes these actions not on his own behalf, but on behalf of his client — which makes him an actor.

195

A lawyer representing a corporation in court is a concrete example of this ambiguous relationship. She is acting on behalf of someone else, and so cannot be properly considered to be an author. But neither does she fit comfortably in the category of actor, since her charge — the corporate person — is an entity most people would consider incapable of autonomous behavior such as issuing orders.

Readers may object here that the lawyer is actually following the instructions of, say, the corporation's vice president for legal affairs, who as an autonomous human being can properly be considered the author. But, as I've been arguing throughout the book, that vice president is not really an author, because whatever he does must conform to the goals and aims of the corporation that employs him. He is, in other words, an actor. This applies all the way along the chain of command, up to and including the CEO.

Ultimately, the corporation seems, once again, to be the author — which is impossible. Impossible, that is, unless we consider the corporation to be an autonomous agent capable of making decisions on its own. Thus, in this riddle I see further evidence that the corporation is indeed an autonomous agent operating in the world.

But this is less than a completely satisfying answer to the question, Who *is* the author — the morally responsible individual — in cases where corporations are being represented (representing themselves?) in the world? It seems to me that, because corporations owe their existence to the authority that grants their charter to operate, that authority must, to some degree, bear authorial responsibility for corporate actions.

The granting authority is of course the state. This relationship was explicitly recognized in the early history of corporations, when state charters were very specific in detailing what business undertakings a corporation could engage in (usually a single project). In earlier times, a corporation might be chartered to build a bridge or dig a canal or to engage in trade with a foreign land, and the chartering governments were willing to accept authorial responsibility within that limited range of actions. But governments were *not* willing to accept responsibility for any and all enterprises that a corporation might decide to undertake, and charters would be withdrawn where the corporation stepped outside its bounds. This basic delineation of ethical responsibility has been lost sight of in an era when corporations are chartered to engage in any and all business enterprises, at their own discretion.

In light of this, I want to suggest that it is a mistake to try to locate comprehensive ethical responsibility for the actions of modern business corporations exclusively in any or all of the three areas usually identified as morally culpable — that is, with either the corporation per se, the people working within the corporation, or the shareholder/owners. Some portion of responsibility for unethical actions must also lie with the government under whose jurisdiction corporations are chartered to carry on business.

The state is an author and therefore morally culpable in two senses: it is the creator of the corporation and thus an author in the same sense as is the paterfamilias in Roman law, and it also employs the corporation as its agent for the specific purpose of facilitating the operations of the economy, in the manner discussed in chapter 7.[2] This second relationship is directly analogous to that of a plaintiff hiring a lawyer, or a homeowner hiring an architect. It is more than Hobbesian dogma, it is simple common sense that in cases where an actor or agent is employed to do something, the author is to some degree responsible for the actor's actions.

The picture is clouded somewhat by the fact that actors, in the traditional Hobbesean construction, are also autonomous persons (as is a stage actor) and thus ethical creatures in their own right. They are capable of deciding between right and wrong, and whether to follow orders. Should they do something wrong in carrying out an author's instructions, they will inescapably bear some portion of the moral responsibility.[3] To apply this reasoning to the corporate setting would mean that, should a corporation do wrong in carrying out its state-chartered role, it must share responsibility with the author/state.

Things are becoming a bit clearer.

Or not. When you stop to think about it, it is apparent that we do consider corporations to be ethical entities, at least in some measure. We expect the cable company to provide us with clear TV pictures in return for paying our bill each month, and are rightfully indignant when it does not. We blame the corporation for behaving unethically. We expect the oil company not to pollute the ocean when it is granted offshore drilling rights, and we are morally outraged when it does. Furthermore, modern corporations behave much more like authors than actors in their day-to-day operations. Once they have received their multipurpose charters, they act with almost complete autonomy, restrained only by the law. They defend themselves vigorously against state regulation and other forms of "interference" with their freedom to act in their own best interests. They hire lobbyists to promote their interests in government circles. They routinely make autonomous decisions — closing or relocating factories, laying off large numbers of workers, developing new technologies and suppressing others — that have enormous import for society.

It might be argued, then, that we *can* sensibly hold corporations, in and of themselves, ethically responsible for the wrongs they commit, because they exercise intentionality and agency.

That is, they decide what they want to do and do it, and thus qualify as moral agents in these two important respects. But at the same time it remains doubtful whether corporations can be accused of knowing right from wrong, which is the ultimate requirement of moral agency. Corporations do not operate in the human world of moral thought. They conduct their affairs in a world defined by charters, laws, regulations, and other legal devices that have no necessary bearing on morality. In this world of law, they are not expected to act ethically — just legally.

Moral responsibility, most philosophers would argue, is strictly a human attribute. Since corporations, as cybernetic mechanisms that exhibit a high degree of autonomy, seem to fall somewhere between the category of human and machine, we would have to look to science fiction for what guidance there may be on this question.

In Isaac Asimov's classic treatment of the ethics of robotic creatures, moral behavior is programmed into the machine in the form of the First Law: "A robot may not injure a human being, or through inaction, allow a human being to come to harm."[4] Corporations have no such ethical imperative embedded in their charters (Why not? we might reasonably ask), though they are subject to the law. The law, unfortunately, is a purely reactive tool, coming into play only after an offense has been committed.

Perhaps the most sensible course of action in the case of the miscreant corporation is simply to ignore the tangled issue of culpability and act as we would with any other machine: if it has the potential to do harm, closely regulate its manufacture and/or use. In the case of the corporation, that would mean exercising some meaningful regulation over its license to operate — its charter — up to and including revocation. In Asimov's story "First Law," a robot who disobeyed the first law saw herself and all of her kind immediately and permanently withdrawn from service.

The other alternative would be to continue to treat corporations as natural persons and ascribe to them moral agency. That would solve the problem of locating culpability, but perhaps at too great a cost. As natural persons, corporations have, as we've seen, enormous legal powers to defend themselves against prosecution. And it is unclear why, as tools devised for a specific social purpose, they should continue to have this power. We do not, after all, grant other tools and machines in our lives such enormous authority.

As noted, shareholders, the owners of corporations, enjoy freedom from financial liability under the law. In other words, liability for any damage caused by the corporation or any breach of civil law is limited to claims on the assets of the corporation itself, rather than those of the shareholders. But do they also enjoy a holiday from *ethical* liability? As the owners, they might be expected to bear full ethical responsibility for the corporation's actions. The corporation, after all, carries on business on their behalf: shareholders are clearly authors in this sense.

But if that's the case, they are surely a strange breed of author. Shareholders typically hold their stock for only a few months and during that time take little or no interest in the operations of the corporation. Typically, they hold their shares through some sort of mutual fund, which is managed by another corporation, or through their pension plan, managed by yet another corporation. Those who hold stock speculatively normally do so for an average of three months, and are interested exclusively in its return on investment. Annual meetings long ago devolved into pro forma affairs in which corporate directors vote proxies on behalf of millions of disinterested shareholders.[5]

It seems nonsensical to call these shareholders authors and

to hold them responsible for the corporation's actions. Nor, obviously, are they actors in Hobbes's definition. They seem to be a form of ethical parasite on the system, draining off returns on investment, but making no contribution to supervision and ineligible to assume any moral responsibility.

Limiting liability to the corporation itself is a relatively recent development, and was seen at its inception as a radical departure from past practice. Prior to the twentieth century, corporate owners, shareholders, were expected to supervise the use of their money. When harm was done, the law extracted damages from them, *proportional to their holdings*. This was the original idea behind "limited liability." The modern condition of *complete* immunity from legal prosecution allows shareholders to invest in and earn money from corporations while being completely free from liability for harm caused by the corporation in the course of its activities. This removes a major incentive for shareholders' interest in supervising the corporate decision-making process. The effect is reinforced by the fact that corporations themselves are often shareholders in other corporations. This further distances the human actor from corporate risk taking and malfeasance.

The legal scholar T. A. Gabalon notes that "regardless of the legal effect on policy, the fact that limited liability is enshrined in the law can inflict a separate harm by shaping values and social reality."[6] In other words, it may contribute to a general lowering of standards for ethical responsibility in society. Psychologist Dennis Fox takes up this point, concerned about "the psychological costs when real persons are motivated only by profit, undeterred by either legal or moral constraints." He argues that limited liability doctrine has served to narrow the distinction between real and corporate persons. "Just as corporations have escaped the legal requirement that they serve a public function, individuals under corporate capitalism are encouraged to seek profits despite the public good. The parallel should not be surprising, perhaps. If the amoral corporate person is a social good, after all, then why not the amoral individual motivated only by higher dividends?"[7]

Only in the atypical case of the shareholder who owns a significant block of shares in a corporation does it seem realistic to assign ethical culpability. A shareholder in this position has a clear ethical responsibility to take an interest in what the corporation does. In this case, the owner/shareholder will typically have knowledge of the corporation's operations, and be in a position to either cajole corporate management or dispose of her shares should she become aware of unethical activities. We can call these "responsible owners." The reality of the system as it is currently constituted, it would seem, is that only in the case of responsible ownership can the shareholder reasonably be held morally culpable.

Of course, it is possible to argue that, theoretically, anyone purchasing shares in a corporation, no matter how few and no matter through what intermediaries, thereby becomes an author and therefore has a moral responsibility to make herself aware of the ethical aspects of the company's operations. And knowledge, of course, imposes moral responsibility to act.

The logic of the argument is flawless, but in its practical application it is fraught with difficulties. Most of these involve corporate secrecy, both about current product formulations and future strategies, each of which is legally protected by the alleged need to compete through product exclusivity. Corporations abhor the idea of letting the competition know what they're up to, and business law respects that abhorrence.[8]

Finally, we need to recall that institutional shareholders, now the controlling factor in the stock market, will invariably operate as "rational economic agents," and have no interest in their holdings beyond the returns they produce. If those returns decline, the rational course of action is frequently not to mount a shareholder revolt or attempt to exercise corporate control by some other means, but simply to revise the portfolio. In general, it is a rare occurrence for shareholders to interfere in the management of modern business corporations, which is testified to by the lavish news coverage such events generate when they do happen.

What about the humans working within the corporation, especially those cadres of professional managers that became a feature of corporate life in the last century? Can ethical responsibility for corporate wrongdoing reasonably be charged to them, particularly in light of the fragmentation of responsibility that is typical of large enterprises?

This fragmentation, encouraged on the plant floor as a means of boosting productivity, becomes unavoidable in bureaucratic management simply due to size and complexity. In big corporations large numbers of people are involved in every task, so many that no one can reasonably claim authorship of any act or decision. Responsibility floats freely.

And yet, managers *can* be held responsible, because they are actors (on behalf of the corporation, as author), and actors who commit wrong, even though acting under an author's instructions, must share responsibility.

Workers, too, are actors, even though their work is, if anything, even more fragmented. Workers normally find themselves completely interchangeable, with similarly trained colleagues who may number in the thousands. "Each [worker's] role has a brief attached which stipulates exactly what job is to be done, how and when. Every person who knows the brief and has mastered the skills which the job requires can do it."[9] (Dennis Gioia, whom we met in connection with the Pinto tragedy, might have called these briefs "cognitive scripts.")

The important conclusion is that nothing would change if I declined to do some job. Some other person, trained to be interchangeable with me, would step in to fill the gap according to the corporate script or brief. Or so we tell ourselves when confronted with a moral dilemma on the job. However, though we may wish to tell ourselves that responsibility rests with the role and not its performer, the fact is we cannot avoid the responsibility of actors.

Culpability varies of course according to the degree of freedom of action available to actors — slaves, for example, bear but little responsibility for carrying out orders. Corporate employees and managers are not slaves (though they do face serious consequences for failure to obey orders, as detailed earlier). But to the extent that they are fully informed of the consequences of their actions, or in a position to *become* fully informed, then workers and managers must accept full moral responsibility for unethical actions they undertake or take part in on behalf of the corporation.

Note, as well, that ethical responsibility is not a determinate sum: each willing party to a consciously immoral act will be fully culpable, no matter how many participate. There is always enough blame to go around!

But culpability cannot stop there. It must be extended to the ultimate author, which, as we've seen, is the state.[10] Those who are culpable in cases of corporate immorality are the corporation itself, the humans working within the corporation, "responsible owners," and the state and its agencies to which it assigns the responsibility for corporate creation and regulation. Ethical censure must fall upon each of them. The public's moral indignation can and should be focused on government as well as the usual corporate suspects, both on the public servants who have roles as actors, and the politicians acting as authors of action taken by any state. If they are incapable of supervising corporate operations closely enough to ensure ethical operation, then *they have a moral responsibility to create the conditions for such supervision.* This could be, for example, direct government regulation or imposed industry self-regulation. But it must be effective if government is to behave in an ethically responsible way.

Citizens, too, inevitably bear moral responsibility for the misdeeds of corporations chartered by their governments. Citizens are, after all, the ultimate authors of government action in a democracy — government of, by, and for the people. Remote as most citizens are from the misdeeds of corporations they may never even have heard of, culpability is inescapable. Their moral responsibility extends to ensuring that corporate malfeasance is punished, if only for the sake of deterrence. As a practical matter, this can be accomplished through electing the right representatives. It can also be done by citizens acting responsibly in their role as consumers. Products and services that are harmful to people and the environment will not be produced if there are no buyers for them.

Finally, it is worth reiterating that as entities created to be the perfect "rational economic agent," corporations, through their PR spokesmen and the public statements of their senior officers, dispense advice of all kinds in a special way. The so-called rational economic agent is an ethical egoist, whose one and only obligation is to promote for himself the greatest possible balance of pleasure over pain — "pleasure" being defined in terms of material wealth. This carries with it the further inescapable implication that not only as an actor, but *as an observer and advisor*, the economic agent makes moral judgments and dispenses moral observations and advice according to what is to his own advantage. But not just moral advice — economic, political, social, cultural, aesthetic advice as well are to be treated as having an essentially self-serving goal.

This is no small consideration, given the frequency with which corporate spokespersons are asked for advice by governments and the media, and corporate-sponsored research institutes offer policy prescriptions. *It is simply unrealistic to expect that advice to be unbiased and geared to the public interest.* If it serves the public interest, it will be by coincidence, because corporations have no interest in the public interest.

Operations Research pioneer Sir Stafford Beer has provided a useful archetype for the corporation as a single-minded, self-obsessed entity in his classic analysis of bureaucratic institutions (a class that, of course, includes corporations). Beer asserts that bureaucratic institutions have self-preservation and growth as their primary goals and produce the social benefits that arise out of their activities "simply as by-products of their major bureaucratic undertaking, which is to produce themselves."[11] Institutions that are successful at the business of self-production or self-creation, Beer says, achieve a kind of long-term stability that in dynamic systems is called homeostasis. A key characteristic of homeostasis is that the system holds a critical output at a steady level. A boat's autopilot is such a system, adjusting the rudder and holding the vessel on course (the critical output) through corrections prompted by feedback from compass readings. But, as Beer says, bureaucracies are a special kind of homeostatic system in that "the output they hold steady is *their own organization.* Hence every response that they make, every adaptation that they embody in themselves, every evolutionary mutation that they spawn, is directed to survival. [This] rather well explains why we cannot change our institutions very easily. Their systematic organization is *directed, not primarily to our welfare, but to their own survival.*"[12]

In the end, the real problem seems to be that neither citizens nor legislators have a clear idea anymore of where to attach moral responsibility where corporations are concerned. And that confusion has led to paralysis when faced with the enormous and growing problem of corporate wrongdoing on every scale. Whether intentionally or not, as a device for obscuring moral responsibility, for keeping culpability forever afloat and never anchored, the modern business corporation has been dismayingly successful.

Philosopher Elizabeth Wolgast, in an elegant allusion to the mythical ring that granted its wearer invisibility and thus made his crimes unsolvable, asks with Plato whether blamelessness equates with an absence of moral responsibility: "Treating corporations like persons is morally hazardous. For the fiction of a person without any moral dimension is a modern Gyres ring, an invitation to act without accountability."[13]

# 14

## Common Sense About Corporations:
## Some "Irrational" Conclusions

*Between public madness and that treated by doctors the only difference is that the latter suffers from disease, the former from wrong opinions.*

— Seneca

*It may well be that rhetoric will follow reality, that we will find some painless way of rationalizing the arrangements in our midst. But as yet no philosophy has been created that mingles men and machines as joint participants, nor is it clear that American inventive genius will be able to adjust the vocabulary of democracy so as to allow corporate institutions to assume the role of just plain folks.*

— Andrew Hacker

IT OFTEN AMAZES ME how we deny the most basic observations of life because they do not fit with what we call common sense, or conventional wisdom.

Conventional wisdom, it turns out, is largely a compilation of notions about the world that were concocted three hundred years ago, and have been mostly discredited by more recent science and philosophy. I have already mentioned some of these:

the idea that science is our only route to reliable truth about the world; that humanity is steadily making progress through technology; that "progress" is inexorable and unavoidable, so that the future will be better than the present, which is better than the past. That old ideas are therefore inferior to new. That it is possible to have a science of humanity and of society that is as precise and mathematically definable as Newton's physics. That what cannot be observed is necessarily less real than that which can, or as Lord Kelvin, the nineteenth-century British physicist, put it: "Whatever exists, exists in some quantity, and can therefore be measured." That material wealth is the proper measurement of happiness.

For me, the most obvious of truths is that people are not innately and consistently selfish, as is claimed in the Rationalist market ideology and in current economic theory. Or as the eighteenth-century philosopher David Hume put it, swimming against the stream, "There is some benevolence, however small . . . some particle of dove kneaded into our frame, along with the elements of the wolf and the serpent."

The idea of universal ethical egoism has been contradicted for me at every level of experience, beginning with the Darwinian notion of ruthless, selfish competition for survival. My wife and I live with four cats, all of which were adopted as kittens. To watch those animals interact is to understand that their behavior is anything but "bestial" as Hobbes would have used the word. Rough-and-tumble play stops abruptly when anyone cries "uncle." They wait patiently for food to be placed in their individual bowls. They share favorite window perches and sleeping spots. Earlier, when our children were young, we had two other cats and a dog who ate, slept, and even fished together in our pond in friendship and cooperation. These animals almost never behaved selfishly, or egoistically.

I ask myself, Is it likely that we are less ethically endowed at this very basic level than our domestic animals? Of course, this is an absurd question for the social scientist and evolutionary biologist, who warn us sternly not to anthropomorphize animal behavior. Animals, they will tell us, are incapable of purposeful behavior. They do what they are programmed to do by genetics and stimulus-response mechanisms. What may have the appearance of happiness or sadness or grief or joy or love or expectancy or disappointment is simply the visible manifestation of highly determined bodily responses to various environmental proddings.

But simply watch any mammal over an extended period of time (and I specify mammals only because we have a close physiological affinity and therefore a better understanding of them) and the idea that they are essentially unreflective, unpurposeful machines becomes absurd. Why, then, should we assume, as Hobbes did, that life for humans in a state of nature was one of constant warring, one against the other, of "continual fear and danger of violent death, and the life of man solitary, poor, nasty, brutish, and short." For Hobbes, the fruits of reason — arts, letters, society — seem to be the sole determinant of a worthy life. No wonder the aboriginal peoples being contacted around the world in his era were thought of as subhuman "savages." Such was the parochialism of the Rationalist mind.

Lately we have been feeding a variety of wild animals at our country doorstep: raccoons, skunks, feral cats, a fox. To see those animals interact is, for a Disney-generation observer, a revelation. One night, for instance, we watched, fascinated, as a raccoon waited impatiently for a skunk to finish at the food bowl, and finally walked up and shouldered it out of the way. The raccoon was twice the weight of the myopic skunk, but that did not keep the skunk from pushing its snout back into the bowl. There was no drama, histrionics; no bloodshed. A few weeks later we witnessed a similarly decorous confrontation between one of the stray cats and one of the skunks. In the early summer, mother raccoons began bringing their children and we have had as many as a dozen of these attractive creatures, along with a couple of skunks, feasting on organic dog food and peanuts at the same time, without serious incident.

These little tableaux opened my mind about the lives of animals in the wild, and subsequent reading about animal symbiosis and cooperation has confirmed my suspicion that altruistic behavior is common among the so-called lower species. The pups of the African meerkat, to cite a famous example, remain in their colony of birth to help raise younger pups, assisting with feeding, babysitting, guarding, and other activities, as opposed to immediately dispersing to reproduce elsewhere. Research has identified well over three hundred birds and mammals, including African wild dogs, chimpanzees, kookaburras, pied kingfishers, and Seychelles warblers, that help out in the same way, delaying their own chances at reproduction. Our own wild raccoons seem to form long-term bonds of friendship (or perhaps it is sibling companionship), and we watch with warm hearts as they tenderly groom each other after enjoying a bowl of kibble.

When I was a television news producer I noticed that video from the most terrible disasters had one thing in common — people running *toward* the scene of the calamity, to try to help. Of course, on our newscasts we would focus on the victims of the disaster, and if it was man-made, on the perpetrators. We focused, in other words, on the unfortunate and the aberrant. The much larger numbers of helpers and caregivers were too *normal* to be news. And I would often ask myself, why do we identify humanity so strongly with the criminals, rather than the helpers?

Wherever I have traveled in the world I have found ordinary people to be extraordinarily kind and generous, the exceptions

211

being those in official positions whose duties and training require of them that they behave "efficiently" and "effectively" according to some bureaucratic or commercial program. On rare occasions I have been harassed in one way or another by the very poor, usually in Third World countries, who have seen me (correctly) as representative of their exploiters. But in general, and regardless of geography, I have found people to be prone to behave decently and humanely toward me rather than otherwise. I know of no one who has traveled widely who would be unwilling to confirm this experience.

I have presented other, perhaps more persuasive evidence in earlier chapters, but these bits of highly unscientific corroboration support, in my mind at least, my intellectual conviction that the Rationalist, Utilitarian picture of human beings as ethical egoists is false. Hobbes was wrong about humankind it its primitive state, as current anthropology and archaeology can attest. The Rationalists and the Utilitarians were wrong to think that moral behavior is something created by society and its institutions, and that without those institutions we would revert to Hobbesian bestiality.

Darwin, in his turn, was wrong to picture life in nature as unrelenting callous competitiveness in the pursuit of self-interest: cooperation is at least as common, and altruism is far from rare. These are observable facts, certainly in human society and, the evidence would suggest, among other animals as well. The ultimate reasons for unselfish behavior are, for our current purposes, unimportant — we can even accept the Behaviorist's insistence that altruism must ultimately redound to the benefit of the altruist, and it remains true that the fundamental premise of Rationalist economic theory, which might be called the "beggar-my-neighbor principle," is in error.

Why, then, do we make "common sense" of the idea of innate human selfishness and deny the existence of the moral impulse? Why do we assert the need for a market system that is based on the "reality" of these false concepts? Why do we accept the power and influence of corporations that support and feed into that reality but have no interest in genuine human welfare? Why do we, with each passing year, find ourselves increasingly in the position of working for the market and the corporation, rather than having them work for us? Why have we let our tools get the upper hand?

Of course, humans always adapt, to some degree, to the technologies they use. It is said that in domesticating animals, for example, humans domesticated themselves, switching from an adventurous life of hunting and gathering to a more secure, sedentary life of farming and animal husbandry. The invention of the stirrup changed the nature of land warfare, as radio transformed naval conflict. The adoption of the factory system of production, and power sources like the waterwheel and the steam engine, transfigured European society, depopulating the countryside and crowding the cities.

Humans have accordingly adapted to the social technologies invented by the Rationalists of the eighteenth and nineteenth centuries, most notably to the technologies we call the market and the corporation. That adaptation has involved our becoming, as nearly as possible, "rational economic agents." We have trained ourselves to be self-interested and self-indulgent, to obey the work ethic and the consumer ethic. "We live and die rationally and productively," laments Herbert Marcuse. "We know that destruction is the price of progress, as death is the price of life, that renunciation and toil are the prerequisites for gratification and joy, that business must go on, and that the alternatives are Utopian."[1]

This training has taken place against the grain, and in the

213

face of enormous resistance, of riots and insurrections and sabotage. We now look upon that resistance as not just futile, but immoral: the Luddites in nineteenth-century England who protested the dehumanizing impact of factory life are dismissed as criminally obtuse, and anyone who confesses to being content with what is sufficient and unwilling to work and earn and consume beyond that level of sustenance is dangerously antisocial and morally impaired by sloth. Ambition, for its own sake, is a virtue, as is material possessiveness, even though the modern idea of private property is only as old as John Locke (1632-1704). All of this is directly at odds with conscience, folk wisdom, and the accepted moral traditions of Western (and Eastern) society going back to Socrates and beyond.

Socrates, the first moral philosopher, believed that the most important philosophical question was not, How does the world work, but How should men live? The answer to that question depends importantly on how we define "men," or humanity. Socrates and succeeding generations of moral philosophers, prior to the seventeenth-century scientific revolution, were virtually unanimous in thinking of humans as spiritual beings, made in God's image. With the scientific revolution that changed: humans were now essentially mechanical entities, to be identified, successively, with currently popular technologies — mechanical clocks, steam engines, and, eventually, digital computers.

How mechanical or artificial persons should live is quite a different question from how human beings ought to conduct their lives. More correctly, how mechanical persons conduct their lives is not a moral question at all, because mechanical lives are deterministic lives — they do not involve autonomous choice, or free will. And there can be no moral choice without free will. To ask how a machine *ought* to live its life is a senseless question. The machine has no choice.

To berate corporate managers and employees about behaving ethically on the job is of little practical value. Corporate workers are under contract, written or implied, to further the aims of the corporation. And even in its broadest construction the idea of morality involves some concept of human interests, while the moral ethos within which the corporation operates is restricted to contractual obligations and rewards. To ask corporate employees to behave in accordance with authentic moral values, as opposed to the synthetic ethical standards of the corporate machine, is to ask them to invite dismissal and replacement.

In the perfectly efficient corporation, there is no room for human moral qualms, unless they happen to coincide with corporate aims. Of course, few corporations are one hundred percent efficient, and employees can sometimes get away with obeying their moral impulses, doing what is right rather than what is merely profitable. In the long run, though, the corporation will identify and eject what it sees as malignancy.

It seems to me to be a mistake to criticize corporations for behaving immorally or unethically and go no further. Corporations do what they are designed to do. If what they do does not serve human interests, then we ought to change the way they operate. They are our creatures, and therefore we bear the ethical responsibility for their depredations. We cannot reasonably expect them to consider the human interest in their actions if we do not force them to do so through law and regulation. If we allow them to subvert or escape regulatory supervision, then we are again ethically responsible, because to try to avoid unnecessary expense is simply their nature.

Humans who work within the corporate person in whatever capacity are in an ethically difficult position. They cannot escape moral culpability. This is because they are morally conscious entities, a status that corporate persons do not enjoy. Corporate

215

workers cannot escape accountability with the tawdry phrase, "I was only following orders." That much, at least, was established by the sorry history of the twentieth century.

I said at the outset that it is an error to think of corporations as human beings writ large. I hope that by now it is obvious why this is the case: corporations are not in any meaningful sense "managed" by humans. Nor do they, in their autonomous operations as human avatars — mechanical representations of the "rational economic agent" — embody anything like the full range of human attributes. In fact, they mimic only what is least desirable in the human psyche.

It is also an error to try to deal with corporate persons as individuals. Corporations are highly social creatures, and draw on one another's support in ensuring that the legal and regulatory environment in which they operate is friendly and accommodating. Corporations constitute a kind of diaspora, a worldwide tribe sharing the same basic history and values and practicing the same rituals. They are, however, an alien tribe, and they have more in common with one another than they do with the race of humans.

We ask the advice of corporations at our peril, because, as perfect ethical egoists, anything they tell us will be self-serving. This may occasionally mesh with the human interest, but only by coincidence. The only reliable advice we can count on from corporations is advice on how to help them improve their profitability.

Corporations should not be charged with the responsibility of administering aspects of human life that properly have nothing to do with profit. They should not, for example, be involved in any aspect of the democratic process. They should not be involved in education at any level. They should not be involved in health care. They should not be involved in the administration of social services. They should not be involved in the administration of justice. Why? Because they are incapable of understanding and conforming to higher human aspirations and needs, and to try to impose regulation of sufficient complexity and comprehensiveness to ensure that they do not compromise those values would be virtually impossible from an administrative point of view, not to mention the enormous expense of supervision and enforcement. Better to leave these areas to government, and to nonprofit organizations, both of which are administered by humans in the human interest.

Nor should corporations, as they are currently constituted, be involved in the arts and media, except as arm's-length donors. Few artists can resist the temptation to shape their creations to please the source of their livelihood, as was well understood by Renaissance painters and sculptors who relied on the generosity of their patrons, often against their better judgment. When it comes to maintaining artistic integrity, pleasing a human patron or a human institution such as the Church is one thing — pleasing a corporation with its corporate values and aesthetic is quite another.

Corporate sponsorship of programming on broadcast or electronic media of news, information, and entertainment should be either prohibited or severely restricted (as it is on public broadcasters around the world), because corporations invariably put profit before quality. Competition, which is supposed to ensure quality in a market economy, fails to do so in commercial radio and television because, though there is certainly competition, it is for advertisers rather than listeners and viewers. Many a television program, popular with critics and viewers, has been scrapped by networks because it did not please advertisers. The advertisers who are the subject of competition among broadcast media are almost invariably other corporations whose values and aesthetics are corporate and not human. "High quality" in commercial broadcast media is measured in terms of the response of advertisers and not audiences. What is judged to be good programming is thus programming that serves corporate, rather than human, interests. On the rare occasions when, due to some accidental alignment of benign circumstances, great programming is produced by commercial media, it is rightly deemed a small miracle.

The notion of restricting corporate sponsorship of electronic broadcast media may seem a hopelessly utopian idea, but it was widely accepted in the early years of radio, nowhere more so than in the United States. Opinion both in government and in the general public was heavily in favor of financing radio programming through endowments or foundations or taxes, rather than through advertising. In 1922, Herbert Hoover, then U.S. commerce secretary and later president, expressed the majority view in these words: "The ether is a public medium and must be used for the public good. It is quite inconceivable that it should be used for advertising." David Sarnoff, president of RCA (and later NBC), argued strongly that advertising would destroy radio's potential for education and quality entertainment. He believed that programming should be financed at arm's length by radio manufacturers like RCA, GE, and Westinghouse. An industry-sponsored blue ribbon panel looking into the state of radio in 1925 reported, "There is a natural conflict of interest between serving the broadcast listener and serving the advertiser. . . . The listener desires a program of the highest quality as free as possible from all extraneous or irrelevant material, particularly such as may be psychologically distracting from an artistic performance because of its commercial tinge."[2]

These ideas were swept aside when AT&T, then in the radio

as well as the telephone business, discovered the bonanza of revenue awaiting companies that put together networks of stations (linked by telephone lines) capable of reaching very large national audiences and therefore of enormous interest to corporate sponsors.[3]

The first and most important step in dealing with the problem with corporations is to realize that there is nothing "natural" about the market and nothing "natural" about the corporation. Both are technologies, tools we've designed to do a job, and both could be replaced or modified. Indeed, they ought to be changed, because as human constructs, they were created centuries ago to achieve laudable human goals, but using assumptions about the nature of humanity and society that are no longer (and in fact never were) appropriate, applicable, or credible. For the past hundred years, we have been compensating for the widening chasm between reality and those antique suppositions by trying forcibly to adapt human behavior and expectations to the Rationalist economic framework, instead of vice versa. The work ethic and the consumer ethic have been deployed in that cause and mightily reinforced by modern media.

The corporation is a living example of the misguided notion of the value neutrality of technology — the idea that our tools bear no normative content, that they are simply neutral devices for doing work and that any good or ill that comes from their use is the sole responsibility of the user. There are no good or bad technologies, according to this view, only good and bad users. This is an argument familiar to Americans in the rhetoric of the National Rifle Association, which advertises that "Guns don't kill people, people do." Well, of course, the handgun and the assault rifle are designed to do nothing *but* kill people and in that important sense they do embody ethical thought, built right into their mechanism. Similarly, the automobile is replete with built-in cultural notions peculiar to Western modernity — ideas of freedom and individualism, among others. The technologies that took men to the moon incorporate cultural ideas about the importance of making that trip, concepts that other cultures may not share.

The tools we build reflect in direct and obvious ways the society that builds them, from the decision to construct them at all, to the ways in which they are made to interact with the humans who must operate them. Some tools, for example, act as extensions of their operators, conforming to human mental and physical capacities; others require their operators to adapt to the machine's requirements. The early Apple personal computers, creations of gamers and hackers, represented the former attitude; earlier "mini-computers," and the early IBM PCs, were products of military R&D and a culture of elitist engineering expertise, and showed it in their massive operating manuals and inscrutable user interfaces. In this, and in many other ways, the technologies, which are products of our culture, in turn shape that culture through their employment within it.

The automobile, once again, provides an obvious example: once it had been produced and accepted by North American society (for social reasons), it transformed the social and physical environments in profound ways that encouraged — indeed, made mandatory — ever wider adoption. Once a luxury, it became a necessity. And to use a more contemporary example, the technologies of genetic modification and cloning bear within them the cultural assumption that humanity is capable of guiding its own destiny as a species, and the destiny of the earth's other species as well. Some would argue that these technologies incorporate a fatal hubris; others see them as reflections of a natural and unavoidable human destiny.

But the recognition that culture plays an important role in the determination of technology is a relatively new one. The assumption made by the designers and promoters of the modern business corporation was that it would be a morally neutral machine, whose impact on society would be governed and ameliorated by the larger mechanism of the market economy. It was a product of the broader Rationalist determination to face the "fact" that people are incorrigibly selfish and greedy, and rather than try to change that fact (which as a "law of nature" was anyway unchangeable), to build institutions that would make use of it in promoting social good. The corporate machine was never morally neutral, nor could it have been. There is no escaping that it was designed to institutionalize and rationalize the vice of avarice, and it does this with wicked effectiveness.

I have described the corporation as sociopathic in its disregard for human goals and values; others have pointed out that in its behavior it fits World Health Organization criteria for defining the psychopath. These "psychological" diagnoses can be amplified by the observation that the scientific Rationalist intellectual milieu that spawned both the market and the modern business corporation bears a remarkable affinity with what we now classify as paranoia. The paranoid's thinking is characterized by a fear of being controlled by others, and his attention to the minutest detail of his environment is scrupulous and obsessive. Nothing, no detail, however tiny, is ignored. He must know everything, and everything must fit:

> The paranoid delusion suffers not from a lack of logic but from unreality. Indeed, its distortion derives, at least in part, from the very effort to make all the clues fit into a single interpretation. . . . For the paranoid, interpretation is determined primarily by subjective need — in particular, the need to defend against the pervasive sense of threat to one's own autonomy. . . . The

world of objects that emerges is a world that may be defined with extraordinary accuracy in many respects, but is one whose parameters are determined principally by the needs of the observer.[4]

This definition seems to me to explain the Behaviorist impulse to reduce *everything*, without exception, to physics. It explains the Victorians' acceptance of a description of social development and of morality that flies in the face of logic, but at the same time provides a tidy justification for imperialism, social injustice, and the market. It explains how the modern business corporation, as a creature of Rationalism, interacts with the world.

And, of course, in "explaining" all of that it explains nothing, rather merely describes it and gives it a medical name. But in doing this it provides a valuable service because it helps us to see the object of our attention more clearly, from another perspective. If we can begin to see the corporate person as a sociopathic entity spawned by a paranoid hallucination, then we can begin to see some of its manifestations — the work ethic, the consumer ethic, WTO-style globalization — for what they are: symptoms of a delusional understanding of the world.

Anyone who doubts the importance of perspective or point of view in the real world beyond theory and academic musings should consider the case of the environmental movement that has grown up over the past forty or fifty years around the issue of the destruction of the global ecosystem. Two of the central myths of the late-twentieth-century environmental movement were the so-called tragedy of the commons and the claim that Christianity was essentially incompatible with proper environmental stewardship. I use "myth" here in the pejorative sense of a false account. The influential essay "The Tragedy of the

Commons," by Garrett Hardin, was published in *Science* in 1968. At its core was this story:

> Picture a pasture open to all. It is to be expected that each herdsman will try to keep as many cattle as possible on the commons. Such an arrangement may work reasonably satisfactorily for centuries because tribal wars, poaching, and disease keep the numbers of both man and beast well below the carrying capacity of the land. Finally, however, comes the day of reckoning, that is, the day when the long-desired goal of social stability becomes a reality. At this point, the inherent logic of the commons remorselessly generates tragedy. As a rational being, each herdsman seeks to maximize his gain. Explicitly or implicitly, more or less consciously, he asks, "What is the utility to me of adding one more animal to my herd?" This utility has one negative and one positive component.
>
> 1. The positive component is a function of the increment of one animal. Since the herdsman receives all the proceeds from the sale of the additional animal, the positive utility is nearly +1 (plus one).
>
> 2. The negative component is a function of the additional overgrazing created by one more animal. Since, however, the effects of overgrazing are shared by all the herdsmen, the negative utility for any particular decision-making herdsman is only a fraction of -1 (minus one).
>
> Adding together the component partial utilities, the rational herdsman concludes that the only sensible course for him to pursue is to add another animal to his herd. And another. . . . But this is the conclusion reached by each and every rational herdsman sharing a commons. Therein is the tragedy. Each man is locked into a system that compels him to increase his herd without limit — in a world that is limited. Ruin is the destination toward which all men rush, each pursuing his own best interest in a society that believes in the freedom of the commons. Freedom in a commons brings ruin to all.[5]

Hardin draws several conclusions about the need for draconian regulation of both pollution and population, but these need not concern us here. What is significant in the present context is

Hardin's basic premise that "rational" human beings always act to maximize their own self-interest. This is the basic assumption of Rationalist institution builders, and the tragedy of the commons makes no sense without it. But as I have argued, the presumption of ethical egoism is mistaken.

Nevertheless, the story does seem to ring true when we look around at what is happening in the world. Fisheries and farmlands are being exhausted; toxic chemicals are to be found in every corner of the globe; species are vanishing at an accelerating rate; global warming is melting polar ice caps; rain forests are being decimated; fish stocks are collapsing; there are holes in the ozone layer; and so on. As noted, the root of this seeming paradox is that, while humans may not be ethical egoists as Hardin presumes, the corporations that conduct most of the world's business are. Where corporations are involved, the tragedy of the commons is not just a possibility but an inevitability.

It is critically important to understand this distinction, because if we assume, as Hardin does, that the environmental problem is a problem of innate human behavior, then we will direct our search for solutions to the wrong place. Furthermore, we are likely to cause widespread skepticism about the possibility of finding solutions at all, because everybody knows that "human nature" is notoriously difficult to change. This was in fact the response to Hardin's article when it first appeared. Environmentalism replaced economics as the "dismal science" in the minds of many in the West, and in the developing world his prescription for rigid laws governing population growth was widely interpreted as incipient racism.[6]

If, on the other hand, the solutions to the problem are seen in the context of closely regulating the activities of business corporations, then policy initiatives are not hard to imagine. Implementing them will undoubtedly be difficult, given the formidable collective strength of the corporate tribe, but certainly not impossible. What is necessary is political will in governments of the leading industrial nations, and that must come from the people. It will never be there so long as there is a fundamental misunderstanding of the nature of the problem as human nature rather than the nature of corporate persons.

The second defining myth of the environmental movement is contained in a famous essay by Lynn White, Jr., published in *Science* in 1967, "The Historical Roots of Our Ecologic Crisis." White, like Hardin, writing only a decade or so after the emergence of the corporation in its fully mature form, blames the environmental crisis on Christianity, which "in absolute contrast to ancient paganism and Asia's religions . . . not only established a dualism of man and nature but also insisted that it is God's will that man exploit nature for his proper ends. By destroying pagan animism, Christianity made it possible to exploit nature in a mood of indifference to the feelings of natural objects." White went on to say that since "our present science and our present technology are so tinctured with orthodox Christian arrogance toward nature . . . no solution for our ecologic crisis can be expected from them alone." He proposed instead that "the remedy must also be essentially religious, whether we call it that or not. We must rethink and refeel our nature and destiny." He famously proposed that the environmental movement adopt as its patron saint Francis of Assisi.

Subsequent discussion (and there was a great deal of it) established that White, while a respected historian of technology, was no theologian, and had failed to appreciate the complexities of Christian attitudes to nature. Once again, though, that is of peripheral interest here. What is significant is that White's essay led environmentalists away from the scent of the real quarry, in pursuit of a prescriptive dead end — the remaking of mainstream

Christianity. It is not Christianity or any other religion that ultimately can ensure that we treat the rest of nature with the respect it deserves: it is the moral impulse, our innate compassion for the Other. That impulse must be acknowledged, and listened to.

And it is not the Christian attitude to nature that has created the environmental crisis, any more than the Buddhist or Confucian attitude. It is, primarily, the corporate ethic of pure and boundless egoism, supported by the antique Rationalist idea of the market as an autonomous, automatic manufacturer of Good. The corporation has extracted, distilled, and concentrated the essence of human selfishness and acquisitiveness, enormously amplifying the range and depth of immorality deemed acceptable, even admirable, in human affairs. To the corporation, vice is virtue and virtue is vice, and that is the Orwellian message with which consumers of corporate media, worldwide, are bombarded all day every day. This is what we designed corporations to be, and they are doing what we built them to do. But no one, certainly none of the early Rationalist designers, suspected they could become so good at it.[7]

Without wishing to carry what is essentially a rhetorical device too much further, I cannot resist noting that another characteristic of the paranoid is that they "exhibit remarkable consistency and coherence in their belief systems." At the same time, "it is extremely difficult to convince such people that they have made an error in reasoning."[8] Reform, which is urgently needed, will not come from within the corporation or from its ideologically committed allies. All we can expect from them is more of the same. It would be a denial of their DNA to do anything else.

Nobody expects the bulldozer or the nuclear reactor to reform itself: it is strange indeed that we demand it of the tool we call the corporation. The responsibility is ours, collectively, and we can best respond to the challenge through government. A detailed program for reform is beyond the scope of this book, and beyond my competence as well. But the outlines of what needs to be done are clear:

- Corporate personhood (the "natural personhood" that bestows access to human rights) was never granted by public consent and has turned out to be a very bad idea. It needs to be withdrawn through legislation.

- Like armies, corporations are a necessary evil, and in constitutional terms, the corporation ought to be treated as we treat the military. Strict observance of government authority and strict subordination to the government's will is needed. (Recall, though, that by "corporation" I mean large, publicly traded business corporations and not the smaller, private variety that constitute the vast majority of businesses.)

- The moral liability of corporate officers and workers needs to be clearly codified in law. And not just for crimes *against* the corporation (as in the Enron/WorldCom-inspired Sarbanes-Oxley Act) but for crimes *of* the corporation.

- Corporations have grown too big and powerful. We need legislative limits on their size and wealth. Rural municipalities where I live place load limits on country roads during the spring thaw to keep them from being ruined by heavy trucks and machinery. The limiting of corporate gigantism should be no more controversial than this sensible policy in aid of preserving the public domain from

227

damage by private interests. Our culture reacts strongly against government interference with rights of the individual, so it is important to emphasize the obvious: limiting corporate growth would not restrict the rights of individual human beings in any way.

- The notion that the advice of corporate leaders should be sought in connection with global economic agencies like the World Trade Organization and the World Bank, international trade agreements, national budgets, economic forecasts, and the like is dangerously outmoded. Modern business corporations, by their nature, give untainted advice only when it comes to improving their own profits. They will not give advice, no matter how necessary or obvious, that can lead to impairment of their financial position. They are, in short, not to be trusted as objective advisors.

- Corporate charters ought to specify the business goals for which the company was established. This will go some way toward ensuring that corporations are concerned with the products and services they produce, rather than simply with the revenue they produce. It will also give state regulators more control: the law needs to provide for the withdrawal of corporate charters in cases of serious corporate crime. This kind of "capital punishment," it seems to me, is ethically justified where it concerns inanimate entities like corporations.

Measures such as these will result in a market populated by much larger numbers of small to medium-sized companies competing for customers. It is this process, and not the alleged efficiencies of monopoly and oligopoly, that is the bedrock justification for market capitalism. Such a program of reform is not radical, it is conservative.


One writes books such as this in hope that the ideas they contain will be widely discussed and perhaps even acted upon. To the extent that this book is noticed by the organs of corporate business, the suggestions for reform I've made here will assuredly be dismissed as impractical, dangerous, wrong-headed, and, yes, *irrational*. But that is my point. We have suffered enough of the social engineering practiced by our Rationalist forebears and their present-day admirers. It is time, once again, to pay heed to Socrates's admonition that the important questions are not about how things work, but how we ought to live.

# Acknowledgments

MUCH OF THE RESEARCH FOR THIS BOOK was done while I was Maclean Hunter Chair of Ethics in Media at Ryerson University in Toronto. I am grateful to the Ryerson School of Journalism and its faculty for the opportunity to teach and do research for two years in a field in which I have an abiding interest, and to the many students who helped me hone my ideas. I am also indebted, as always, to my Canadian editor and publisher, Patrick Crean, and to the legendary Richard Seaver, my American publisher at Arcade, for their interest in and support for my somewhat unorthodox take on the world.

# Notes

## Introduction

1. Danny Hakim, *New York Times Service*, August 22, 2005.

2. This activity has been widely documented, but the best summary is provided by Ross Gelbspan, "Snowed," *Mother Jones*, May/June 2005.

3. Ibid. Gelbspan reports:

> In the early 1990s, when climate scientists began to suspect that our burning of coal and oil was changing the earth's climate, Western Fuels, then a $400 million coal cooperative, declared in its annual report that it was enlisting several scientists who were skeptical about climate change — Patrick Michaels, Robert Balling, and S. Fred Singer — as spokesmen. The coal industry paid these and a handful of other skeptics some $1 million over a three-year period and sent them around the country to speak to the press and the public. According to internal strategy papers I obtained at the time, the purpose of the campaign was "to reposition global warming as theory (not fact)," with an emphasis on targeting "older, less educated males" and "younger, low-income women" in districts that received their electricity from coal, and who preferably had a representative on the House Energy and Commerce Committee.

*Notes*

# 1. A Pilgrim's Progress

1. R. H. Tawney, *Religion and the Rise of Capitalism* (London: Penguin, 1966 [1924]), 52. Emphasis added.

# 2. The Fable of the Bees

1. For an exhaustive and thoroughly exhilarating treatment of this enormously important transition, see Hans Blumenberg, *The Legitimacy of the Modern Age* (Cambridge, Mass.: MIT Press, 1988), esp. chap. 5.

2. To which William Blake replied: "May God us keep / From single vision and Newton's sleep." Letter to Thomas Butts, November 22, 1802, in Alicia Ostriker, ed., *William Blake: The Complete Poems* (New York: Penguin, 1977).

3. R. H. Tawney, *Religion and the Rise of Capitalism* (London: Penguin, 1966 [1924]), 43-44.

4. Blumenberg, *Legitimacy of the Modern Age* (Cambridge, Mass.: MIT Press, 1988), 370.

# 3. Machine-Made Morality

1. Determinism is the theory that every event, act, and decision inevitably follows from — is determined by — prior conditions that are independent of the human will and therefore unalterable. It is a theory of how and why things happen. The early Rationalist thinkers were strongly deterministic. That is, they believed that most, if not all, events and decisions in life are determined by laws of nature that operate independent of human will.

2. Zygmunt Bauman, *Work, Consumption, and the New Poor* (Buckingham, UK: Open University Press, 1998), 5-6.

3. "Neither Charles Kingsley nor Friedrich Engels, neither Blake nor Carlyle, was mistaken in believing that the very image of man had

been defiled by some terrible catastrophe. And more impressive even than the outbursts of pain and anger that came from poets and philanthropists was the icy silence with which Malthus and Ricardo passed over the scenes out of which their philosophy of secular perdition was born." Karl Polanyi, *The Great Transformation: The Political and Economic Origins of Our Time* (Boston: Beacon Press, 2002 [1944]), 102-3.

4. It would take John Maynard Keynes's ideas of deficit financing to snap the industrialized world out of the depression cycle.

5. Richard Lewontin, *The Doctrine of DNA: Biology as Ideology* (London: Penguin, 1993), 10.

# 4. The "Science" of Selfishness

1. Adam Smith, *An Inquiry into the Nature and Causes of the Wealth of Nations,* ed. R. H. Campbell and A. S. Skinner (New York: Clarendon Press, 1976), 146.

2. Natural theology is the discipline that deals with knowledge of God derived from reason, as opposed to being acquired through revelation. It tries, for instance, to establish the existence of God from the study of the world He created.

3. I have followed one academic convention and ignored others in using the terms *ethics* and *morality* and their variants interchangeably throughout the book. Academic conventions are fine in their place, but here, to give the words separate meanings would merely be confusing. One is a Greek root, the other Latin: they both refer to the Good.

4. Bertrand Russell, *History of Western Philosophy* (London: George Allen Unwin, 1961), 744.

5. Politics was similarly captivated. Thomas Jefferson wrote that the only aim of government is "to secure the greatest degree of happiness possible to the general mass of those associated under it." And John Adams writes, in *Thoughts on Government:* "The form of government which communicates ease, comfort, security, or, in one word, happiness,

to the greatest number of persons, and in the greatest degree, is the best."

6. William Stanley Jevons, *The Theory of Political Economy*, Reprints of Economic Classics, ed. A. M. Kelly (Cambridge, Mass.: Harvard University Press, 1965).

7. This and subsequent Jevons quotations are taken from David F. Noble, *Beyond the Promised Land: An Essay on the Passing of the Modern Myth* (Toronto: Between the Lines, 2005).

8. Quoted in Philip Mirowski, *Machine Dreams: Economics Becomes a Cyborg Science* (Cambridge: Cambridge University Press, 2002), 100.

9. We can see the same logical inconsistency that Russell notes in connection with Utilitarianism, that if everyone automatically, by natural law, acts in his own self-interest, it makes no sense to say that he *ought* to do so.

## 5. Ethics and the Market

1. Adam Smith, *An Inquiry into the Nature and Causes of the Wealth of Nations*, ed. Edwin Cannan (New York: Modern Library, 1937), 14.

2. Ibid., 423. Emphasis added.

3. Notice the important fact this implies, that not only as an actor but as an observer and advisor the economic agent makes moral judgments and dispenses moral observations and advice according to what is to his own advantage.

4. Paul Heyne, *The Economic Way of Thinking*, 4th ed. (Chicago: Science Research Associates, 1983), 4.

5. Campbell McConnell, *Economics*, 8th ed. (New York: McGraw-Hill, 1981), 141.

6. Karl Polanyi, *The Great Transformation* (Boston: Beacon Press, 2002), 257-58.

7. For many children of the twentieth century, the idea of objective accounts of well-being sets off alarm bells about authoritarianism and paternalism of the kind that characterized the worst of the administrations of Communist Eastern Europe. If what I think is good for me can be wrong according to some "objective" standard, then doesn't that open the door to some central authority telling me what I can and can't do with my life?

At least three points can be made in this connection. First, as I will discuss in the next chapter, the idea of objectivity (or absolutism) in values does *not* imply infallibility. We can believe in objective truths while at the same time accepting that we do not know (and perhaps cannot know) with certainty what they are. Properly construed, "objectivity" implies an obligation to listen to and explore alternative perspectives, because they may bring us closer to that objective truth.

Second, objectivism or absolutism does *not* say that what people want is irrelevant to their well-being. Saint Augustine himself, obviously a believer in objective truths, conceded that happiness can be contingent on a person's getting what he wants, though with an important reservation: "All that are blessed have what they will, although not all who have what they will are forewith blessed. But they are forewith wretched, who either have not what they will, or have that which they do not rightly will. Therefore he only is a blessed man, who both has all things which he wills, and wills nothing ill" (Augustine, *De Trinitate).* No one can be happy if what she has is of no value to her, or if she cannot have what *is* of value to her. But at the same time it is entirely possible to be in error about what is actually of value, and to mistakenly value things that will bring unhappiness. Thus, the fact that people are unhappy if they don't get what they desire does not necessarily mean that they are happy if they do. Put another way, getting that which is personally endorsed as valuable is a necessary, but not sufficient, condition for happiness.

A third point is that the very process of making considered choices about one's individual welfare is an important constituent of human Good. It is good for us to struggle with these questions — it "develops character." As we'll see in the next chapter, it is the process by which we identify who and what we are as individuals. And what makes choosing so difficult is that it is not simply a matter of selecting from an array of options, as economic theory would have it, but of *discovering what is of value*. It follows, then, that a good society is one that gives people the opportunity to learn about and reflect upon questions of value rather than one that dictates the answers, as did the pre-1989 Eastern European economies.

# 6. What It Means to Be Moral

1. Harold A. Herzog, Jr., "The Moral Status of Mice," *American Psychologist*, June 1988. Dr. Herzog is associate professor in the Department of Psychology, Western Carolina University, Cullowhee, North Carolina. His essay was written while he was on sabbatical leave at the University of Tennessee.

2. Terry Eagleton, *Ideology: An Introduction* (London: Verso, 1991), 165.

3. The idea was elaborated a century later by David Hume in his *Treatise of Human Nature*, 1739-40.

4. Noam Chomsky, *Language and Problems of Knowledge* (Cambridge, Mass.: MIT Press, 1988), 152. And later (p. 161): "The evidence seems compelling, indeed overwhelming, that fundamental aspects of our mental and social life, including language, are determined as part of our biological endowment, not acquired by learning, still less by training, in the course of our experience."

5. Larissa MacFarquhar, "Profiles: The Devil's Accountant," *New Yorker*, March 31, 2003, 64ff.

6. Zygmunt Bauman, *Postmodern Ethics* (Oxford, UK: Blackwell Publishers, 1998), 32.

7. Ibid., 13.

8. I have addressed this question at length in *Galileo's Mistake* (Toronto: Thomas Allen Publishers, 2001; New York: Arcade Publishing, 2003).

9. John Polkinghorne, *Belief in God in an Age of Science* (New Haven, Conn.: Yale University Press, 1998), 15.

10. Robert Kane, *Through the Moral Maze: Searching for Absolute Values in a Pluralistic World* (New York: Paragon House, 1994), 74-75.

11. This naturally assumes the real existence of Good (and bad). To go into this issue further would require a long excursion into metaphysics, which is beyond the scope of this book. I hope I can safely assume that the great majority of readers will have no trouble accepting good and bad as real distinctions having real ethical meaning and addressing real-world circumstances. In any system of understanding there must be some basic, foundational concepts that cannot be defined in terms of other concepts. In other words, understanding has to begin somewhere, upon some foundation which must be accepted on faith. As perhaps the ultimate abstraction in philosophy, Good stands outside any possibility of concrete definition. Ultimately, the existence of Good can only be established through a leap of faith. Some might say it is something that exists only so long as we will it to, and vanishes otherwise. Others would insist that it exists always, as an overriding reality, as in Plato's "ideal forms" — that landscape of perfection, of which the reality accessible to humans is but a shadowy sketch — and that when we deny its existence on grounds that it is an "irrational" concept, we are willfully denying truth. I find myself on the side of Plato in this. Good seems to have a kind of existence analogous to the tenuous nature of quarks, mesons, and other quantum entities, which, physics says, must be observed in order to exist as anything other than a possibility, a potential, but which nevertheless are real.

12. Thomas Nagel, *The Last Word* (Oxford, UK: Oxford University Press, 1997), 141.

# 7. The Rise of the Modern Business Corporation

1. Following the Supreme Court ruling, Nike settled the lawsuit privately.

2. Summary descriptions were routinely ignored by corporations, despite several court rulings that "object clauses" must be adhered to. In 1966 the courts abandoned this position when the Court of Appeal in *Bell Houses Limited v. City Wall Properties Limited* approved an objects clause giving the corporation power to: "carry on any other trade or business whatsoever which can, in the opinion of the board of directors, be advantageously carried on by the company in connection with or as ancillary to any of the above businesses or the general business of the company." In 1989 a new Companies Act effectively eliminated the requirement to state the firm's intended sphere of activity in its charter. The power to determine what activities a corporation might legally engage in was transferred from the courts to the corporation.

3. I mean here ownership in the proprietary sense, exemplified by company founders. The late-twentieth-century practice of incorporating share ownership in the pay package of senior corporate officers has given these managers a more direct interest in the company's performance. However, the result has often been that corporate managers, increasingly nomadic in their employment, become interested in short-term goals designed to maximize share price (e.g., through layoffs and mergers), rather than goals that add genuine long-term value to the enterprise. The managers are merely behaving, as might be expected, as ethical egoists. It should also be noted that these managers exercise their power over corporate decision making not through their stock holdings, which seldom amount to a significant percentage of total equity, but through their management positions.

4. Under the American Constitution, corporations are creatures of the state governments.

5. *Marshall v. Barlow's*, 436 U.S. 307 (1978). See also *Colonnade Catering Corp. v. United States*, 397 U.S. 72 (1969) (exception for the liquor industry); *United States v. Biswell*, 406 U.S. 311 (1977) (exception for firearms industry); *Donovan v. Dewey*, 452 U.S. 594 (1981) (exception for mining industry). Exceptions in these cases were based on the long prior history of government regulation.

6. *First National Bank of Boston v. Bellotti,* quoted in Mayer, "Personalizing the Impersonal: Corporations and the Bill of Rights," *Hastings Law Journal* 41 (March 1990): 633.

7. Paul Hawken, *The Ecology of Commerce* (New York: Harper Business, 1993), 109.

8. First Amendment right to commercial speech, *Central Hudson Gas and Electric Corp. v. Public Utilities Commission,* 1980 (corporations' right to commercial speech protected); First Amendment negative free speech right, *Pacific Gas and Electric Co. v. Public Utilities Commission,* 1986 (corporations have a negative free speech right not to be associated with the speech of others); Fourth Amendment freedom from regulatory searches without warrants, *Marshall v. Barlow's Inc.,* 1978; Fifth Amendment freedom from double jeopardy, *United States v. Martin Linen Supply Co.,* 1977; *United States v. Polk and Co.,* 1971, asserted the "fundamental principle" that corporations enjoy the same Seventh Amendment rights as human individuals to trial by jury; Seventh Amendment right to trial by jury in a civil case, *Ross v. Bernhard,* 1970.

9. Christopher Caldwell, *The New York Times Magazine,* December 12, 2004, 102. Caldwell writes: "The Inglewood referendum won't be the last time voters are invited to trade citizen rights for consumer rights — and no one should make any glib assumptions about which of those rights Americans hold more dear."

10. Michael Mandel, *The Charter of Rights and the Legalization of Politics in Canada,* 2nd ed. (Toronto: Thomson Education Publishing Inc., 1994), 231ff.

11. The concept of corporate personhood was written into Canadian business law with the passage of the Canadian Business Corporations Act of 1981.

12. Mandel, *The Charter of Rights,* 328-29.

13. Supreme Court of Canada, Committee for the Commonwealth of Canada, 1991, in Mandel, *The Charter of Rights,* 295.

14. Mandel, *The Charter of Rights,* 234.

15. Ibid., 239.

16. Abraham Lincoln's letter to Col. William F. Eakins, November 21, 1864.

17. Both quoted in Harvey Wasserman, *America Born and Reborn* (New York: Collier Books, 1983), 89-90, 291.

18. Alfons J. Beitzinger, *Edward G. Ryan: Lion of the Law* (Madison: State Historical Society of Wisconsin, 1960), 115-16. From an 1873 address to the graduating class of the University of Wisconsin Law School.

19. Grover Cleveland, "Fourth Annual Message to Congress, 3 Dec. 1888," in *Messages and Papers of the Presidents*, ed. James D. Richardson, vol. 8 (Washington, D.C.: Government Printing Office, 1989), 773-74.

20. Brandeis, in *Liggett v. Lee*, 288 U.S. 517 (1933).

21. Joel Bakan, *The Corporation* (Toronto: Viking, 2004), 36-38.

22. Ibid., 38-39.

23. Milton Friedman, "The Social Responsibility of Business Is to Increase Its Profits," *New York Times*, September 13, 1970, 32.

24. Theodore Leavitt, "The Dangers of Social Responsibility," in *Ethical Theory and Business*, ed. Thomas Beauchamp and Norman Bowie (Chicago: University of Chicago Press, 1979), 138.

25. David Olive, "IPO Challenges Google's 'Do No Evil' Directive," *Toronto Star*, August 18, 2004.

26. In both of these high-profile cases, the professional managers brought in after going public eventually realized that the corporations would do better financially by remaining associated with their founders.

27. David Olive, "Googzilla," *Toronto Star*, Sunday, September 4, 2005.

28. J. K. Galbraith, *The New Industrial State* (Boston: Houghton Mifflin Company, 1967), 50.

29. As early as the mid-twentieth century serious concern was being expressed over the consequences of the near-complete elimination of the partnership, sole proprietorship, and other means of majority ownership of American business corporations. "If we . . . consider that management in most large companies eventually reaches a position where, to all intents and purposes, its power over the organization is beyond review, there are likely to be consequences of the utmost seriousness in both the moral and economic spheres that will encourage the demand for government control." Ernest Dale, *The Great Organizers* (New York: McGraw-Hill, 1960), 185.

30. Galbraith, *The New Industrial State*, 77ff.

31. Doug Henwood, *Wall Street: How It Works and For Whom* (London: Verso, 1997), 270ff.

32. Ibid., 291.

33. Aristotle, *Politics*, 1300b.

34. Peter French, *Collective and Corporate Responsibility* (New York: Columbia University Press, 1984), 102.

35. Jack O'Dwyer, "PR Industry's Amicus Brief Has a Flaw," ReclaimDemocracy.org, http://reclaimdemocracy.org/nike/pr_brief_retort_kasky_nike.html.

36. "Frito-Lay Adding Broccoli to Its Chips While Cutting Bad Fat," *Toronto Star*, September 25, 2002.

37. "Kraft Cooks Up a Plan to Avoid Obesity Lawsuits," *Toronto Star*, July 5, 2003.

38. Trans fats were introduced following World War One as a cheap substitute for animal fats. These oils have been processed with hydrogen gas to make them solid at room temperature and delay spoiling. Governments in the United States and Canada have not required trans fats to be included in nutritional labeling. (They are found in hydrogenated and partially hydrogenated oils and in shortening, which *are*

included in labeling.) This has allowed manufacturers to reduce "fat" content listed on labels by substituting trans fats for other fats and oils, a practice widespread in the industry. Harvard University researchers concluded in 1994 that 30,000 premature coronary deaths in the United States each year could be attributed to trans fats. The food industry disputed the study. The U.S. Academy of Sciences advised in 2002 that there is no safe level for trans fats in food. "Kraft Move to Slim Down Opens New Front in Fat War," *Toronto Star*, July 25, 2003.

39. Dr. Bruce Holub, quoted in ibid.

# 8. Who's in Charge Here?

1. The idea is not unique to me: it can be found as early as 1964 in Andrew Hacker's essay "Corporate America," the introduction to *The Corporation Takeover*, ed. Andrew Hacker (New York: Harper & Row, 1964).

2. J. Doyle Farmer, Alletta d'A. Belin, "Artificial Life: The Coming Evolution," in *Proceedings in Celebration of Murray Gell-Man's 60th Birthday* (Cambridge: Cambridge University Press, 1990).

3. Quoted in Doug Henwood, *Wall Street* (London: Verso, 1997), 299.

4. http://www.house.gov/commerce_democrats/legviews/ 109luhr1640-mtbc.shtm.

5. CNNMoney.com, August 2, 2000.

6. D. McCabe and L. K. Treviño, "Academic Dishonesty: Honor Codes and Other Situational Influences," *Journal of Higher Education* 64 (1993): 522-38.

7. D. McCabe and L. K. Treviño, "Cheating Among Business Students: A Challenge for Business Leaders and Educators," *Journal of Management Education* 19, no. 2 (1995): 205-18.

8. Choosing "to kill several people [was] something that [Ford executives] would . . . not choose to do in their private capacities." Thus, "an organizational rationality . . . need not be the simple sum of its

members' or leaders' rationalities." Paul Brietzke, "A Law and Economics of Coercion," paper presented at a symposium on Law and the Legitimation of Violence, held at State University of New York, Buffalo, March 1988, 6, quoted in Elizabeth Wolgast, *Ethics of an Artificial Person: Lost Responsibility in Professions and Organizations* (Palo Alto, Calif.: Stanford University Press, 1992), 87.

9. "Ford Rejected Advice on Recall: Papers," *Toronto Star*, May 3, 2004.

10. Michael White, "Verdict Finds GM at Fault for Burns," *Associated Press*, July 10, 1999.

11. In theoretical terms, the trouble with externalizing costs is that, for the market to function efficiently in setting prices so that competition can do its quality-optimizing trick, all costs of production must be included in the selling price.

12. Zygmunt Bauman, *Work, Consumerism, and the New Poor* (Buckingham, UK: Open University Press, 1998), 53.

13. Among the best of these is Linda K. Treviño and Katherine A. Nelson, *Managing Business Ethics: Straight Talk About How to Do It Right*, 3rd ed. (New York: Wiley, 2004). See 36-45, 243-44.

14. He tells his story in "Pinto Fires and Personal Ethics: A Script Analysis of Missed Opportunities," *Journal of Business Ethics* 11 (5, 6): 379-89; and in "Reflections," in Treviño and Nelson, *Managing Business Ethics*, 129-32.

15. J. S. Coleman, *The Asymmetrical Society* (Syracuse, N.Y.: Syracuse University Press, 1982); H. C. Kelman and V. L. Hamilton, *Crimes of Obedience: Toward a Social Psychology of Authority and Obedience* (New Haven: Yale University Press, 1989).

16. J. Tomkins, B. Victor, and R. Adler, "Psycholegal Aspects of Organizational Behavior: Assessing and Controlling Risk," in *Handbook of Psychology and Law*, ed. D. K. Kagehiro and W. S. Laufer (New York, Springer-Verlag 1992), 523-41.

17. David Luban, *Lawyers and Justice* (Princeton, N.J.: Princeton University Press, 1989), 123. In a similar vein, the judge in the Dalkon Shield intrauterine birth-control device lawsuit (the device caused widespread sterility among its users) found responsibility often impossible to pin down: "The project manager for Dalkon Shield explains that a particular question should have gone to the medical department, the medical representative explains that the question was really in the bailiwick of the quality control department, and the quality control department representative explains that the project manager was the one with the authority to make a decision on that question. . . . It is not at all unusual for the hard questions . . . to be unanswerable by anyone from Robins [the manufacturer]." Quoted in Luban above, *Lawyers and Justice*, 124.

18. The question might be asked, Why didn't the U.S. government take similar legislative action? The answer appears to be that Washington is more susceptible to lobbying on behalf of the corporations involved, some of America's largest.

# 9. The Corporate Worker's Dilemma

1. David F. Noble, *Progress Without People: New Technology, Unemployment, and the Message of Resistance* (Toronto: Between the Lines, 1995), 43.

2. David F. Noble, *America by Design: Science, Technology, and the Rise of Corporate Capitalism* (Oxford, UK: Oxford University Press, 1977), 82.

3. Ibid., 82.

4. Ibid., 179.

5. Philip Hancock and Melissa Tyler, *Work, Postmodernism and Organization: A Critical Introduction* (London: Sage, 2001), 40.

6. Quoted in Seymour Melman, *Profits Without Production* (New York: Knopf, 1983), 106.

7. Robert Jackall, *Moral Mazes* (New York, Oxford University Press, 1988), 203-4.

8. Noah Kennedy, *The Industrialization of Intelligence* (New York: Unwin Hyman, 1986), 251.

9. Quoted in Stewart Ewan, *Captains of Consciousness: Advertising and the Social Roots of Consumer Culture* (New York: McGraw-Hill, 1976), 18.

10. Linda K. Treviño and Katherine A. Nelson, *Managing Business Ethics* (New York: Wiley, 2004), 210-11. Dunlap later found himself in hot water with the U.S. Securities Exchange Commission over accounting practices that overstated Sunbeam profits and paid a fine of $500,000.

11. Note, however, that primitive Fordist/Taylorist management techniques continue to be employed by First World corporations in their Third World workplaces.

12. Hancock and Tyler, *Work, Postmodernism and Organization*, 100.

13. *The Cambridge Dictionary of Philosophy* (Cambridge: Cambridge University Press, 1995), 625.

14. Paul du Gay, "Governing Organizational Life," in *Consumption and Identity at Work* (Thousand Oaks, Calif.: Sage Publications, 1996), 58.

15. Ibid., 73.

16. Simon Head, *The New Ruthless Economy: Work and Power in the Digital Age* (Oxford, UK: Oxford University Press, 2000), 163.

17. Ibid., 165.

18. Ibid., 166.

19. Ibid., 98.

20. Ibid., 109.

21. Ibid., 124. Author Simon Head makes a point in this respect that deserves the attention of all who concern themselves with the debate over private versus publicly funded medical care: "For-profit MCOs [Managed Care Organizations — that is, corporations such as Aetna and Humana that supply for-profit medical care to corporate employees at

corporation expense] make money when their average spending per enrolled patient falls below the average value of the premiums they receive from employers. The less an MCO spends on its patients, the greater its profits, and the greater the shareholder value it contributes to its investors. The industry uses the phrase 'medical losses' to describe the payments it has to make on behalf of its sick customers, and this choice of words reveals much about how the industry regards such payments. An MCO's 'medical loss ratio' calculates the payments to MCO customers as a percentage of total revenues, and is an amount that MCO managers try to keep as low as possible. But an MCO's 'medical loss' may be a patient's lifeblood, literally" (p. 120).

22. Ibid., 187.

23. William H. Davidow and Michael S. Malone, *The Virtual Corporation: Structuring and Revitalizing the Corporation for the 21st Century* (New York: Harper Business, 1992), 6.

24. Ibid., 191-92.

25. Ibid., 192.

26. Ibid., 198.

27. See Zygmunt Bauman, *Work, Consumption and the New Poor* (Buckingham, UK: Open University Press, 1998).

28. Charles Taylor, *The Malaise of Modernity* (Toronto: Anansi, 1991), 40, 18.

29. Erich Fromm, *Psychoanalysis and Religion* (New York: Bantam Books, 1950), 86.

30. Quoted in Herbert Marcuse, *One-Dimensional Man* (New York: Beacon Press, 1964), 33.

31. Ibid., 33.

32. *The Icon Critical Dictionary of Postmodern Theory*, ed. Stuart Sim (Cambridge: Icon Books, 1998), 220.

# 10. Artificial Ethics for Artificial People

1. Curtis D. MacDougall, *Interpretative Reporting* (New York: Macmillan, 1972), 4.

2. It's worth noting in passing that objectivity, as journalists use the word, and neutrality, which is usually what is meant, can at times be in opposition: "Objectivity is not neutrality . . . if you take a series of descriptions of an event — millions of people died; millions of people were killed; millions of innocent civilians were massacred — then assuming all are true, each is more objective and less neutral than the last; it is more objective because it gives a fuller account of what occurred, excluding more misconceptions; and it is less neutral because it paints what occurred in a more gruesome light." Andrew Collier, *In Defense of Objectivity and Other Essays* (London: Routledge, 2003), 139.

Thus, if the real goal of journalism is the truth, then objectivity can often be a barrier: "As one moves away from neutral descriptions, one arrives at fuller and more objective accounts of the social world." John O'Neill, "Commerce and the Language of Value," in *Defending Objectivity: Essays in Honor of Andrew Collier,* ed. Margaret S. Archer and William Outhwaite (London: Routledge, 2004), 82.

3. Andreas Eshete, "Does a Lawyer's Character Matter?" in *The Good Lawyer*, ed. David Luban (Princeton, N.J.: Princeton University Press, 1986), 227.

4. "The Gambler Who Blew It All," *Newsweek*, February 4, 2002, 18-24; "Cliff Was Climbing the Walls," *Newsweek*, February 4, 2002, 24.

5. Ibid., 13.

6. Ibid., 27.

7. Viktor Frankl, *Man's Search for Meaning* (New York: Washington Square Press, 1963), 106-7.

8. A notable exception is the Association for Computing Machinery (ACM) Code of Ethics and Professional Conduct, which, before moving

on to specifics, exhorts its members to comply with a set of "general moral imperatives." It states, "As an ACM member I will . . . contribute to society and human well-being; avoid harm to others; be honest and trustworthy; be fair and take action not to discriminate; honor property rights including copyrights and patents; give proper credit for intellectual property; respect the privacy of others; honor confidentiality." The code is reproduced in Deborah G. Johnson and Helen Nissenbaum, *Computers, Ethics and Social Values* (Upper Saddle River, N.J.: Prentice Hall, 1995), 598-600.

9. This and succeeding quotes are from John Ladd, "The Quest for a Professional Code of Ethics: An Intellectual and Moral Confusion," in American Association for the Advancement of Science (AAAS), *Professional Ethics Project: Professional Ethics in the Scientific and Engineering Societies*, ed. Rosemary Chalk, Mark S. Frankel, and Sallie B. Chafer (Washington, D.C.: AAAS, 1980), 154-59.

10. Ibid.

11. From Maxwell Taylor, "A Do-It-Yourself Professional Code for the Military," *Parameters: Journal of the U.S. Army War College* 10, no. 4 (December 1980): 11, in Elizabeth Wolgast, *Ethics of an Artificial Person: Lost Responsibility in Professions and Organizations* (Palo Alto, Calif.: Stanford University Press, 1992), 23.

12. Ibid., 23.

13. Thomas Donaldson and Thomas Dundee, "Values in Tension: Ethics Away from Home," *Harvard Business Review*, September 1996, 54.

14. http://www.ci-pinkerton.com/workplace/alertline.html.

15. Other, frequently hilarious, examples of corporate commitment-speak are supplied in Don Watson's *Death Sentences* (New York: Penguin, 2005), chap. 2.

16. Zygmunt Bauman, *Postmodern Ethics* (Oxford, UK: Blackwell Publishers, 1998), 32.

# 11. Consumerism and the Corporation

1. The political scientist C. B. Macpherson made the important observation that in modern market societies "every expenditure of energy is considered to be painful, to be, in the economist's term, a disutility. This assumption, which is a travesty of the human condition, is built right into the justifying theory of the market society. The market society, and so the liberal society, is commonly justified on the grounds that it maximizes utilities, i.e., that it is the arrangement by which people can get the satisfactions they want with the least effort. The notion that activity is itself pleasurable, is a utility, has sunk almost without a trace under this utilitarian vision of life." C. B. Macpherson, *The Real World of Democracy* (Toronto: CBC, 1965), 38.

2. Especially recommended are Stewart Ewan's *Captains of Consciousness: Advertising and the Social Roots of Consumer Culture* (New York: McGraw-Hill, 1976); and *All-Consuming Images: The Politics of Style in Contemporary Culture* (New York: Basic Books, 1988).

3. This, and following quotations, are from Roland Marchand, "The Great Parables" in *Advertising and the American Dream: Making Way for Modernity, 1920-1940* (Berkeley: University of California Press, 1985).

4. Quoted in Ewan, *Captains of Consciousness*, 22.

5. Whiting Williams, *Mainsprings of Men* (New York: Charles Scribner's Sons, 1925), 192.

6. Herbert W. Hiese, "History and Current Status of the Truth in Advertising Movement as Carried on by the Vigilance Committee of the Associated Advertising Clubs of the World," *Annals of the American Academy of Political and Social Science*, May 1922, 211. Quoted in Ewan, *Captains of Consciousness*, 19.

7. Ewan, *Captains of Consciousness*, 91-92.

8. Zygmunt Bauman, *Postmodern Ethics* (Oxford, UK: Blackwell Publishers, 1998), 183.

9. Ibid.

# 12. Risky Business

1. The case is made convincingly in the thousand pages of Edward Hooper's *The River: A Journey to the Source of HIV and AIDS* (Boston: Little, Brown and Co., 1999). Hooper suggests that the HIV-AIDS pandemic began when HIV was accidentally introduced into hundreds and perhaps thousands of Africans during vaccinations of over one million people, mostly children, against polio in 1958 and 1959 in Rwanda-Burundi and selected centers in the Congo. The vaccines had been manufactured using tissue from chimps infected with a simian variant of the virus, which was able to jump the species barrier.

2. See, for example, the case of asbestos producer Johns Manville, in chapter 8.

3. Langdon Winner, *The Whale and the Reactor: A Search for Limits in an Age of High Technology* (Chicago: University of Chicago Press, 1986), 143-44. Emphasis added.

# 13. Who Do We Blame?

1. See chapter 10.

2. The father, as head of the household, was held to be responsible for the actions of all other household members, including spouse, children, slaves, and retainers. Elizabeth Wolgast, *Ethics of an Artificial Person: Lost Responsibility in Professions and Organizations* (Palo Alto, Calif.: Stanford University Press, 1992), 13.

3. Exactly what portion will depend to some degree on the conditions of coercion under which they operate. Soldiers facing death for insubordination share less responsibility than lawyers, who are free to drop their clients if asked to behave unethically.

4. Isaac Asimov, "First Law," in *The Rest of the Robots* (New York: Panther Books, 1968). Asimov's Three Laws of Robotics were laid down in 1941. The other two are: "A robot must obey the orders given it by hu-

man beings except when such orders would conflict with the First Law"; and "A robot must protect its own existence as long as such protection does not conflict with the First and Second Laws."

5. Andrew Hacker, "Corporate America," in *The Corporation Take-Over* (New York: Harper & Row, 1964), 9.

6. T. A. Gabalon, "The Lemonade Stand: Feminist and Other Reflections on the Limited Liability of Corporate Shareholders," *Vanderbilt Law Review* 45 (1992): 1429.

7. Dennis R. Fox, "The Law Says Corporations are Persons, but Psychology Knows Better," *Behavioral Sciences and the Law* 14 (1996): 349.

8. This is one of many ways in which the system militates against ethical behavior. The obvious, if radical, solution is to make corporations perfectly transparent. Whether governments any longer have the power to enact the necessary legislation and defend it against the inevitable court challenges is highly questionable.

9. Zygmunt Bauman, *Postmodern Ethics* (Oxford, UK: Blackwell Publishers, 1998), 19.

10. In a democracy the state is the people and politicians represent the people, subject to periodic elections. To call the state an author is thus not completely accurate. The ultimate author of anything the state does is the people. But just as in the case of a person engaging another person to do something, the actor may sometimes do things the author had not wished or anticipated. In those cases, the author is in some measure responsible for those actions, but not entirely. Some blame, perhaps a preponderance, must clearly fall on the actor as well. Citizens are thus only partly responsible for the ethical misdeeds of government, which must share culpability.

11. Sir Stafford Beer, *Designing Freedom* (Toronto: CBC, 1974), 77.

12. Ibid., 71. Emphasis added.

13. Wolgast, *Ethics of an Artificial Person*, 95.

# 14. Common Sense About Corporations

1. Herbert Marcuse, *One-Dimensional Man* (Boston: Beacon Press, 1964), 145.

2. This and the previous quotation are taken from *Spirit of the Web: The Age of Information from Telegraph to Internet* (Toronto: Key Porter, 1999), in which I provide a more complete discussion of the commercialization of broadcast media.

3. The reason newspapers avoid similarly overt advertiser control over content is that readers can pick and choose what they want to read simply by scanning stories and flipping pages — the content is randomly accessible. One is not compelled to read through advertisements in order to get to the end of a newspaper story. Advertising and editorial content are, to some extent at least, separate and distinct in the reader's experience. The other important difference between print periodicals and broadcast media is that most newspapers and magazines derive significant income from subscriptions and newsstand purchases. This further insulates them from advertiser influence.

4. Evelyn Fox Keller, *Reflections on Gender and Science* (New Haven: Yale University Press, 1985), 121-22.

5. *Science* 162 (1968): 1243-48.

6. See my *The Plot to Save the World* (Toronto: Clarke, Irwin & Co., 1973).

7. Some will want to make the point that communism certainly had no truck with corporations but was nevertheless at least as guilty of environmental crime as the corporate-dominated West. This is certainly true, but neither did communism, in its scientific fetishism, recognize anything so decadently irrational as the notion of a moral impulse. If anything, communism as it was practiced in Eastern Europe and Asia was the embodiment of what White had mistakenly attributed to

Christianity — that is, an utter hubristic arrogance in the face of nature. It was based not on religion, but Rationalism.

8. L. J. Cohen, "Can Human Irrationality Be Experimentally Determined?" *Behavioral and Brain Sciences* 4: 317-70, quoted in Philip Mirowski, *Machine Dreams: Economics Becomes a Cyborg Science* (Cambridge: Cambridge University Press, 2002), 341.

# Index

# Index

# Index